GREER, SC

The Center of the Universe

by Leland E. Burch

illustrations by Suzanne Greene

photography by Eddie Burch

ISBN-10: 1481955616
ISBN-13: 9781481955614

Library of Congress Control Number: 2013900722
CreateSpace Independent Publishing Platform
North Charleston, South Carolina

Foreword

Greer, S. C. is the greatest small town in the world—period. Here's proof: First, Greer cares. This was evident over a century ago when Greer established one of the state's best public school systems and municipal utility services. In 1938, caring citizens launched Greer Relief and Resources to provide food, medicine and clothing for people trapped in emergency situations. Greer Community Ministries was founded in 1972 to provide Meals on Wheels to elderly, homebound residents. And in 1990, the Greer Soup Kitchen was started to feed the hungry.

Greer is the site of a modern day miracle, the Greer Christian Learning Center. The community built this facility to offer Bible studies and life lessons for more than 500 students participating in one of the nation's most outstanding Released Time programs.

Greer is the home of Kids Planet, a world-class handicapped accessible playground built by volunteers.

Left Field occupies a large slice of our Field of Dreams. It was the hangout for our Strategic Planning Committee that met once a month for three years and never planned anything; it's the city's water reservoir that was used as a private airport by the pilot of a pontoon-equipped airplane; it's where Presbyterians can park in No Parking Zones on Sundays; it's the only downtown business district with traffic signals installed backwards. And that's only the beginning.

In the 1880s, the Southern Railway was building tracks from Charlotte to Atlanta, but the town of Reidville objected—farmers feared the locomotives would scare their goats. Thus, the tracks were diverted seven miles to the north, through farmland owned by Manning Greer. A depot quickly followed, and the City of Greer was incorporated in 1886.

Greer's location is ideal. Thus, the Greenville-Spartanburg International Airport was built in Greer in 1962. That was the key factor in recruitment of BMW that made Greer the North American home of the world's most prestigious automobile manufacturer. Greer then became the fastest growing city in South Carolina, exceeding both Greenville and Spartanburg in land mass by the year 2000.

When Greer residents were tempted to let this success go to their heads, I felt it my duty to jump up and say, "Hey! Wait just a minute!" I did this through my weekly newspaper column where I used hyperbole, occasionally mixed with bits of humor and gems of wisdom, to deflate huge egos and over-hyped accomplishments.

This is a collection of columns, written when I was editor of *The Greer Citizen* newspaper, that focuses on my hometown. I took up writing "Off the Record" when my father, Edd A. Burch, passed away in 1985. He started "Off the Record" as Editor of *The Dalton* (Ga.) *Citizen,* and continued the column when he purchased *The Greer Citizen* in 1942.

Over the years, the columns garnered awards from the South Carolina Press Association, and thousands? of readers requested that I publish them in a book. Actually, it was more like one person, Suzanne Lanford Greene, who made me promise to compile this book.

Suzanne Greene

Dedicated to Suzanne Greene

You would not be reading "The Center of the Universe" except for Suzanne Lanford Greene. But that is just one reason why this book is dedicated to her memory. A little background...

...for the better part of the Twentieth Century, youths who grew up in Greer left to find fame and fortune elsewhere. The pastures were much greener in other areas, especially for those pursuing professional careers. Over time, Greer lost numerous gifted young people. But there were notable exceptions, those who returned home after college and helped build this community to greatness. One of the most remarkable of these was Suzanne Greene.

The demands upon Greene as a housewife and mother of three make her accomplishments all that more remarkable. The gifted and widely acclaimed artist somehow found time to paint—often in the wee hours of the morning. Her watercolors were widely exhibited and won numerous major awards. The South Carolina Watercolor Society honored Greene with the Artists Excellence Award and Best in Show for three consecutive years.

Late in life, Greene turned her attention to the history of womankind and spent several years compiling her own original art for a yet unpublished book that expresses feminine wholeness and spirituality.

Had she left Greer, Greene might have found fame and fortune in the trendy art circles of New York City or San Francisco. Instead, she poured every ounce of her remarkable talent back into her hometown. Greene produced numerous art works that she freely gave to churches, charities and even the city government. She never sought to make a quick buck for herself.

Greene's original art can be found hanging in local professional offices, financial institutions and other commercial establishments. Many Greer residents have Greene's watercolor paintings prominently displayed in their homes. The owners especially treasure these pieces because they knew the artist who painted them from her heart.

Had Greene not chosen to return to her roots, Greer would be a much poorer community today. And I would have never undertaken this book without her encouragement. Before she passed away on July 6, 2004, Greene created three dozen sketches to illustrate a book of my newspaper columns and then made me promise that I would actually publish the book. Despite dragging my feet, I have assembled this book of columns on many aspects of life in Greer. I believe Suzanne Greene would enjoy this book, and hopefully the tribute "Greer Has Lost a Great Treasure" that appears in the chapter titled People Worth Remembering. I hope that you also enjoy this book.

- Leland Burch

Table of Contents

Greer Assets and Notables

There Is No Other Greer - April 10, 1996

The Greer Citizen newspaper has been accused of keeping alive the myth: there is no other Greer. So says Tom Greer in a letter from his mountaintop home in North Carolina. Like the Grinch who stole Christmas, this gentleman has punctured our pride with his claim of finding five other Greers in the United States.

In answer to his contention, I say "there is no other Greer like this Greer. We may be imitated, but we have never been duplicated."

If you ask Dr. Wilson Nelson, pastor of the Greer First Baptist Church, he will tell you that this Greer is the 'Center of the Universe.' And nobody has been able to disprove Nelson. When the strongest telescope imaginable has been invented, you will be able to stand on the South Main Street overpass, point it toward the heavens and on a clear day see the back of your head!

But there's no need to wait until the year 3000 for such proof. If you look about you, you will see all kinds of evidence to confirm that Greer is, indeed, the Center of the Universe. Here are some clues:

Defense lawyers have discovered a source of milk and honey at the corner of Main and Poinsett Streets in downtown Greer. It is the Police Department.

This is the only place in the world that has a Monument to the Phantom Farmer. It is known as Square One.

This is the only Greer that has a web site on the Internet. It can be accessed at www.redneck.com.

This is the only place in the world that turns senior citizens into world-class sprinters. They have to be in order to survive crossing Trade Street between the blinks of the traffic lights.

There is no crabgrass growing in our Field of Dreams. Unfortunately, we can't play on the field because of the traffic.

Only in the Center of the Universe would a drag strip often be the hottest topic of conversation.

BMW has begun a five-year plan to gain acceptance into the Center of the Universe. They have dispatched ambassadors to Pelham and Apalache and stationed an advance scout in the lobby of Wal-Mart.

Greer is known for family togetherness. That's because most families must huddle around the only TV set they can afford.

Once upon a time, the anxiety level was high in the Center of the Universe. Then Prozac was mistakenly added to our water supply instead of fluoride, apparently because of the confusion with all of those other Greers out there. Although we get more cavities in our teeth now, we feel better about ourselves.

We are incurably optimistic. Greer residents actually believe a new high school will be built, and the Strategic Planning Committee will produce a plan before the turn of the century.

Greer is the birthplace of downsizing. Weight Watchers continues to meet every third Tuesday night in the Center of the Universe.

Greer is the home of the Miss Universe Pageant. Until now, however, it has been known as Miss Le Flambeau.

There is some dispute about whether Bullock's Barber Shop or the New Dixie Restaurant is the center of the Center of the Universe. Unfortunately, the issue will not be resolved this year since neither shrine is among the stops scheduled for the Family Fest Historical Tour.

It says in my notes that if you need further proof, then stand in the middle of the eighth green at the Greer Country Club. It is the only place in the universe where you can be assured of not being hit by a golf ball.

Seeking Greer - June 3, 1998

W. L. "LeRoy" Jones recently made a special trip to the newspaper office just to offer a suggestion. He wants us to print something that will inform people where Greer is located. "I read things, like letters to the editor signed by people with Greer addresses, and I don't know where it is anymore," Jones said.

I've given Jones' request considerable thought, but I haven't figured out a way to fulfill his wishes. Describing Greer is exactly like what happens in the parable of the three blind monkeys trying to describe an elephant. No three people describe Greer in the same way.

If, as pastor Dr. Wilson Nelson likes to say, "Greer is the center of the universe," then perhaps we should print a map of the cosmos, or maybe just the Milky Way, and identify the dot that represents Greer. It would be helpful for UFOs searching for the center of things. Greer might even become the subject of an X-Files episode. If, as development specialist Peter McCord says, "Greer is Going Places," then maybe we should put someone on its trail to find out where it is headed.

Greer has managed to dodge every tornado. Which is good because Greer has not had to be declared a disaster area. Even so, Greer can be found on most maps, but you can't figure it out. The outline of the city limits looks like one of those inkblot tests.

Consider this: the new Greer High School is out of town, but Riverside High is inside the city. And Greer's water reservoirs are in Blue Ridge.

The BMW plant is completely surrounded by the Greer City Limits, but the company advertises that it is located in Spartanburg.

Greer's City Limits also surround the jetport, but it is known as Greenville-Spartanburg International Airport. The weather bureau is housed at the airport and acknowledges on weather radio that it is broadcasting from Greer. The irritating thing about weathermen is that they are right sometimes.

4

There are people who live in subdivisions that have a Greer address and a Greer telephone exchange number, but think they are in downtown Greenville. We note in the daily papers that The Eastside extends from Bob Jones University to Spartanburg, but it doesn't include Greer—at least those of us who are "po but proud." Then there are some folks with Taylors addresses who will swear they live in Greer.

If you need directions, Greer is the only place in the universe where all east-west traffic is directed into the parking lot of a restaurant (Ryan's).

A professional soccer team calls Greer its home. But the locals have never heard of soccer.

Someone once said that living in Greer is like living in the funny papers. Where else would a public official be investigated for taking a marijuana plant home (from the police evidence locker) to show to his neighbors? That may have happened 20 years ago, but Greer hasn't changed. Greer is still a place where you can have fun, as long as no one suspects that you are having a good time. Then you have to leave town, like to go to the movies.

There you have it, Mr. Jones. I guess the only thing you could say for sure about Greer is that it must be a state of mind.

Greer Mill Was Ahead of Its Time – Jan. 31, 1996

Last week was one of the worst in recent memory. In addition to the deaths and serious illnesses of some very close friends; our son tore the clutch out of his car, which had to be towed 60 miles for repairs ($459); a daughter-in-law wrecked her car, which forced her to cancel our grandchildren's birthday party in Columbia; and the Greer Fire Chief lost his job for making a gloomy prediction in our newspaper.

Then came Friday. On a day so cold and dank that lawyers kept their hands in their own pockets, it was announced that the old Greer Mill would be shut down next month.

It was there that I got my start on the road to success, working the third shift during the summers when I was in college. Getting a job in the mill was a great stroke of luck. I stepped up from earning 50 cents an hour working in the peach shed to $1.30 an hour in the Preparation Department on the second floor of Greer Mill.

I may be afflicted with Old Timers Disease, but I remember those days well. I worked with many "salt of the earth" folks at Greer Mill. There was "Shorty" McCallister who seemed to be such a part of the mill that you would think that it had been built around him and his elevator. Mack the 'second hand' was stuck with repairing the machinery that I broke. The shift supervisor, a preacher on weekends, nearly lost his religion when I took 3 a.m. naps behind mountainous cardboard boxes full of wooden quills.

Believe it or not, Greer Mill was on the cutting edge of things back in the fifties. I can remember…

…when textile workers wore white socks before Ronnie Bruce made them fashionable. We also wore blue jeans before such garments were discovered by Paris fashion designers and marketed with sexy television commercials.

….when we were the only people in the world who had ever heard of Junior Johnson—outside of his own family.

6

...when we were brown bagging before the country club set discovered the practice. We brought tomato sandwiches to work in brown bags.

....when the weave room could be heard for blocks around, and everyone who worked inside was stone deaf. You had to go up to the third floor to carry on a conversation. Today's looms are much quieter, but employees are required to wear earplugs—so they still can't hear anything.

....when the plant was recognized for setting a safety record with one million man-hours without an accident. We devoted an equal amount of hours to smoking cigarettes, and still managed to turn out a massive amount of cloth that went into dress uniforms for the U.S. Army.

That was before some Harvard Business School-types took over. They hung up "no-smoking" signs, removed the old equipment, and installed new knitting machines. A few weeks later, the world market for knit fabrics went into the dumper.

The plant recovered years later when the knitting machines were sent to the recycling heap. Then came the Desert Storm War, and Greer Mill operated overtime to make fabric for U.S. Army combat uniforms. When we won the war without taking a single casualty, there was no more need for uniforms, except to replace those lost in luggage on airlines.

Greer Mill has not outlived its usefulness. The times have just now caught up with it.

I Really Miss the Old Library – Aug. 21, 1996

Greer's new Jean M. Smith Library opened last September, and the response has been overwhelming. Three times as many people are using the new library now than before. It has twice the books as the old library, plus new attractions including videos, compact disks, computers and even a fireplace.

While I am grateful for the new library, I must confess that I really miss the old Davenport Memorial Library on School Street. I grew up in that library. That may account for why I know everything that is worth knowing, and why I am willing to share my knowledge every week in the newspaper.

The old library had many benefits that have been lost in the gloss and glitter of the new one. For one thing, old Davenport was convenient. I only had to walk half a block from the newspaper office. In fact, old Davenport reminded me of my office because every time I sneezed, it raised a cloud of dust.

When visiting the old library, I did not have to fight crowds to look for books. The reason being that nobody could get a parking place near old Davenport, so they didn't bother to go there.

A trip to old Davenport was like having a free membership in a health club. You got a lot of exercise going up and down those steps. You could even go inside with mud on your shoes. Mud was the same color as the floor. But the new library has fancy living room-style carpet, and you don't dare soil it.

Like any Hot Spot convenience store, old Davenport offered a quick stop. The new book always sat out by itself on a special shelf. If it was not there, you knew immediately that someone else had beaten you to it and you would have to come back another day.

The new library has so many new books that you don't know where to begin looking. You could spend hours in there searching and miss your favorite TV shows. Unless I live to be 125, I don't have enough time left to read all those books.

I considered the books in old Davenport to be safe. You could always tell because they were tattered and torn. Many people had read them, so I figured they must be really good books.

But most of the books in the Smith Library look new and unread, maybe not even touched by anyone—like those bargains going for $1.98 at the Book Barn.

I always enjoyed talking to Joada (Hiatt) the Librarian at old Davenport. She could find any book instantly (they were all within an arm's length of her desk.) In the new library, you must use a computer to find a book. The computer not only tells you the location of the book, it also overloads you with information like the number of term papers the author has written. If the book you're seeking happens to be in the building, then you have to use a map to find it. But don't ask Hiatt. She is occupied supervising dozens of assistants who are moving in endless circles from return carts—to shelves—to checkout and back again.

I wonder if we made a mistake by cutting corners on the tin roof of the new library and using the savings to buy all those books. I have been told that the new libraries planned for Travelers Rest and Mauldin will have genuine copper roofs with very few books so that patrons will not be overwhelmed with reading material.

Our new library's tin roof is painted green. I will admit that it reminds me of the grass growing out of the roof of old Davenport.

My greatest disappointment is that the new library doesn't smell like the old one. Old Davenport had a distinct odor of musty books— an odor usually reserved for such revered places as the Biltmore Castle. I wish we had splurged for the additional $25,000 that it would have cost to add Old Book Musk scent to the paint for the new library.

Top Ten for Hysterical Preservation – June 26, 1996

Did you know about the architectural and historical research project that is underway in Greer? A team of special investigators is compiling a survey of Greer's ten most popular buildings and/or places that should be preserved.

Compiling such a list has been a real problem for me because I like everything in Greer. After weeks of fretting about it, I have finally narrowed down my Top Ten List of places for the Hysterical Preservation Register. They are:

The Greer Country Club. This golfing mecca was carved out of solid rock in 1954, and it took every bit of the next 40 years to get grass to grow on the granite. Not only did that feat qualify to become one of the Seven Wonders of the World, it also is interesting to note that the country club was built before neighborhoods organized and railed against developments like rock quarries and high schools.

Taylor's Peach Shed. Another monument to the good old days— way back when real peaches grew in Greer. Those peaches produced real fuzz that, I'll bet, is still pilled six feet deep in places under the old wooden floors of the shed. Global warming, ozone layer, ice storms, floods and other acts of irresponsible weathermen have ruined our peach-growing climate.

Alta Cunningham's. I'm referring to the original Alta Cunningham store of the 1950s. And that was when the original Miss Alta, the owner, was already an old lady. It was the only store in the world that never had a sale—even the dresses that were still in stock from the 1930s and 40s (which may still be in some corner of the attic) carried the original price tags. Of course, those styles will probably come back sooner or later.

Trade Street Railroad Crossing: The world's largest speed bump that is responsible for Greer's having more auto parts stores per capita than any other city in the country.

Tab's Flea Market – offers a real-life game of "chicken" for daredevils crossing East Wade Hampton Blvd. in search of bargains.

Trade Street Parking Meters – Long gone, they once gave downtown Greer an air of big-city class. Furthermore, the nickels and dimes those meters sucked up helped keep taxes low.

New Dixie Restaurant – The only restaurant in the world where the customers get personal service from the waitress, cook dishwasher, cashier and owner—one in the same person, all at the same time.

Lake Cunningham – The world's only lake that is so shallow you can walk across it.

Bullock's Barber Shop – The cultural center of the universe. It must be, because time stands still in this place—especially for anyone who is in a hurry. Bullock's also is the only place in the world where you can find out (whether you want to or not) which football teams are going to win next weekend.

The Den – of the Greer Lions Club. The Lions are a captive audience, if there is one. The door to their meeting room cannot be unlocked from the inside. Thus, on Tuesday nights you can hear those Lions roar—when they can't get out the door because they have been locked inside!

Taking Inventory – Nov. 29, 2000

In his inaugural sermon on Sunday morning, our church's new youth minister, Rev. Wayne Cole, suggested that everyone should take an inventory. While folks in Florida have been counting ballots like mad, Cole's message is that we must not be outdone. The least we could do is count our blessings since this is the Thanksgiving season.

I think we should go one better and take an inventory of the entire community because I suspect a good many things are missing or have been misplaced. I have come up with a partial list of assets which were once in Greer's inventory:

The S.C. Shamrocks – After the city spent $10,000 fixing up the old Greer High football stadium for soccer matches, only three paying customers showed up, and the Shamrocks team disappeared—vanished without a trace.

The investigative team from Unsolved Mysteries also is looking for the **S.C. Seminoles**. You may remember that this team started playing football in that same stadium back in September and hasn't been heard from since.

Jazz & Candlelight – This downtown revitalization project folded when the city council voted to ban the consumption of alcohol on the sidewalks. I personally miss the candlelight more than the booze because at least you could see how to get around after dark on Trade Street.

GARP (the Greer Aristocratic Redneck Parade) – was an organization known for throwing black-tie galas to raise money to support the budding artists among us. It disbanded because, take your pick: (a) our budding artists had no talent, or (b) Smith & James men's store no longer rents tuxedoes.

Square One Farmers' Market – this was a good idea that never got off the ground because farmers refused to come to town. Which was a downer for classes of school kids that made field trips to Square

One to see and touch a real farmer. Today, these students are bussed instead to the Greer Heritage Museum to examine the faded photograph of a farmer.

Movie theaters – can be found if you look far enough back in the dustbin of Greer history. In the 1950s, there were five of them: The Grand, Greer and Rialto indoor theaters in downtown Greer, and the outdoor drive-in theaters, the Greer and King Cotton. What happened to the movie theaters? Obviously people stopped going to the movies when television came along with entertainment that was free—albeit the fare is much worse. But then, no one ever accused Greerites of being choosy about entertainment.

This brings us to the **Strategic Planning Committee**. By my reckoning, this blue ribbon panel of the town's leading citizens never planned anything. But they were considering looking into the need for a movie theater at their last meeting, back in 1994.

Life in Greer

Dollar Daze – Feb. 20, 1991

Dollar Days in downtown Greer is my favorite event of the year. Not only does the big February sale mean that winter is nearly over, there is a chance you can go shopping and come out ahead.

I don't mean like you can get something for half price. I mean like you can steal a pair of $100 shoes for $25. At least that's what I thought until a couple of weeks ago. Then I discovered there is no such thing as a $25 pair of shoes this side of the Goodwill store. Even worse, shoes in my size are nearly extinct.

Since my motto is "why buy something now when you can wait and get it on sale," I had been biding my time for months in anticipation of Dollar Days. In the meantime, the leather on my old shoes was wearing so thin that I had to put on an extra pair of socks just to keep my feet warm. I even took my old loafers to the Dixie Shoe Shop for recapping, but there wasn't enough of them left to support a piece of new leather.

That is the background of how I spent most of the Dollar Days weekend in downtown Greer matching wits with Gene Collins at Bailes-Collins and with Paul Smith, Jr. at Smith & James.

Smith had everything in the store on sale except shoes, which he claimed were already a bargain at the regular price. Amazingly, Smith did have two pairs of shoes available at my maximum price of $25.

One was a mismatched pair, with a size 8 left shoe and a size ten right shoe in the same box. The other pair appeared to be a half-century-old World War II style left over from the Tillotson Brothers Men's Store era.

That jolted me into the painful reality that I was going to have to fork out more cash than I had planned to acquire a pair of shoes that fit my feet. Then I remembered our company's annual financial report and decided that I could not afford anything more than a box with a picture of a shoe on it. When I made that decision, Smith became so depressed about the recession in the shoe business that he went home with a headache.

I didn't fare much better up the street. "We have the shoes you want but not your size," declared Gene Collins. "Bailes-Collins stocks shoes for the big and tall, not the short and fat."

"But my size is average," I protested.

"Nobody is average any more," Collins declared.

I checked out his claim at the famous name department store, and their shoe sales person put it a little differently. "People in Greer are funny. Not one is average. Besides, most people don't walk anymore. They park in the handicapped spaces, and their feet have become big and tall from lack of use."

The shoe section in the supermarket was even worse. They did have one pair of shoes my size, but I did not think that pink and green sneakers would look good with my navy blue suit.

After getting an installment loan at the bank, I returned to the Dollar Days scene to make a down payment for Collins to order a pair of shoes for me. He said there had a been a price increase while I had been away to take out the loan. That's when it hit me that the reasons hamburgers are so cheap is because the leather is the most expensive part of the cow.

So I dashed back to Smith & James to have another look at the World War II brogans. But someone, apparently banking on that model coming back in style when we go to war again, had beaten me to them.

The sight of a senior citizen lying in the floor, kicking and screaming prompted co-owner Bernard Price to scurry to the back room and start shuffling around. Eventually he produced a pair of shoes ordered for another short, fat size customer who had never returned to pick them up. Mumbling something about never again having another Dollar Days sale, Price reduced the pair of shoes on the spot, emptied my wallet, and pushed me out the door.

Now, if my old shoes will only hold out a few more days, I can save the new ones to break out at church this Sunday.

CSI SSI– Mar. 26, 2009

Until the spare time that came with the title of "Editor Emeritus," I never had the opportunity to do much investigative reporting, known in some circles as "muck raking." Now folks are suggesting all sorts of such research to keep me busy. One project is CSI SSI.

I plunged into this dish of alphabet soup at the request of Lance Owens, proprietor of SSI - Savvy Seniors In (search of the Fountain of Youth). It seems that bath towels are disappearing from SSI at the alarming rate of one a day.

After posting notices everywhere urging patrons to return the terrycloth towels, Owens approached me. "As a last resort, I want you to get on the case. Otherwise I'm going to have to put a guard on the door," he said.

Being a helpful type, I agreed even at the expense of putting off my doctoral degree studies on the flavor of cheese that the moon is made of.

My head was soon filled with ideas. Most of these, however, Owens rejected out of hand, especially when I suggested that he switch to 40'x40' towels—towels so large that when patrons began lifting them, they would no longer need to work out.

He also rebuffed my idea that SSI should simply give towels away, and then nobody would want them. As a bonus, it would bail out the defunct textile industry. "I'm not the federal government!" Owens screeched.

"Then use paper towels instead. Only the tree huggers would complain about seeing an entire forest wiped out," I suggested. "And you could reduce the size of your staff—the two people who wash, dry and fold towels 24-7. Or you could implant each towel with a cell phone that would sent you a text massage when it left the premises," I continued helpfully.

"That would be so expensive that it would only be a couple of weeks before we were all eating cat food," Owens responded.

"Well, how about reaching out to the towel thieves by forming a klepto support group," I suggested.

"How about you giving this some more thought," he countered.

That led to the idea of permanently attaching department store-type magnets to each towel to set off an alarm when one walked out the door. Of course, the washer-dryer would have to be replaced every week, but it would serve as a huge advantage to be armed with one of these during a towel fight in the locker room.

Owens also dismissed the notion that the towels are being pirated to make costumes for the hit TV show *Dancing with the Stars*. Only one towel would have been necessary to outfit the entire cast.

Racking my brain, I recalled having "accidentally" brought home an SSI towel one day last year. "What are you doing with this towel?" my wife asked as I came through the door.

Thinking quickly, I said, "Well, if you like this one, I was planning to gift wrap a box of them to celebrate our anniversary. This is the year for textiles, isn't it?" I asked.

"No, she huffed. "Not only are these towels stamped 'Property of SSI', they also don't match our décor. If we were to start using these towels, we would have to redecorate the bathroom. Then the rest of the house would look shabby, so we would have to repaint. And Ben Hannon hasn't returned our phone calls in years because he hasn't forgotten the last time when we had him experiment with 85 shades of yellow before finding just the right paint for each room."

This was quickly becoming a greater challenge than facing the federal government in reigning in AIG (Arrogance, Incompetence & Greed). Just when I had given up on getting a bonus and, as a last resort was about to notify the CIA that the towels are being stolen to make turbans for members of a local terrorist cell, I solved the mystery.

A quick trip to the new City Hall complex (after 5 p.m. when everyone had gone home) confirmed my suspicions. Thousands of SSI towels had been stuffed under the new lake in City Park now in its fifth year of renovation. No wonder the pond won't hold water! The towels are soaking it up.

There must be a reason for this, so I began quizzing *The Greer Citizen's* investigative team. Jim Fair suggested that the Commission of Public Works must be creating a new reservoir under the pond. If the drought continues much longer, they will simply wring out the towels to refill Lake Robinson. But I couldn't confirm this by asking Jerry Balding, because he recently retired. Took his ball and left the playground.

Summoned to Serve – Feb. 21, 1996

I have just completed a week of patriotic duty—serving on the jury.

I learned that when a jury summons arrives in the mail it is both good news and bad news. Greer is one of the few places that no known excuse can get you out of serving on the jury. But the good news is that Greer juries never try any cases.

Let me explain.

To start, the city summons 300 people to serve on a six-man jury. Right off the bat, that lets the defendant know he is badly outnumbered.

Then each juror has to answer pages of loaded questions like: "Do you believe in the death penalty for jay walking?" After hearing the responses, 99 percent of the defendants plead guilty to avoid getting the chair.

I used the questionnaire to make my own case for getting excused from jury duty. I listed all of my friends who are police officers. Then, at the bottom of the page, I wrote that I preferred leniency, meaning life sentences for anyone convicted of not wearing his seat belt.

I also was the first to raise my hand when no-nonsense judge Hank Mims asked if anyone should be excused from jury duty. I had an appointment with the painless dentist who has a fixation about tinkering with my braces at least once a week.

"You really don't have an excuse, Mr. Burch," Mims declared. "Therefore, do you feel you can be fair and impartial?"

"Of course," I snapped. "Don't you read my editorials?"

But I cannot complain. The judge also refused to dismiss his sister-in-law from the same jury, and she had a real excuse. In so doing he probably wrecked the family's plans for Christmas dinner.

I was about to raise my hand again when the judge asked for a show of those who feared being sequestered. After all, I was sitting next to Chris Harvey who cannot resist repeating Smokey the Bear jokes. But I quickly changed my mind when I spotted the last juror walking through the door. She happened to be a former high school beauty queen.

Knowing full well that the $5 a day paid to jurors would put me in a higher tax bracket, I got my affairs in order and toughed it out for the week. Mainly, I remembered the last trial in Greer was held in 1987, and it was for a juror who did not show up when summoned.

Judge Mims opened court by congratulating us jurors for attaining the highest (non-elected) office in the land, without campaigning.

"Yeah," I said, "and I bet those candidates running for president in the New Hampshire primaries would love to know our secret."

After that, we had to report to court at the crack of dawn each day in the unlikely event some defendant actually wanted to take the risk of going to trial before the jury.

Finally on Thursday, the prosecutor brought in a motorist who was charged with double parking. The case ended in a mistrial when the jury failed to return from lunch. It seems the clerk sent them out to eat at the Copper River Grill, and they are still waiting to be served.

John Rollins, Jr., the public defender, never got to deliver his closing argument. We could overhear him rehearsing in an adjoining room, repeating over and over, "if it doesn't fit, you must acquit," as if committing it to memory.

A Half-Day in the Life of Greer - Feb. 19, 2003

(I suspect that it was done on purpose, but *The Greer Citizen* was ignored in the revenue enhancing publication "A Day in the Life of Greer" which was distributed recently by the big daily newspaper to the west. To rectify that snub, I am revealing the intimate details of what happens at this place. So much goes on, though, that I had to cut the material in half which accounts for the title: "A Half Day in the Life of *The Greer Citizen*.")

7:30 a.m. – As co-owner, Walter Burch has the privilege of opening the office and sweeping the floor. It can be rewarding, however, since he usually finds several pieces of loose change.

8:05 a.m. – Employees begin bouncing in the door, totally excited since it is publication day. Walter heads for the law office of Ronnie Bruce who is brewing free coffee.

8:40 a.m. – Walter makes his way to Citizens Building and Loan, where free coffee is also being served. He complains to Robert Lynn about the quality of coffee that Bruce is serving.

8:50 a.m. – I arrive, half asleep after having worked past midnight on the sports section. When I check the E-mail, the computer crashes, forcing me to start over.

8:55 a.m. – Lori Sondov is confronted with having to input a raft of faxes containing obituaries of people who took advantage of the mortuary's President's Day Clearance Sale. The sheer volume crashes her computer.

8:59 a.m. – Julie Holcombe puts in a call to mayor of Duncan to get his comments about assistant town clerk resigning.

9:18 a.m. – I answer the first of two dozen phone calls from information seekers. This person wants to know the population of Greer. I don't have the answer, however, for at any moment in time the actual number depends upon whether the traffic lights on Wade Hampton Blvd. are green or red.

9:20 a.m. – I continue pressing on toward the deadline, gathering bits of information about the new GHS Health Care campus and the looming war between the City of Greer and the Taylors Fire District.

9:55 a.m. – Theresa "Granny" Williams arrives, hung over from a six hour Tuesday night meeting of the Blue Ridge Water Board.

9:56 a.m. – "Granny" phones a friend and begins delivering blow-by-blow details of the water board meeting.

10:03 a.m. – A spy from a daily paper comes in and asks for a copy of today's paper. Jamie Zaeger tells him it is not ready. The man asks what she knows about the big hospital announcement, and she replies "nothing." He then asks for a copy of the front page. She says the page is not ready. He demands to know when it will be ready, and she says, "it depends on whether or not the press breaks down." When the pest finally leaves, she declares, "What part of no did he not understand?"

10:06 a.m. – Preston Burch is dispatched to take photo of Humvee that crashed into Tyger River Fire Department.

10:07 a.m. – Walter gets in line at the post office with a check to pay for mailing the newspaper in case it actually comes off the press.

10:08 a.m. - Lois Stringer puts together the last of 60,000 inserts that will go inside this week's issue.

10:09 a.m. - Julie Holcombe puts in a second call to Duncan mayor.

10:12 a.m. – The press breaks down while printing the sports section.

11:01 a.m. – Walter makes it to the window of the post office.

11:06 a.m. – Granny's water board report is interrupted by a call to make plans for attending "Cory, Cory's" basketball game on Saturday.

11:21 a.m. – Writing headlines is not going well, especially for the hospital story. Something about my first draft: "Health Care Costs Skyrocketing and Greer to Get More of It" just doesn't sound right. When I start over, my computer crashes again.

11:32 a.m. – Eddie Burch finishes writing the account of last night's city council meeting that erupted into a war of words.

11:39 a.m. – Granny hangs up and dials the first of six local restaurants to get today's lunch menus.

11:55 a.m. - Granny discards all menus and orders a hot dog from Rosie at the Green Top service station.

11:56 a.m. - Granny puts in emergency call to her chiropractor. She complains of arm weariness as result of repetitive lifting of the company's ergonomically challenged telephone receiver.

11:58 a.m. - Press repairs completed, Lois Stringer puts number 1,402 of the stack of inserts into a sports section. The paper is now two hours behind schedule, but it is the earliest we have been late.

11:59 a.m. - Julie Holcombe gives up after another unsuccessful attempt to reach the Duncan mayor.

12:01 p.m. – Walter finishes affixing advertisements to the front section pages using duct tape. No ads have ever been lost with duct tape. (Note: The stories, photos and headlines must be arranged on the pages. They can be moved around and positioned in various places using wax instead of tape. The downside of using wax as an adhesive is that the material is prone to fall off the pages. And that sends everyone scrambling in a desperate search through the debris on the cutting room floor.)

Sometimes items simply vanish into thin air. Today, the photo of a concert soloist has mysteriously disappeared. If it doesn't turn up we must decide whether to use the story without the photo or hold it until next week to allow seven full days for the search to continue.

Laying out the pages is a great deal more difficult than anyone would think. Unlike a jig-saw puzzle, nothing ever seems to fit without considerable editing. Entire paragraphs are often whacked out of stories.

The greatest challenge is deciding what to print because there is never enough space for everything. Today, a blue ribbon investigative piece about how sofas have invaded front porches in the Victor community is yanked to make way for the announcement of a new medical campus in Greer.

12:03 p.m. – Walter heads out the door to get a haircut at Bullock's Barbershop.

12:04 p.m. – Kris Gordon leaves to deliver tear sheets (copies) of ads that customers have placed in the newspaper. With only two stops, she should be back soon.

12:06 p.m. – Another phone call is added to the stack of messages for Angela Mathis. The calls could have been forwarded if only Angela had taken her cell phone to the tennis court.

12:17 p.m. – A loud chain saw-like noise erupts from the front office. We rush out to discover that Granny Williams has dozed off at her desk. Awakened by the activity, Williams complains, "I couldn't sleep last night, but I sure can now."

12:33 p.m. – The Mayor of Duncan returns Julie Holcombe's phone call. She refuses to talk to him.

12:48 p.m. – The singer's photo is still missing. The story is replaced by an update of activities at the Jean M. Smith Library.

1:11 p.m. – The suggestion of lunch sets Julie Holcombe's stomach to growling. "I'm sorry," she says for the 23rd time in an hour.

1:38 pm. – As the layout process nears completion, lines (borders) must be taped around the photos that do not accompany articles. This is done to avoid confusing our long-suffering readers into thinking that a train wreck has something to do with the school lunch menus. Katie Smith, Julie Holcombe and Lori Sondov try to squeeze into the women's restroom at the same time to avoid this tedious chore.

1:50 p.m. – The last page goes to the dark room to be photographed for printing. This is somewhat earlier than usual, which is a bad omen. Like the timing of peaches from blossoms to the harvest, the earlier the pages are pasted up, the later they come off the press.

1:58 p.m. – Walter's turn finally comes to get in the chair at the barbershop.

1:59 p.m. – The editorial staff goes to lunch

Final Chapter Half Day in the Life... Feb. 26. 2003

2:43 p.m. – All employees gather around the ancient printing press and stare at it, waiting to see if it will start cranking out newspapers. The scene is reminiscent of World War II photos of prisoners staring at cattle cars before being loaded for the German concentration camps.

2:55 p.m. – The press sputters and runs in fits and starts, producing several hundred pounds of "spoiled" copies – papers that are mostly solid black with ink or totally blank. This waste fills a six-by-six foot cubic box with newsprint that keeps the city's recycling business going.

3:15 p.m. – The first good copy comes off the press.

3:16 p.m. - With the sound of a loud firecracker, the web breaks. (The web is the continuous sheet of newsprint that travels through the printing press.) It breaks every week at precisely this moment. In fact, this is how the new clock at Poinsett and Main is calibrated.

3:34 p.m. – After the web is duct-taped together, the press starts running again.

3:35 p.m. – An ear-piercing grinding noise, like a giant dentist's drill, fills the air as the press screeches to a halt. The gear assembly has locked down, causing the drive line to separate. Like when the transmission falls out of your car, this breakdown will take time to repair.

3:36 p.m. – Walter posts a notice on the front door stating that the paper will be one hour late.

3:39 p.m. – A salesman appears, trying to sell us a new press. Walter informs the salesman that they don't make presses like they used to, comparing our press to another fine machine of the same era, the Model T. Ford. It will get you there—eventually, Walter claims, while showing the salesman the door.

3:40 p.m. – Jamie Smith calls Katie Smith to discuss renting a movie tonight.

3:43 p.m. – Katie calls Jamie with a list of her movie choices.

4:30 p.m.- Walter changes the sign on the front door to announce that the paper will be ready at 5 p.m. Several dozen customers, who have been waiting just inside the front door, become restless.

4:31 p.m. – Having arrived at work a half hour early so she could get off early, Donna Dawley begins to pout.

4:35 p.m. – Joel FitzPatrick's final thoughts are X-rated because he will be so late delivering papers that he will miss playing pseudo ice hockey on roller skates at the Cannon Street gym.

4:37 p.m. – Lori Sondov rushes out the door after receiving an emergency call from the day care center saying that her daughter has taken a spill.

5:10 p.m. – Walter changes the front door sign again, stating the paper will be ready in another 45 minutes. Most of the remaining customers start drifting away.

5:26 p.m. - Theresa "Granny" Williams phones Belk's to inquire what time the Senior Citizens Day Sale ends.

5:46 p.m. – Walter is getting nervous. The company has a policy of buying pizza for all employees when the press is not running by 6 p.m.

5:47 p.m. – Lori returns with daughter in tow. She is nursing a hangnail.

6:01 p.m. – No paper yet. The only question now is whether to order pepperoni or sausage pizzas. If the press, coveted by The Smithsonian, doesn't start by midnight, then we will have to send out to the Aweful House for breakfast.

6:02 p.m. - Granny volunteers to pick up the pizzas.

6:05 p.m. – Kris Gordon returns with a tale of woe about getting lost on Main Street in Landrum.

6:06 p.m. – Katie Smith calls Jamie Smith to say that she may not be home before the Blockbuster movie rental store closes.

7:45 p.m. – Granny returns with the pizzas, having been delayed by a detour to check out the sale at Belk's.

7:46 p.m. – But there's no time to eat. The press starts running. Everyone hustles to start putting the papers together.

7:46 p.m. – Granny remembers she had not paid her electric bill and dashes out the door to the Duke Power office on the corner.

7:50 p.m. – It's Walter's turn to shine. He begins gluing address labels on papers by hand using the "Wing Mailer" as has been done every Wednesday since 1925. As long as something works, why change?

7:59 p.m. – The high school kids start loading bundles of stamped papers for a trip to the Post Office in the company's vintage 30-year-old Chevy pickup truck. Our un-rock-like Chevy looks and runs like a burned out charcoal briquette, but it knows the way to the Post Office by heart.

8:14 p.m. – Lois Stringer disappears when a nine-foot high stack of papers that she is putting together collapses in a landslide.

8:17 p.m. – Hope springs eternal. I sit down at my computer to start working on next week's paper, thinking that it might actually come out on time.

Bullock's Barbershop

The Last Stand – May 20, 1987

Some of you may have thought that Jim Bakker and Jessica Hawn or perhaps Gary Hart and Donna Rice were the hottest items in the news in the headlines of 1987. Well, you would be wrong.

The really big news is that the courts have ordered the Rotary Club to admit female members. And if the Rotary can be made to accept women, can the Lions and Kiwanis be far behind?

When women begin taking over civic clubs, men's lib will have been dealt a serious, if not fatal, blow. That will leave only a shrinking number of barbershops as the last bastion of male supremacy.

Even now, an increasing number of lady barbers are cutting men's hair and vice-versa. One of the few remaining holdouts is Mike Bullock who is preparing for a last stand against the feminist movement from behind the brick wall in his barbershop on Trade Street in downtown Greer.

Ordinarily, Bullock does not make headlines. Just the opposite. Bullock usually gathers the news while standing and listening for hours to all sorts of tall tales, gossip and virtues of the Carolina Gamecocks football (or Clemson Tigers, depending on who's in the chair).

Every Tuesday afternoon, we rush a reporter over to the barbershop and Bullock passes on all the latest news. That's how we stay on top of things at *The Greer Citizen*.

This week, however, Bullock himself is the news. One of our correspondents just walked in with word that Bullock is remodeling the barbershop, apparently getting into the Main Street USA Revitalization swing of things.

Not only that, our source says Bullock is planning to upgrade his line of services. No, he's not installing a shoeshine stand because no Greer resident would wear shiny shoes. The big news is that Bullock is building a tanning booth in the back room.

Our reporter believes that Bullock's tanning booth will be in great demand because of its numerous features. There will be a one-arm section for truck drivers who want their right arm to match the tan left one, and a no-arm booth for golfers who wear alligator shirts. The longest lines are expected to form for the neck-down booth. That's where red necks can become red all over. Obviously, Greer will never be the same.

I Hate It When Bullock Goes on Vacation – July 17, 1996

The old men started gathering at daybreak on Monday. They unfolded nylon-webbed lawn chairs and plopped down on Trade Street to set watch. This happened at an almost leisurely pace, for the panic had subsided. Mike Bullock was scheduled to arrive at 8 a.m. to open the barbershop.

Bullock had been away on vacation for a week and, like an eclipse of the sun, everything had stood still in Greer during his absence.

I hate it when Bullock goes on vacation. He spends the following six months trying to catch up with the multitude of men who have fallen behind keeping their locks trimmed. That means a minimum of two hours is required to get a hair cut. That length of time, by the way, is how the city arrived at allocating two hours of free parking on downtown streets. Unfortunately, the city fathers have not taken the next step and installed a bench outside the barbershop to handle the overflow.

Sometimes the size of the crowd in Bullock's waiting room can fool you. Sometimes there are several men who have just come inside to sit around and shoot the bull.

"I hope all of you aren't waiting for a haircut," declared J.D. Owens as he headed for the last empty seat on Thursday. But that was not the case. All ten occupying the seats were waiting on the big chair.

It's not too bad today," observed Billy White. "I've only had to wait an hour and 45 minutes so far."

"I hadn't meant to take the morning off from work, but it looks like I just did," said another friend (who would be in serious trouble if I shared his name), as he emerged from the big chair at high noon.

I had arrived just ahead of a man who claimed that he had driven 25 miles from Lake Bowen for a hair cut. "Why don't you take appointments?" the man complained to Bullock.

"Because I would have to hire a secretary to answer the phone," Bullock explained, never even looking up from contemplating the finishing touches of a flat-top style that another barber would need surveying equipment to create.

The phone rings away as callers anxiously inquire about the number presently waiting for haircuts.

One young mother called to check on her son whom she had deposited in the waiting room two hours earlier. With a haircut thrown in, Bullock is operating the most economical baby-sitting service in town.

I decided that a cottage industry could spring up for those willing to sit still by the hour and hold places in line for paying clients.

The passage of time in the barbershop is marked by a 1950s-era wall clock with an advertisement for Beason's Jewelers, a small business that was once a landmark across Trade Street. The clock even provides light. It shines through a large gap in the face, which is probably the only reason that George Beason ever parted with it.

The barbershop furniture is indestructible, although OSHA may require Bullock to install seatbelts to prevent customers from sliding into the floor when they fall sound asleep while waiting. Still, customers flock in undeterred. Bullock's would be the last place in town to be evacuated in the path of a hurricane.

Hair care merchandise is displayed on an antique desk. (I had plenty of time to take a mental inventory). Bullock has enough combs (three dozen) and ten hairbrushes. But I became concerned about the supply of hair tonic. The stock was down to just one bottle of royal purple-colored Sure-Lay, the forerunner of Castrol GTX synthetic motor oil, and three bottles of Lucky Tiger, which was my favorite when I was in the eighth grade in the 1950s.

Eventually I moved on to better things, including writing this column and catching up on the latest sports news. It seems that Clemson is negotiating with the Dream Team (of Johnny Cochrane and F. Lee Bailey) to coordinate the football defense this fall.

Obviously, I get a lot done while waiting at Bullock's. I hope he doesn't spoil things by deciding to take appointments.

Economic Crisis in Downtown Greer - Jan. 19, 2005

Downtown Greer is caught up in the throes of the greatest economic crisis since the police drove shoppers away by marking tires and writing parking tickets. Last Monday, Mike Bullock raised the price of a haircut in the Center of the Universe.

At first, I thought Bullock must have ESP because I happened to have an extra dollar in my pocket when I walked into the barber shop and saw the large sign posted on the Pepsi vending machine stating simply: "Hair Cuts Increase $1."

Bullock blames the increase on the fact that downtown Greer has evolved into an upscale retail venue catering to the more affluent. If Gerard's can charge $20 for a plate of spaghetti and the Great Bay Oyster House can serve a $7.50 hamburger, then haircuts should cost more as well, he reasons.

In other words, a domino effect is occurring in downtown Greer, sort of like a California mud slide without the mud.

Paying $1 more for a haircut may not seem like a lot, but I figure that it amounts to $800 over a lifetime. Which is equal to a handful of nights out on the town in Greer. Fortunately, or more so unfortunately, I don't have that many haircuts remaining. Even so, I am having to decide what must be sacrificed, as a person on a fixed income (no pay raise in six years), to afford a haircut.

I may have to postpone buying an I-Pod for 15 years. Or refill empty bottled water containers from the bathroom faucet instead of buying fresh bottles from the company vending machine.

Bullock's sign does not state the cost of a haircut, only the amount of the price hike. And so, one of the many newcomers spilling into town from New York, Chicago, etc. may just plunk down $30 plus $1; or $40 plus $1; etc. having been accustomed to paying such prices for a trim. Then Bullock can afford to start closing on Fridays as well as Saturdays.

In Bullock's defense, a haircut is not the only amenity that comes with visiting the barbershop. While relaxing for a couple of hours waiting to be ushered past the brick wall to the barber's chair, customers are regaled with Ken Emery's tales of delivering newspapers and his cheap customers who won't leave a tip.

Adding spice to the entertainment, such characters as Ronnie Bruce, Tommy Williams and Steve Brown drop in to needle Emery about his record as the poorest football prognosticator in the Greer Touchdown Club. Occasionally, J. Van Collins stops by to seek donations for his favorite charity--himself.

Nevertheless, the fallout from the price increase has been immediate and downright frantic. On Thursday night, the Greer Kiwanis Club summoned Nicole Southgate to share the warning signs of depression (part of her Miss Greer platform), should it strike those who can no longer afford a haircut.

When he learned of the haircut hike, while sipping free coffee at Citizens Building and Loan the next morning, Walter came running back up the street, nearly out of breath, screeching, "We've got to raise the price of newspapers to keep up." He figures if Bullock can go up 10 percent, then a subscription should cost 20 percent more.

News travels fast. As I was leaving the barbershop, the phone rang. It was Robin Leach pleading to include the barbershop in his upcoming "Lifestyles of the Rich and Famous" PBS documentary on downtown Greer.

And in Washington, D.C., Alan Greenspan got wind of the spiraling haircut prices and called an emergency meeting of the Federal Reserve Board to analyze whether runaway inflation in Greer will infect the cosmetology industry nationwide.

Believe-it-or-Not:
Strange Folks, Events

From John Doe to Hero - June 8, 2005

Everywhere I went in Greenville County for 20 years, I was known as "Mr. Margaret Burch." My wife was well known as a school board member, and I was merely an afterthought. So I can empathize with Ernest E. "Buddy" Clayton who has been known for years in Greer as "Mr. Elizabeth Dillard." That's what happens when you are married to the sister of Steve Dillard and the niece of Senator J. Verne Smith.

I once erroneously referred to Buddy by the name "Mr. Dillard" in the newspaper. And a pastor of our church, Rev. Ray White, introduced him as 'Buddy Dillard' before a crowd of several hundred people attending a regional church event.

Not only did he get no respect from fellow church members, Clayton also seemed unable to establish an identity in the professional world. A pharmacist, he unluckily worked for drug store chains that kept going out of business, chains like Rite Aid, Revco, and more recently, Bi-Lo, which was sold out from under him.

Then everything changed. In a flash, Clayton went from an ordinary John Doe to a genuine hero.

It happened one morning when Clayton, who had been transferred to a Bi-Lo supermarket in Berea, observed a man trying to sneak out the door with a package under his arm. Since the man had not been through the checkout line, the package set off an alarm. Clayton yelled for the man to stop, but the suspect ran.

Clayton followed, carrying a large plastic cup of iced tea that he had been sipping from, even as fellow employees urged him to let the shoplifter go.

Outside, Clayton set the cup on a window ledge and began chasing the suspect. What the shoplifter did not know is that Clayton was a track star in college, and he has continued to run for recreation during his adult life.

"You might as well stop because I can run all day!", Clayton yelled at the thief.

The suspect obviously did not believe him and continued to run for blocks with Clayton in hot pursuit. Eventually, the suspect turned a corner and headed across the street where he happened to crash into the side of a moving car. The impact knocked the thief to the pavement, causing him to drop the five-pound bag of frozen shrimp that he had stolen. Clayton was standing over him in a flash. Soon the assistant store manager drove up (having decided early on in the chase that an automobile was a more efficient means of transportation than shoe leather.)

Within a couple of minutes after that, a police squad car arrived and hauled the suspect off to jail. While the shoplifter was being booked, he asked only one question "who was that man in the white coat?"

Clayton walked (not ran) back to the store, collecting his cup of iced tea on the way. Thus, the news spread like wildfire about how Clayton had run a couple of miles and apprehended a shoplifter without spilling a single drop of tea in the cup he was carrying.

He was somewhat deflated, however, when relating the incident to his wife. "The poor old man was hungry. Why didn't you just let him have the food?", Elizabeth wanted to know.

Clayton said the man should have asked for food, not stolen it. "Too many people shoplift all the time, and we can't allow it," he explained.

Then Clayton's wife scolded him for chasing the thief. "What if he had had a gun? He could have shot you," she pointed out. "That's not worth a bag of shrimp."

"I guess I can't win, either way," Clayton decided gloomily.

Just Call Him Sparky – June 22, 1994

The odds would have been better for my brother-in-law, Gary Griffin, to win the lottery than what happened to him last Wednesday afternoon. He was struck by lightning and actually lived to tell about it.

The electrifying incident took place at the Lakeview Golf Club near Piedmont. It was witnessed by two other golfers who had made a wise decision not to ride in the same golf cart with Griffin.

Griffin should have run for the clubhouse when an angry-looking black cloud appeared on the horizon about 5:30 p.m. But, being the true Scotsman that he is, Griffin did not even think twice about the risk involved in finishing the last two holes on his round. After all, he had paid to play them all.

As he walked off the 17th green, a bolt from above lit up a near-by tree, shot across the grass and zapped Griffin through his metal-spiked golf shoes. The hot charge burned the hair on Griffin's legs and chest as it traveled upward.

Fortunately, Griffin had lost most of his hair over time, so there wasn't much to singe when the electrical charge exited through the top of his head. If Griffin had been sporting a head full of curls, he would have lit up like a Roman candle.

In the spilt second when the shocking experience occurred, Griffin said his life did not flash before his eyes. He merely remembered all the bad golf shots that he had hit that day.

A true Scotsman, Griffin demanded a refund from the golf course because he never completed the round. He was hauled away in an ambulance to the emergency room before he could stagger on to the 18th tee box.

Griffin also considered suing, but his attorney refused to return his phone calls.

The Greer Commission of Public Works (CPW) has ordered limited edition posters showing Griffin holding a lightning rod and advocating recreational electrification. These will go on sale Friday, first come, first serve for anyone who can get through the maze at the CPW.

That's not all. Griffin (now known as Sparky) has suffered considerable emotional trauma trying to figure out why he, of all people, had been struck by lightning. Griffin swears he wrote down his customary double bogey on the scorecard for the 17th hole instead of attempting to fudge with a six.

He also doesn't recall taking money out of the offering plate as it passed by at church on Sunday morning. But his pastor continues to insist that Griffin is a wonderful source of sermon material.

I have figured out that Griffin was struck because he was telling another one of his bad jokes. Not that his jokes are sacrilegious or blasphemous. I think he was being a bore as usual, and God let him have it.

I have never been struck by lightning on the golf course because I never play golf on Wednesdays, and I never play at Lakeview, even though Griffin obviously gets a charge out of the place. And for good measure, I never play golf without taking my preacher along.

No Points for Interior Decorating - Sept. 12, 2001

Men who retire early should be placed in the Witness Protection Program. John Williams comes to mind. The unfortunate man has experienced nothing but trouble since he retired from Roadway Express for the good life on the farm in the Dark Corner. With too much time on his hands, Williams gets into things—not mischief, mind you, but things he wouldn't fool with if he was still punching a time clock.

Last fall during the hunting season, Williams fired so many rounds of buckshot that herds of deer fled from Union and Laurens counties and came this way. More of the frightened animals were killed attempting to cross South Highway 101 than Williams ever brought home strapped to the hood of his '78 Chevy pickup truck.

When the weather turned cold, Williams came indoors and took up another hobby, cooking. As one who is culinary challenged, I can attest that the kitchen is no place for ordinary men. In fact, the kitchen is off limits for Williams whenever his wife, Theresa (better known as "Granny") is at home. But Williams enjoys the kitchen so much that he has refused to hear of Granny retiring from her part time job at the newspaper office. Even so, Granny manages to be at home guarding the kitchen most of the time because she figures out ways to take holidays that we didn't even know existed—holidays such as Groundhog Day and the anniversary of Martha Stewart's divorce.

Amazingly, however, Granny reported for duty last Monday on Labor Day, which is just another working day in the newspaper business. Her husband wasted no time in sneaking back into the kitchen. It had taken several months, but Williams eventually perfected a recipe for cabbage soup, perhaps forgetting in the process that this dish blew up more Europeans than all of the artillery shells that were fired during World War II. Now Williams was ready to try his hand at another delicacy—turnip greens.

Williams wanted results in a hurry, so he dumped a box of frozen greens into an old fashioned pressure cooker. That was the utensil of choice for creating a quick dish before the advent of microwave ovens.

Granny had barely arrived at the office that morning before the phones started ringing off the hooks. Hundreds of people were calling, not to inquire if we were open for business on a holiday, but to report witnessing a strange unidentified flying object streaking across the morning sky.

It wasn't long until a call came from John Williams. There had been an accident on the order of the infamous incident when a little old lady attempted to dry off her rain-soaked poodle in the microwave. The pressure cooker had exploded. Somehow the lid missed decapitating Williams and shot out the window, last seen headed toward Atlanta. The turnip greens had converted the once snow-white kitchen ceiling to a soggy, moss-like green mush.

Granny left immediately to assist with the clean up. The next day, she was late for work. When she finally arrived, Granny explained that not even a pressure washer would blast the turnip greens from the ceiling. Now the rest of the kitchen will have to be painted green to match.

I advised Granny to find the silver lining in the dark cloud. It could have been worse—exploding collards would have provided a powerful fragrance to accompany the new color scheme.

Granny contended that a more thoughtful husband would have cooked a pot roast on the stove instead of turnip greens. Then, if lunch exploded, it would have blended in with the beige color scheme on the walls.

John Williams doesn't get any points for interior decorating, and he is definitely overdrawn when it comes to cooking. But in all fairness, Williams was bored having already watched all of the reruns of Bonanza three times since retiring.

No Good Deed Goes Unpunished – Jan. 29, 2003

Marsha Lurey Strong is one who focuses on shepherding Greer's 'po but proud' in so many ways, serving as either an Indian or a Chief in nearly every worthwhile community cause.

Such a lifestyle can be demanding. In fact, Strong is living proof of the theory "no good deed goes unpunished." An example is what happened during Strong's regular Sunday morning trip to the Publix supermarket in Greenville to pick up the chain's leftover breads, cakes, donuts and other outdated foodstuffs for the Greer Soup Kitchen. She piles the food to the ceiling of her compact car, often leaving barely enough room to get behind the wheel.

Strong had made this trip every Sunday for six years without incident until January 12. That day, Strong arrived at the Soup Kitchen, unlocked the door, set down her purse and headed back to the car to unload the bread. A puff of wind blew the door closed, automatically locking Strong's purse, which contained her cell phone and car keys, inside the building.

So Strong, dressed in her Sunday best, set out in her high-heeled shoes on the one-mile hike to the Greer Police Department to get help.

"Can you give me a key to the Soup Kitchen? I'm locked out," Strong asked the officer on duty when she arrived at the police station 20 minutes later.

"We can't just give the key to anyone," the desk officer said. The U.S. Department of Homeland Security apparently had warned police that in the event of a terrorist attack on the Soup Kitchen, the enemy would likely be disguised in Sunday church garb instead of robes and turbans or military fatigues.

Strong took the denial in the wrong way, assuming the officer thought she intended to burglarize the place. "If I was going to break in somewhere, it sure wouldn't be the Soup Kitchen," she huffed.

"Well, why do you want to get in the Soup Kitchen?" the officer asked.

"Because I have a car full of bread to drop off there," Strong answered.

"Just where is the Soup Kitchen," the officer asked, trying to poke a hole in her story.

"On East Poinsett Street, of course," Strong replied.

Satisfied that he had grilled Strong sufficiently, the officer said, "Okay. I'll call someone to let you in."

His first ten phone calls failed to turn up a single person connected with Daily Bread Ministries that operates the Soup Kitchen.

Finally, Strong suggested "Call Jo Sullivan. I'll bet she will come downtown and unlock the door."

"Can you come to the jail and pick up Marsha Strong?" asked the officer when Sullivan answered the phone.

"I guess so," Sullivan said. "What do you have her for?"

"She's trying to get into the Soup Kitchen," the officer replied.

When Sullivan arrived at the police station, the officer asked "do you feel safe with her in your car, or would you like for a policeman to go with you to the Soup Kitchen?"

"I think I'll be all right," Sullivan replied.

The incident did not sit well with Strong's mother, Leah Lurey, who had baked a cake and delivered it to the police department every Monday morning for the past ten years. Mrs. Lurey launched her homemade cake ministry in a "turn-the-other cheek" response to having been issued a traffic ticket when she inadvertently attached a renewal sticker to the wrong side of the license plate on her car.

Although Greer's Finest have devoured more than 500 of Mrs. Lurey's cakes, without acquiring even a hint of a guilt complex, her strategy had failed to gain an ounce of clout. That prompted Mrs.

Lurey to blurt out "you're the one who arrested my daughter!" when she delivered yet another cake the following morning.

The offending officer, whose name is Custer, wasn't about to come out to confront Mrs. Lurey who stands 4'10" and weighs no more than 85 pounds soaking wet. Custer chose to make his last stand from behind the triple-paned, bulletproof window that guards his office, and persuaded a colleague to go out and collect the cake instead.

The Ambulance Driver – July 26, 1989

I don't know if the incident was a mid-life crisis or a childhood dream come true. At any rate, for one fleeting moment a Greer man discovered his true calling. Put away the books, wipe off the black-board, and stop shuffling the papers, Tommy Hughes. This elementary school principal and former assistant to four area public school superintendents found his place in the sun as an ambulance driver.

This is the true story of how Hughes' neighbor and friend, Sam Clayton, made the dream come true.

Clayton, it seems, decided to cut down a tree that he had been neglecting for years. Armed with a chain saw, Clayton was wearing tennis shoes for the occasion. (I don't know what to think about anyone who saws trees wearing tennis shoes. My personal preference is loafers when handling such difficult outdoor jobs).

Anyway, Clayton began whacking the limbs off a sapling that had sprung up in a flowerbed (many years ago). Not slowing down as he neared the base of the tree, Clayton whacked off the top of a tennis shoe.

Upon realizing that he had chain sawed his big toe, Clayton began screaming for help.

Hughes, being the good neighbor that he is, rushed over to see what the commotion was all about.

He then agreed to drive Clayton to the emergency room, on the condition that they go in Clayton's brand new Jeep Cherokee. Hughes had always wanted to drive a Jeep.

Clayton however, was reluctant to use his wife's new vehicle. But he made the trip riding in the back seat, heels over head so to speak, to elevate his foot in the air over his head to keep from bleeding on the spotless upholstery.

Hughes claims that he did not exceed the speed limit getting to the hospital, but he did run off the road several times, not to mention hitting three nasty pot holes that bounced Clayton off the back seat each time. "I was trying to pick up a good station on the radio," Hughes explained in defense of his driving.

Once the pair had arrived at the emergency room, the ever-helpful Hughes raced inside and commandeered a wheel chair. As soon as he got Clayton seated in the wheel chair, Hughes turned to make sure the new car was safe and secure.

At that fateful moment, the wheel chair broke free. Gathering speed as it zoomed down a hill, the wheel chair slammed into the wall of the emergency room. All the while, Clayton was still holding his injured foot high in the air.

That mishap left Clayton too dazed to sign in with receptionist. But Hughes barely slowed down at the desk anyway. He pushed Clayton straight in to surgery where a team of doctors jumped into action working on the injured toe.

Then, Clayton demanded that the medics get the job done without putting him to sleep. Clayton claimed he wanted to be awake for his high school class reunion that night. I learned later, however, that the real reason Clayton refused an anesthetic was that he didn't want Hughes to drive his new car on the trip home.

The Unhappy Camper – Feb. 14, 1990

If the term "unhappy camper" ever accurately described an individual, that person is Conrad Robertson. And if the following story has a moral, it is that life can be exciting even for the vice president of the oldest, most stodgy bank in the land.

The story begins when Robertson's motor home blew up at a rest stop in Florida. That's right, it exploded with Robertson inside.

No one is sure what happened. The explosion wasn't caused by a buildup of hot air because J.N. McFadden wasn't along for the trip. Thank goodness Robertson wasn't injured, because he was going to need all of his strength to cope with what happened next.

Robertson finally got his motor home into a repair shop on March 10, and was promised the work would be completed in 60 days, by May 10th, just in time for the summer camping season.

But on May 10th Robertson's motor home wasn't ready. As a matter of fact, it wasn't ready on June 10th either.

Then July 10th passed with no camper, and then August 10th came and went, along with the numerous other times in between when Robertson went to the repair shop to check on things. But the manager did warn Robertson that his weekly visits were delaying completion of the shop's repairs!

As of September 10th the motor home had been in the shop for six months, and Robertson was determined to get it back, having already missed an entire summer of camping.

When Robertson finally took delivery of the vehicle, he drove only a couple of blocks before the engine overheated and stalled. It seems the repairman who had drained the radiator, which also feeds a rear bedroom heater, had forgotten to refill the system with water.

After correcting that problem, Robertson noticed that the cabinet doors were flying open as he began rounding a few curves on the trip to his Blue Ridge residence. On closer inspection, Robertson discovered the repair shop had failed to install catches on the new cabinet doors.

Looking inside the cabinets, Robertson observed the unit's wiring harness stretched across the middle of the storage space. The motor home had been rewired with not an inch to spare. Robertson had to splice and lengthen every wire in order to get the cable above the cabinets and out of the way.

While that project was in progress, Robertson discovered that the old wiring had not been entirely removed. Loose ends were protruding from dark corners, under the carpet, etc. Lately, he has taken to touching some of the wires together to see if any lights will come on. If he finds a 110-volt wire, Robertson himself will light up.

Other things have been even more noticeable. Examining the motor home during daylight, Robertson discovered the license tag was missing. It seems that one of the repairmen had "borrowed" the tag to use on a car and "forgotten" to put it back.

The repair shop also misplaced the exterior fiberglass trim panels, which skirted one side and the rear of the motor home. To this day, the panels have not been found.

Glancing at the toilet, Robertson was startled to see the pavement below. It seems that the toilet had not been piped into the unit's sewer tank.

But there was no danger of the hot water heater blowing up again. It hadn't been reconnected either.

To top it off, the firm that "repaired" his motor home has gone out of business and in the process threatened to sue Robertson for having caused them so much grief!

By Truman's Red Glare - Feb. 5, 1997

Truman Henderson's hair is the only thing I've seen that comes close to matching the color of the highly sought Tickle Me Elmo doll. At least it was as of Feb. 1, 1997. That was the occasion of Greer High School's Shakespearean Festival, although Henderson's flaming presence gave it an aura of an MTV production. He stole the show from Macbeth, Romeo, Juliet and all those other 400-year-old characters.

It was just like that time on the same stage, back in the Medieval 1950s, when Henderson beamed, bowed and gathered in a bouquet of red roses following his memorable performance in the high school play.

Fast-forward 40 years to last Friday when dozens of hens, seated around the founding father of GARP, were clucking. They were returning the same type of grief that Henderson has been known to dish out. The ladies were asking pointed questions and offering opinions about his hair. It was a shade of red in the range that is sometimes seen on two other world famous personalities, Sen. Strom Thurmond and NBA star Dennis Rodman.

And Henderson will be raising eyebrows for some time because he bought an expensive dye. It won't wash out.

"Actually my hair didn't start out this color" explained Henderson, recounting the details of the botched hair affair. "I just wanted to blend a little color in with the gray. We kept adding color to it, trying to get the correct shading. But it kept getting worse and worse instead."

Henderson said his mane had absorbed so much dye that it will have to grow out in order to return to its natural color. That could take months.

As for why he took the plunge into the fountain of youth, Henderson explained patiently to dozens of questioners: "I just can't decide what I'm going to do when I grow up."

I will concede that Henderson's excuse sounds reasonable enough. But don't you think it's a little late for him to be having a mid-life crisis? Besides, I'm concerned about his chances of landing the TV commercial role of the speeding driver who the traffic cop can't recognize from the man's gray-haired driver's license photo.

On the other hand, Henderson did not think much of my suggestion that he could wear a yellow suit and sign autographs in front of McDonald's.

Since Henderson is far from being totally gray anyway, the dye job is a waste of money in my book. And what if a groundhog saw his reflection in Henderson's Red Glare the next day? We would be doomed to six more months of winter!

Henderson is one of the few people in Greer who has the luxury of quitting work while he makes up his mind what to do next. I wish I had that kind of nerve. Since I'm still waiting for my ship to come in, I put on my best suit on Sunday for the Super Bowl. I was sure the Prize Patrol was coming to deliver the $10 million check from Publisher's Clearing House, and I wanted to look my best. Somehow they couldn't find my house.

When my prize does arrive, I will become bold and venturesome. I think I will dye my hair too. I haven't done anything so daring since I was in the eighth grade and showed up at school one day with green hair. Next time I will be a blonde. They say blondes have more fun. I'll bet a set of bright yellow locks would get me straight to the chair at Bullock's Barber Shop with no waiting.

Things That Went Wrong

Murphy's Law Strikes – July 17, 2002

One of my golfing buddies brought up the subject of reincarnation the other day. He was speculating that people will return to earth at some point in the future in a new life form, like a gold fish, a pet rock or even another person.

I decided we would make all the same mistakes again if we were destined to live another life. And that would be pretty boring since the one lesson that every ancient person has learned is: "The more things change, the more they stay the same."

I went on to review the list of life's lessons learned. At the very top is: "One can never sit back and bask in the glow of success for very long until something comes along to put you back in your proper place." And, no truer words were ever spoken than "the best laid plans of mice and men oft go awry."

The latter was again demonstrated in the Center of the Universe on a long-awaited day of celebration. After years of planning, raising money and overcoming countless obstacles, the Partnership for Tomorrow finally succeeded in completing the long-awaited Five Points Streetscape. An elaborate, festive dedication celebration had been planned, replete with colorful tents, cloth-covered picnic tables and mouth-watering delicacies prepared by Chef Gerard Cribbin who had just opened Greer's first upscale restaurant, Gerard's. And the new town clock was to be unveiled.

Engraved invitations had been mailed to the cream of Greer society, and everyone from J. Van Collins to Charlie Williams was dressed in his Sunday best for the occasion.

Then Murphy's Law, "Anything that can possibly go wrong will go wrong," kicked into effect.

I must confess that several days earlier, I had become suspicious that something was amiss. I observed that many of the new downtown trees had gotten out of synch with Mother Nature and gone into the autumn mode. Their leaves had started turning brown and dropping onto the new imitation-brick crosswalks.

Given that sign, we should have realized that the meticulous plans for the big event were on a collision course with the prayers for rain that millions had been offering up for weeks. About an hour before the dedication ceremony was to begin, those prayers were answered when the first meaningful rainfall in two months poured from the skies.

Sheets of liquid sunshine washed the ceremony indoors to the second floor of the Chamber of Commerce building. There, dignitaries regrouped and carried on by cutting a ribbon that had been hastily tacked across the fire exit at the back door.

There are many more reasons why the day was forgettable, especially around the newspaper office. Ever since the air conditioning repairman paid another visit to the company and got the cool air flowing again, the outside temperature had been in the balmy 70s for three straight days.

As further evidence of another truism, "bad things always happen in threes," staff member Lori Sondov's daughter, Savannah, accepted an invitation to go roller skating that day and came home with a broken wrist.

And that night, a culvert jumped up and hit the car driven by printing press operator, Wess Skinner. He spent a couple of days in the hospital, delaying the production of school calendars for Visions of Excellence.

None of the above, however, can compare with what happened to Gary Vaughn at the Greer Country Club on the same day. In his best Tiger Woods imitation, Vaughn attempted to whack a golf ball through a clump of trees. But the ball refused to cooperate and centered a tree trunk, caromed straight back and hit Vaughn squarely in the mouth. Vaughn would not have been injured had he kept his head down as golfers are taught. As it turned out, however, the impact knocked out six teeth. Now Vaughn has room in his mouth for an entire sleeve of golf balls.

I know of only one other person who suffered a similar fate on the links. Lynn Bomar once blasted a ball that shot backwards off a tree trunk, striking him in the forehead and knocking him out cold as a cucumber. This also occurred at the Greer County Club, which, by the way, has a special membership rate for ambulance-chasing lawyers.

Riders of the Last Bus – Sept. 27, 1989

A new movie *Riders of the Last Bus*, a real-life adventure series patterned after the Indiana Jones films, was shot in Greer. It features true stories of the Greer Senior Citizens Club that has proven thrills begin at age 65.

Membership in the club isn't for the faint-hearted. It takes a lot of nerve to climb onto the aging Greer City bus for an adventurous journey, not knowing where it will end up or when you will return home.

Something nostalgic lures seniors to the city bus. They are reminded of the "good old days" that their great-grandfathers talked about, because riding the city bus is like riding in a Conestoga wagon. Every bump travels up and down your spine.

One such bus adventure started out as a trip to Gatlinburg, Tenn., on a Thursday morning. Believe it or not, the '76 Bicentennial Bus made it past the city limits and as far as Hendersonville, N.C, in time for breakfast.

Afterwards, those who dined on oat bran were only concerned about making it to the first rest stop. That would have proved to be an adventure in itself, but an even greater thrill was lurking just ahead. The old bus sputtered onward another 20 miles to Asheville where it collapsed in front of a mall.

The city bus refused to budge, no matter what was said or done. In fact, if the senior citizens had traveled in the opposite direction to Charleston instead, our Greer bus would have been a hero. It would have stopped Hurricane Hugo dead in its tracks.

But no such luck. So the Greer senior citizens were marched into the Asheville Mall to wait while the city's best minds attempted to decide what to do.

No reputable Asheville mechanic was willing to risk his reputation on a losing battle with the Greer bus. Eventually, the City of Greer's own mechanic was dispatched to make repairs. It would have been easier to jack up the old bus and drive a new one underneath. Only after the bus got a new fuel pump, new spark plugs and a change of oil did it finally start. By then, it was 6 p.m. which makes "Riders of the Lost Bus" a long running production.

During the nine hours that they were imprisoned in the mall, the Greer seniors had time to memorize the price of every pair of socks in the building. Some got indigestion after eating the mall lunch of a cold fish sandwich and French fries.

Those seniors who paced up and down the mall were cared for by an emergency response team armed with Dr. Scholl's foot aids. But those who developed aching buns from sitting on the hard benches had to fend for themselves.

By the end of the day, the senior citizens had lost all hope of ever visiting Gatlinburg. Yet they were understandably reluctant to climb aboard the city bus for the next adventure—the return trip to Greer.

With that, the city fathers decided to replace the ramshackle bus with a couple of old, worn out vans. That move is aimed at doubling the excitement on the next senior citizens big adventure.

Editor's Career at Low Ebb – Feb. 8, 1995

After 30 years in journalism, I should have progressed up the ladder to something really worthwhile, like being a member of the White House press corps or reporting for *60 Minutes*. Instead, it seems my career has been spent on a treadmill. This shocking truth hit Friday night when I found myself covering a donkey basketball game.

Not only have I failed to attain Pulitzer Prize status, I also haven't learned many of the tricks of the trade. Instead of using a press pass to finagle my way into the game, I paid at the door like everyone else.

"What idiot assigned our sports coverage this week?" I asked myself repeatedly while waiting for the donkeys to arrive. Then, when I went into the men's restroom and looked in the mirror, I recognized the idiot.

I felt better when I returned to the gym and saw how many people were about to be humiliated by agreeing to take part in the event.

I also decided that the sponsoring Greer Community Ministries (GCM) had violated the truth-in-advertising law with the claim that local "celebrities" would participate. The main reason I was there was to photograph Fire Chief Heyward Brissey making a fool of himself. But Brissey, in a bid to gain favor with Republicans in the crowd, invoked the concept of term limits. Brissey limited himself to zero terms. He refused to ride a single round.

Furthermore, such GCM luminaries as J.N. McFadden, Steve McAbee, Johnny Stack, George Gagnon and Jo Sullivan were nowhere to be found. And who told Larry Padgett he was a celebrity, even though he was a last-minute substitute for Ronnie Bruce? Even so, it was the biggest crowd I've seen since I tried to buy a stamp at the post office a few weeks ago.

The 'donkey' basketball billing also took on political overtones when it attracted a bunch of Democrats expecting an election rally. But they weren't disappointed, because Bill Clinton was Master of

Ceremonies. Even though Clinton didn't look like himself, I'm positive he was the MC. Before the game even started, he talked for more than an hour, and didn't say anything.

The absence of rosters added to the confusion. It was impossible to tell the donkeys and celebrities apart.

If that wasn't bad enough, it soon became obvious that none of the donkeys could play basketball. (At least, they showed up—all five of them. Thank goodness it wasn't donkey football).

I learned that the object of the game was for the donkeys and their would-be riders to get from one end of the gym to the other without falling down or stepping in something.

The spectacle of celebrity riders hanging onto donkeys' manes and tails for dear life reminded me of the opening rush at a Big Thursday bazaar. No wonder GCM sponsored the event!

During the halftime break, five volunteers scrambled around on the floor in an adult version of "pin the tail on the donkey." The winner was declared Miss Jackass 1995, and took home a case of canned grits. But the highlight was Mayor Don Wall winning the Donkey Look-Alike Contest.

James Paget stuck around afterwards to interview several donkeys about their ancestral ties to famous Greer families for his upcoming book on genealogy. "James!" I warned, "if this gets out, it won't help your book sales. By the way, please don't mention that I was here."

Greer Has Been Snubbed Throughout History

I Won't Miss the Phone Book - April 19, 1995

I have decided we should change the name of Greer to Rodney Dangerfield, S.C. Like the famous comedian, we don't get no respect.

Just think. Spartanburg County not only claimed the BMW plant, it also restricted our social life by cutting back the hours of operation at the Greer Drag Strip on Saturday nights. And now we suffer the ultimate insult—Ma Bell will no longer print a Greer telephone directory.

How are we going to look up phone numbers of lawyers to defend us from the next lawsuit? Folks are even wondering if the Kiwanis Pancake Supper will be the next to go.

An entire shelf in the new library was reserved for the phone book. Now it will be empty. What a tragedy.

I was hoping the phone company would move forward in a bold new direction by publishing a directory of unlisted numbers. It could be filled with blank pages, and you could write in a phone number whenever you happened to stumble across one.

I was planning to get an unlisted number for our fax machine, which has been receiving junk mail like the post office once delivered.

The fax is much harder on the company's bottom line because it keeps eating expensive paper.

Most of my friends have cell phones, and nobody knows those numbers either. That is another golden opportunity going begging. I won't even mention the crying need for a directory of answering machines, which are the only things that will talk to me anymore.

But we won't even have our Greer directory of ordinary phone numbers. We might as well assume that everyone in Greer has an unlisted number.

If you don't have a computer or time to dial every number in hopes of eventually finding the right person, you are going to have to search the new Greenville phone book. You will have to get past Greenville, Travelers Rest, Easley, Mauldin, Simpsonville, Ft. Inn, Taylors, etc. to find Greer. Instead of calling someone, it may be quicker to just hop in the car and visit in person.

But there is a brighter side to having a bigger phone book. It will eliminate visits to the athletic club. If you pick up the new phone book a few times a day and do a lot of finger walking (just try to find the number of a public school), then you will have had a healthy aerobic workout.

This will enable the phone company to charge extra for pumping you up. Call Lifting charges will be listed on the seventh line of the monthly phone bill, following Call Waiting, Call Girls, Call Forwarding, Call Holding, Call Hang-ups, Caller ID, and Cat Calls.

Still on the bright side, we have a replacement for the long lost Sears catalog. The new phone book will come in handy for those who still use outhouses. People with indoor plumbing can find other uses for the new book such as a barstool, a patio or a hamburger press.

The new phone book is bigger because it has more Yellow Pages from all over. This will give you the opportunity for real excitement by ordering a pizza from a parlor 40 miles away. If it doesn't arrive in

20 minutes, maybe it will be free. Otherwise, you can expect to pay a $25 delivery charge.

The expanded Yellow Pages will allow you to search the entire county for any item. You can plan an all-day outing to buy a loaf of bread in Piedmont, which is 50 miles, there and back.

Actually, I'm just kidding. I really won't miss our Greer phone book at all. I haven't had to use one since the year they took Charlie Williams' picture off the cover. You see, I have my own personal phone book that weighs 2,950 pounds. It is the wall behind my chair in my office. I have scratched every important number on the wall.

My wall book is very convenient. I can see all the numbers at a glance except when I am not in the office. Then I can't remember a single phone number. But my wife can. She is a walking phone directory. So I always carry her with me when I am going to be away from the wall.

I suggest that if you miss having your own Greer phone book, just do like me and get a wall. Or, better yet, get a wife who knows all the numbers.

Greer Folks Must Have Bad Breath – July 3, 1996

It was inevitable, of course. We should have known that the Olympic Torch would not be seen in Greer while crossing America.

You would think that as the Center of the Universe, Greer would get some respect. Not so. Never has gotten any respect, for that matter. Everyone in Greer is still waiting for his 15 minutes of fame.

Did you know:

*When General Sherman came marching through the South during the War Between the States, that he took the time to torch Atlanta and Columbia but did not even stop in Greer?

*Greer was about to become its own county until the idea was narrowly voted down in a referendum in the early 1900s?

*You can no longer board a train in Greer unless you are moving alongside it at 35 mph when the train slows for the Trade Street crossing?

*The airport located in Greer is named Greenville-Spartanburg – except when a Valu-Jet lands, then it is called Greer?

*An oil pipeline has never burst and polluted Maple Creek, although it is unlikely anyone would have noticed if such a catastrophe had occurred?

*BMW built a $600 million automobile assembly plant in Greer and calls it the Spartanburg Plant?

*No one has ever adopted a Greer highway?

*No Greer resident has ever had an action figure modeled after him or her?

*No Greer beauty has ever been crowned Miss America. Once upon a time, Greer did have a first runner up in the pageant at Atlantic City, but she was actually from Berea?

And the list of no respect goes on. Greer is the ultimate proof of such truisms as "if we didn't have bad luck, we wouldn't have any luck at all."

The latest example occurred last Tuesday when the Olympic Torch passed through Greer, shrouded inside a fast moving bus so that no one could see it. That was our punishment because the Greenville County Council had adopted a resolution condemning the gay lifestyle. I believe that an injustice has been done to the people of Greer. We had nothing to do with the anti-gay resolution. Few of us can read and even fewer can write a resolution. Furthermore, Greer people are not gay. Very few, in fact, are even considered to be happy.

Ever since Greer was snubbed by the Olympic torch, we have been running to mirrors to see what is wrong. Attendance has tripled at self-analysis seminars and sympathy support meetings. I have been wringing my hands trying to figure it out. And, at last, I have.

Bad breath is Greer's problem. Everyone has gone for the new fad of eating garlic-laced foods to prevent cancer. One whiff of Greer's breath would have sent the Olympic torch into vapor lock.

Fortunately we are planning corrective measures. An insurance firm has donated a portable breath analysis device to the police department so that Greer's Finest can get garlic-impaired drivers off the roads before they melt down the few traffic lights that are still working.

We may have missed the torch, but everyone who owns stock in Listerine mouthwash can expect a nice dividend check in the mail.

Greer Lifestyle

Two Grumpy Old Men - Aug. 27, 2003

Even after 42 years of pacing up and down the sidelines, I never get tired of high school football. I will get the same rush of adrenalin this Friday night when Greer High kicks off a new season at Dooley Field.

In fact, I am already well into the spirit of things, having taken in several scrimmages and jamborees. As always, half the fun is getting there—especially when Bunchy Godfrey hitches a ride to watch our beloved Yellow Jackets.

A conversation with Bunchy is better than talking to myself, but just barely. Our road trips are like a made for TV movie along the lines of "Grumpy Old Men" rather than "Driving Miss Daisy."

Take the recent jamboree at Daniel, for instance. Bunchy came along, even though I had to make a stop near Belton, which is well out of the way. As we were hashing over the football team's prospects, I asked, "What does Woody say about the Yellow Jackets?"

"Nothing," replied Bunchy, who is a fixture around the Greer High athletic complex this time of year. "Not a single word. Woody is talking about retiring though," Bunchy related.

"Retiring? He's too young to retire," I snorted. "Besides, what would he do?"

"I guess what he always does. He wouldn't change a thing," Bunchy said.

By that time we had reached the south side of Anderson. "If we take this by-pass, I bet we won't have to stop at all the traffic lights," I said.

Yeah, right. Some 15 minutes and 10 miles later we were in the middle of nowhere. "I've never seen this part of the world," said Bunchy. "Where are we?"

"I don't know, but we are getting there in a hurry," I said, looking at the speedometer, which was nudging 60 mph. "Anyway, what would you do if you were in your big rig right now?" I asked.

"Well, I'd stop and look at my road atlas. But we don't have it with us," Bunchy replied.

A few miles farther, we found a convenience store and stopped to ask directions. "The man said go several miles down this road, turn right at a silo, go through the next intersection and disregard the highway signs," Bunchy explained.

Ten minutes later, I asked, "By the way, how many are several miles?"
"I don't know, I forgot to ask," Bunchy replied.

Finally we came to what appeared to be a major highway, "I'm taking this road. It looks important," I said. Five miles further, up popped a sign that stated, "Turn around, road ends in 1,500 feet."

"There's no way this highway is going to run out," said Bunchy of the four-lane road that would do justice to the Verne Smith Parkway. But sure enough, after we topped a hill, the highway disappeared into Lake Hartwell.

Two wrong turns, another stop to seek directions and 45 minutes later, not to mention missing supper, we finally arrived in Central just as the Yellow Jackets were taking the field. "If I hadn't ridden with you, I would have gotten here in time to walk through the gate with the team. Now I have to buy a ticket to get inside," Bunchy grumped.

By 9 p.m. we were on our way home. "Let's get something to eat," I suggested.

"I know just the place in Easley," Bunchy said. "The food is great. I eat at the same restaurant in Greer all the time."

We sat down in a booth at 10 p.m., and Bunchy ordered a Philly cheese steak sandwich. When the food was delivered, Bunchy took one bite and exclaimed, "This is the worst sandwich I ever tasted! There's something wrong with this beef, like the cow had the West Nile virus."

When the waiter eventually returned, Bunchy said, "I don't think much of your food. I had to pull all the meat out, and I wound up with a lettuce and tomato sandwich."

"Would you like to talk to the manager?" the waiter asked. "No thanks," Bunchy said. "Just bring the check so we can get out of here."

When the check arrived, Bunchy laid down a $20 bill. "Would you like some change?" the waiter asked. "Of course!" Bunchy screeched. "My ticket was only $7.95."

"He had a lot of nerve, trying to work me for a $12 tip for the worst food I ever ate," Bunchy declared. "Just for that, I didn't leave him a tip."

An hour later, as we were nearing Greer, Bunchy groaned, "Step on it, Leland. I'm sick as a dog from that food, and I don't know which end is going to go off first. But something is about to happen."

A week later, the phone rang. It was Bunchy. "Leland, can I ride with you to the Byrnes Jamboree? Don't worry. I'll eat supper at home before we leave."

Strange Events in Greer History

Things May Soon Be Back to Normal – Nov. 14, 1992

To Mr. Don Hawkins
    Seattle, Wash.

Dear Don:

You will never believe what happened on Friday, just a week after your visit here. As we were sitting around celebrating the election of Bill Clinton, the end of the depression and living happily ever after, a news bulletin came across the TV screen. The flash warned us not to drink the water.

I almost panicked until I remembered that I haven't drunk water for 40 years. Long ago, I decided that any substance that can rust pipes isn't good for you. So I've drunk nothing but Pepsi Colas since the eighth grade.

Anyway, it seems that too many chemicals got dumped into the Greer water supply. Suddenly, the water was cleaner than ever. And that gave some DHEC authorities an opportunity to demonstrate the importance of their jobs before the new President began cutting their budget.

I must admit that the Commission of Public Works jumped right on the problem—nearly as fast as they send out the monthly bills.

The next thing I know, another news bulletin announced that a computer malfunction was responsible for over-purifying the water. I thought that made sense because computers have been fouling up our lives for years. Computers have put a lot of people out of work, especially in the typewriter and adding machine industry, and that caused the economy to tank.

Just in case there was foul play involved, however, the Greer Police were called to investigate. Lt. Steve Selby took charge immediately. The detective searched attics all over town and did not find a single water pipe.

Then the investigation turned toward Omaha, Neb. Some suspected it was a subversive attempt to lure the BMW plant away from Greer. Our new water might peel the paint right off their cars.

The water crisis impacted our people in a variety of ways:

1. It failed to change my wife's plans not to cook supper on Saturday night.
2. There was a distinct odor in churches everywhere on Sunday morning because no one took their weekly Saturday night bath.
3. Unofficial estimates are that the new water bleached the red out of the necks of 3,118 people.
4. The extra clean water would not freeze. The resulting ice shortage forced several local bars to close. Something like that has not happened since Prohibition.
5. The water did not contaminate the sewer system as many had feared.
6. The community survey, collected today, revealed that 34 percent of Greer residents like the new water better than the old.
7. The other 66 percent wasn't so sure. There was a run on bottled water in the grocery stores, and a black market was quick to spring (no pun intended) up. One fine, respectable wom-

an said she had no choice but to purchase a jug of imported water from drug dealers at a local mobile home park.

8. It took a crisis, but Chicken Lickin' finally got Henny Penny off the front page.

9. The new water bleached the hair of three kids when they were baptized this morning at a prominent local church.

10. In spite of our highest hopes, it was proven that the new water will not kill kudzu. The jury is still out about whether the water will cool global warming.

And that's the way things are in Greer this week. Everything should be back to normal when you return at Christmas.

\- Leland

We Have Dodged a Bullet - Oct. 19, 1994

All of Greer can breathe a big sigh of relief this week. We have just avoided not one, but two major environmental crises.

First, the Town of Duncan has decided not to send its sewage here. That gives new meaning to the old cliché "dodging a bullet."

For reasons I don't quite understand, Greer and Lyman have been locked in a fight over Duncan's sewage. Perhaps another old cliché, "one man's trash is another man's treasure," applies in this case.

I hate to show favoritism, but I'm glad Lyman is getting the sewage. Frankly, I don't think we need any more sewage in Greer. It already gets pretty deep here, especially during election years.

Speaking of flushing forth great leadership, the Duncan Town Council must have needed all the wisdom of Solomon to decide where to send its sewage. At least they did not make a public spectacle of the process by conducting an auction. But they certainly do know how to stay in the headlines.

I think Mayor Randy Richards finally figured that it would have cost more money to build a longer pipeline to send the sewage to Greer. And then he would not have had enough money to pay for the town's new license tag that proudly proclaims: "Duncan - a Sewer-free Community."

At the last minute though, Greer City Administrator Ken Westmoreland confused the issue. He sweetened the pot by offering Richards a free Honey Wagon for emergencies. Greer Mayor Don Wall even went so far as to order a sign erected at the Highway 290 City Limits stating "Send us your tired, your poor, your septic tanks."

But Greer's chances of succeeding went down the drain when Wall flatly refused to release Duncan Police Chief Tommy Brooks who is being held hostage here.

Then there was Greer's air problem. Just one day earlier, the EPA officially declared that the air in Sunnyside is safe to breathe.

We had been holding our collective breath for weeks for fear that the Surgeon General would put breathing on the list of health hazards—alongside calories, caffeine, nicotine, fat grams, wine, women, and song.

Obviously, the air accompanying Duncan's sewage might have created a stink and led to another round of EPA testing. And it was difficult enough for the EPA to test the air the first time. There were many problems, including noise pollution, to overcome.

Researchers agree that the least amount of noise in Greer occurs between 4 and 6 a.m., which is between the time that one Robbie Gravley post-game show ends and the next Robbie Gravley pre-game show begins. During the 22 hours of the broadcast, spectators at the Greer Dragway have complained about not being able to hear the race while the radio is on. And the control tower at the Greenville-Spartanburg Airport is often unable to hear incoming jets.

But being the blue chip agency that it is, the EPA discovered there is more in the air than noise. Investigators found traces of Air Jordan, Air Mail, and Air Wick hovering over our fair city.

Because EPA technicians were unable to see the air, it is not clear if the Sunnyside air is just passing through or if it is en route from Greenville to Spartanburg or vice versa. "It depends on which way the wind is blowing," the report says.

"You win some, you lose some," a disappointed Mayor Wall said yesterday, still weak from the excitement. "If only we could have gotten Duncan's sewage, then we would have charged them enough money to build a dome over Greer and keep all this air to ourselves."

Massage Parlor Ban Outrageous – Sept. 7, 1994

This is an official notice to rally those thousands? of people who have expressed shock, even outrage, over the news that Greer may be denied the constitutional right to have massage parlors. Citizens – we must fight back!

Since the news broke last week, I have been organizing for battle. I am circulating a petition demanding that our city council vote down any ordinance that would ban massage parlors. And I need volunteers. Anyone who wants to join me in this crusade should dial my toll-free number, 1-900-SLEAZE.

It is hard to believe that our city administrator, Ken Westmoreland, could be so shortsighted as to propose banning massage parlors. Such a negative, hardheaded stance will surely stunt Greer's big city growth!

I assume that Westmoreland never watches television. If he did, the first picture Westmoreland would see in any newscast from New York City is Times Square with its dozens of massage parlors. Time Square has a lot of other attractions that Greer has never dreamed of, but I say let's take the temptations one at a time. They are more enjoyable that way.

Westmoreland must not realize that massage parlors are absolutely vital, and much less costly than silicone implants, to fulfilling his dreams. How else is he going to inflate Greer to a larger size than Greenville or Spartanburg, and eventually into another Atlanta?

All studies show that once a city has a massage parlor, people start flocking in from far and wide, nearly matching the pigeon population. The downtown becomes vibrant—er, make that vibrating. Then the big insurance companies and international banks will start throwing up 40-story office buildings around them.

No, Virginia. A small town doesn't get to be an Atlanta without having a red light district. And you don't have a red light district without massage parlors. Granted, many consider Greer is a red light district now, but the only things our red lights stop are cars. Massage parlors will stop people.

I must confess that I have never been inside a massage parlor. I'm past the age of being tempted, even if one were to open up across the street. But I still have my imagination. I imagine massage parlors could be beneficial in many ways, for instance:

*Massage parlors would give people a place to go on days when the flea market is closed.

*Massage parlors could provide a public service by helping over-worked executives forget their business problems—until they have to explain their whereabouts after arriving home from work six hours late.

*Massage parlors will attract thousands of tourists who will visit the new BMW plant to take delivery of new cars. The massage therapy program will help these folks take their minds off worrying about making the steep monthly payments required to drive a Beemer.

*Massage parlors could ease the pain of old men who fall out of trees and hurt themselves, men like Rusty Foxhall.

*Massage parlors could give preachers something to talk about—other than politics.

*A massage parlor would be useful for shining certain heads, like that of a prominent alumnus of The Citadel.

*Speaking of head cases, massage parlors would relieve over-crowding at Bullock's Barber Shop.

*Perhaps the Spartanburg County Library Board would donate a book or two for massage parlors. It would encourage people to read while lounging around.

*Massage parlors could force Greer to change its new slogan from "Going Places!" to "Where's the Rub?"

Stud Muffin May Strike Up the Band! – July 25, 2007

Being as old as dirt, I remember the old days when it was hot news if Greer Police had to investigate more than half a dozen crime incidents in a month.

On occasion, someone was put behind bars to sober up after consuming one beer too many at the Sanitary Cafe. Less frequently, a watermelon was stolen from a back yard garden. And before my time, city cops occupied themselves by keeping tabs on the bootleggers who drove into town from the Dark Corner with loads of illegal whiskey in gallon jugs. The outlaws' vintage Thirties model Fords had been beefed up with heavy duty springs in the rear end to keep the trunks full of moonshine off the ground. Their V-8 engines had been "souped-up"—the better to outrun the cops.

The biggest thing in the 1950s was the night the late Chief Parks Boozer was stuffed upside down into a 50-gallon trashcan by an exceptionally strong man who was feeling no pain. This was outside the Carolina Lunch, a dive that once occupied a building that has since become a vacant lot adjoining Justin's Steak House in the 100 block of Trade Street.

In the early 1960s, I recall gawkers coming from miles around on the day that a car that ran up a guide wire on a phone pole and remained there, perfectly balanced—in front of the police station on Randall Street, no less.

Believe it or not, an even bigger deal occurred one Sunday morning in the 1990s when a rookie cop issued tickets to First Presbyterian Church members who had parked on the yellow curb along South Main St.

When it comes to 21st century crime, there seems to be nothing more astounding than the sort of incidents in Greer that make the 11 o'clock news, while similar incidents in surrounding cities go unreported. Since swarms of media types have Greer under a microscope, one would have thought an ax murder had occurred when a giant blueberry muffin was stolen recently from the parking lot of the Bloom supermarket on West Wade Hampton Blvd.

It proved there's a lot of truth in the old adage: "the more things change, the more they remain the same"—especially in Greer. It was like the 1980s when a pair of huge plastic bulls disappeared from the roof of the Bi-Lo supermarket at the A&G Shopping Center.

Following the muffin theft, the TV News on the Downside issued a helpful Crook Tracker Alert, warning viewers to put their brownies and cookies under lock and key

Police Chief Dan Reynolds, who is looking for every excuse to get away from the golf course, called a news conference to ask the public to be on the lookout for anyone who may have experienced a sudden and massive weight gain.

The city's elite SWAT unit set up road blocks to stop and inspect vehicles for evidence, like loose blueberries that may have tumbled out of the muffin and are rolling around in the trunk.

SLED brought Crime Dog to the scene to sniff a trail of crumbs on West Wade Hampton Blvd.

When those efforts failed to turn up the stud muffin, Chief Reynolds went so far as to assign the entire detective department to stake out local dentists' offices in case the culprit came seeking new dentures after chewing through the 200-pound muffin.

When I heard that a reward had been posted—a gift certificate for lumber at Home Depot to make your own muffin—I jumped into the fray by starting my own investigation. I discovered that the stud muffin thief did a great favor for the City Codes Department. The stud muffin was actually in violation of the city's sign ordinance, and a codes enforcement officer was en route to have it evicted when he received a call informing him of the theft.

Eventually, an eyewitness came forth to report seeing the stud muffin in the back of a pickup truck that was headed up Highway 101 North toward Blue Ridge. Authorities now believe the stud muffin is expected to become the next drum major who will lead the Blue Ridge High School band to another state championship.

Greer Etiquette

My Table Manners Never Improved – Jan. 28, 1999

While conducting research for this book I came across my first grade report card, thanks to my mother who never threw anything away and passed on that same gene to me.

The report card is historic evidence that people never change. That is, I personally have not made any progress in 70 years.

The back page of the report card is devoted to the teacher's comments. Mrs. S.B. (Christine) Hutchings, overcome by the shock of 25 noisy, squirming six year-olds, was unable to make a comment during the first two reporting periods. By Christmas, though, she had summoned up the courage to write the following on my card: "on next report, I shall make a notation on table manners." That was her warning of an impending black cloud on my horizon, a hint of things to come that easily beat the 15-minute Super Doppler storm warning by 30 days.

On the fourth period report card, Mrs. Hutchings wrote: "Leland needs to increase his speed in all of his work. He is careless with food at the lunch table, spills it on table and floor."

Speed. I never found any except at a NASCAR race. I was cast in the role of the turtle in our first grade play about the tortoise and the hare fable. We even had a pet rabbit in Mrs. Hutchings' class, but I wasn't allowed to go near it for fear that I would be a bad influence. That was in 1946. Years later, people didn't get the newspaper on time because I still had only one gear—low.

My table manners haven't improved much either. Which is why we have not been invited out to a dinner party since 1973.

During lunch recently, my wife groused "I put four salt and pepper shakers on the table at every meal, and they always end up on your place mat."

She went on to recite the litany of my poor manners that she has committed to memory. I pled guilty to pouring enough salt on my food to clog the arteries of six people, so I need the shakers handy.

I still spill things, but our 65-pound lap dog, Brooks, never fusses. He thinks I am dropping him a treat, and keeps the floor spotless.

My table manners were ingrained before I ever climbed the front steps of Central Elementary School. I can remember sitting at the dinner table for hours while my mother begged, prodded and even threatened me for not eating the food on my plate. The only items that were exempted were my mother's potato salad, which my dad said wasn't fit to eat because the potatoes weren't mashed, and English peas that he referred to as 'China Berries.'

I was required to eat everything else, including boiled okra which I considered to be incredibly slimy—it makes my skin crawl. I submitted to a switching rather than eat it. I even ignored my mother's constant reminder about millions of children in China starving to death. "They would give anything for the food on your plate," she would declare.

One day mother changed pace and fried the okra for lunch. I did not like it either, just knowing that it was okra. But she was determined I was going to eat fried okra—or else. So I sat at the table for several hours just staring at my plate. Finally, around 3 o'clock, I stuffed the okra in my pockets and announced, "I have a clean plate." I was rewarded with a bowl of rice pudding at supper. Then I got a blistered bottom when my mom removed my clothes for a bath and the okra spilled out of my pockets.

Even now at mealtime, I still think about those poor starving Chinese – if only I could give them my bowl of grits and gravy or the huge slice of chocolate cake that I am consuming on their behalf. If only, then maybe I would not have to keep buying new and larger trousers.

Eventually, just like when I was six years old, I put those thoughts out of my head and dished out a scoop of ice cream to go with the hunk of cake. Then I cleaned my plate.

Good Manners Have Never Gone Out of Style
- June 28, 2011

Anyone who thinks good manners have gone out of style doesn't know Sylvia Jones. She recently prevailed upon my wife to instruct a class in etiquette for youths at Mayfield Chapel Baptist Church.

Inviting my wife to talk about etiquette was like throwing a life preserver to a drowning person. It renewed her outlook on life, giving her a second chance to succeed after having failed to instill some class into her husband and four male offspring. Not to mention the grand-children, two of whom she once treated to a week's worth of behavior adjustment at Millie Lewis Fashion School—to no avail.

My wife got the Mayfield Chapel kids' attention by inform-ing them that they must exhibit the very best manners should a prospective employer ever invite them to lunch at an upscale res-taurant. I never had such an opportunity since none of my em-ployers would have driven past The Clock where a wide variety of etiquette can be observed. But her advice about proper attire and behavior brought back memories. My dad would grouse "get your elbows off the table!" and "put your glass on the table!" (if it was near the edge).

My mother would kindly point out that it is not proper to begin eating until the hostess starts – no matter how hungry you may be. And do not spear a chicken leg with your fork while everyone has their heads bowed and eyes closed for the returning of thanks.

We were not allowed to wear caps or hats in the house—let alone at the dinner table. We could not leave the table during the meal with-out being excused. Unless we had a sudden call of nature, that is, which would spoil everyone's dining experience if left unanswered.

My all time favorite etiquette tip was provided by the late Dr. Warren M. Snoddy who said just before grace, "okay, let's all turn over our glasses of milk and get it over with."

The Mayfield Chapel kids were extraordinarily mannerly. They were all ears when my wife said that "if someone asks for the salt, then pass the pepper at the same time, even if both weren't requested. They are married."

Some upscale restaurants do not provide salt and pepper since it would insult their overpriced chef. A cardiologist's dream patient, I sprinkle salt on everything to start each meal.

My wife did not go into etiquette for same sex marriages—like which partner should hold the chair for the other. Nor did she explain the technique for using a left hand dessert fork.

As luck would have it, I soon got an opportunity to exhibit my revitalized etiquette skills at Greer's most upscale restaurant. Financial status got in the way of table manners in a roundabout fashion when I had to swallow my pride and order the smallest steak on the menu. Actually it was half a steak in an appetizer-size dinner, one of the few menu items that does not require a banker to co-sign for paying the check.

I recalled that my wife had taught the Mayfield Chapel youth to slice bite size portions, one slice at a time, from your cut of meat. I did not need an engineering degree to determine that my steak would need only one cut—in half—to become bite size. The knife provided was larger than my steak, but I gave it a go and missed the steak, which caused the knife to bounce into the air like a majorette's baton. I was unable to catch the twirling knife, so it hit the floor with a resounding clatter.

"Do not pick it up," my wife commanded. "Remember, I told the students that is bad manners. Wait until the waitress comes along, and she will pick it up. Then ask for another knife."

While I waited, I fretted that another patron would innocently step on the knife, sending him into a backward summersault that would instigate a lawsuit. But manners prevailed when the waitress eventually spotted the knife and carted it away. By then I had already consumed my steak—in a single bite.

City Council Shenanigans

Behind the Bushes – Feb. 3, 1988

Twisted grins, floating eyeballs and pigeon-toed gaits. Such symptoms have been observed among City Hall employees since Charlie Williams was elected to the City Council.

Williams, it seems, has turned City Hall upside down with a new policy. After an extensive study, Williams decided that city employees were wasting too much time making trips to the restroom. As an exercise in efficiency, Williams established a new restroom procedure for employees.

His plan calls for each employee to be allocated 20 restroom trip tickets on the first day of each month.

Williams also had the restrooms equipped with a computerized voice identification system, and each employee was required to provide two voiceprints, one normal and another under extreme stress.

When a ticket is deposited in a reader at the restroom door it will activate the voice recognition system and allow the employee to request admission.

Williams said that if an employee uses all of his 20 tickets before the end of the month, the restroom will not open, not even for a voiceprint, no matter how loud the employee screams.

Another feature of Williams' restroom plan was equipping stalls with timer paper-roll retractors. If the stall is occupied for more than two minutes, an alarm will sound. Then, after a 30-second grace period, the roll of paper will retract into the wall, the toilet will flush automatically and the stall door will fly open.

After that, if the employee is not out of the stall within another two minutes, a general alarm will sound, calling Greer police officers to respond with weapons drawn, to escort the employee to a formal hearing to face charges of killing time. When that occurs, any restroom tickets that the employee has left will be forfeited for the remainder of the month.

If there is a second offense, the employee's restroom privileges will be suspended for a period of six months.

Williams said that in the event of a third offense, all City Hall restroom privileges will be permanently suspended and the employee "is on his own."

Just two weeks into the new restroom regulations, the city council has called an emergency meeting for tomorrow night to consider planting bushes around the building.

We Should Sell City Hall – Sept. 25, 1996

People are continually asking, "what is the problem between the City Council and the Commission of Public Works?" I have asked the same question myself. No one knows the answer, not even those on the front lines.

What I do know is that the city is going broke unless the CPW comes across with a million bucks. To make matters worse, the Strategic Planning Committee has been no help, having been preoccupied with seeking a cure for earwax build-up.

So I have stepped in and taken charge of worrying about how to solve this crisis. After wringing my hands for weeks, I have come to the conclusion that we cannot afford to lay off police officers. If no one is available to run the radar, then property taxes will become the city's only source of revenue.

What we really need are ideas to raise money. We do have some valuable assets to use, including the Police Department. As good will ambassadors, I'm sure that Greer's Finest would be agreeable to selling magazine subscriptions. This is truly a win-win proposition. Every motorist that is pulled over for speeding would gladly subscribe to anything to avoid getting a ticket. And filling out the paperwork would fulfill police officers' cravings to take names and license numbers.

If worse comes to worst, someone has suggested printing $10 bills on the city copier. With City Administrator Ken Westmoreland's photo on the funny money, no less. I would like to see the faces of city employees like Phil Rhoads when they open their pay envelopes and find the boss staring at them.

I think it makes more sense to go ahead and sell City Hall, however. Don't laugh. City Hall has the potential for many uses. Its central location would be ideal for another bingo parlor to counter-balance the grove of them on the east side of town. Bingo would provide weekend recreation and entertainment now that Clemson and USC have both ceased playing competitive football.

Once we sell City Hall, we pocket the savings, step back and allow Habitat to build a new house for the homeless (that will be the city council) absolutely free. Trust me. They will call it Habitat for Hardheads.

The Comedy Channel has not yet picked up on city council meetings. But once they do, I believe these sessions can be packaged and sold like hot cakes in sets of 13-week episodes.

Parking meters should be installed in downtown Greer. If that doesn't bring in millions, the city can always rent spaces on the sidewalk in front of Bullock's Barber Shop for those waiting in line.

Even though they can't take credit for this mess, I think we should trot out some of our famous former city council members to help raise funds. Shirlee Rollins, who hasn't pounded the pavement in five years, could come back to lead a walk-a-thon like the March of Dimes does so successfully. Charlie Williams could pose with people for photographs, like the Indian Chief in Cherokee, N.C.

Then too, the city council could have a yard sale. I don't know whose yard would be sold, but there are some nice ones available. We could advertise the sale on the Internet, except that Greer is the only city ever to be denied a home page.

Probably the fastest way to wealth would be to get a scandal going and sell it to one of the supermarket tabloids. As luck would have it, there may be a story waiting to be uncovered since the downtown pigeons have gone missing and the mayor has a new shotgun.

Greer Cooks, Dishes

Pass the Butterfingers - Oct. 9, 1991

I don't think the mayor has signed a proclamation yet, but all citizens will be mandated to observe National School Lunch Week, Oct. 14-18.

I can't add anything to what the mayor says about school lunches except to note that most kids still turn up their noses at the food.

We probably did the same thing in my day, although I really don't remember school lunches being all bad. That could be because I try to put dishes like Chicken Michelin out of my mind and concentrate on the good ones.

My most vivid memory of elementary school lunches was lima beans and cornbread. The kitchen staff must have been getting paid by the hour, because they cooked those beans for days, far beyond the well-done point. The beans that wound up on our plates could have passed for green grits.

By the time I got to high school, the cafeteria had invented a true delicacy—homemade yeast rolls. They might as well not have bothered cooking the rest of lunch. The only thing needed to fill an empty tummy was a yeast roll that you filled with molasses after poking a hole in it. Everyone who downed more than one of those goodies was shot for the rest of the day. We always slept right through the seventh period history class.

If you thought lunches tasted bad back when you were in school, consider that today's lunches probably have no taste at all. Schools have been ordered to reduce the fat, salt, sodium and sugar that go into a meal. In other words, dietitians have been told to take the flavor out, which is like scraping icing off the cake.

Nutritionists are actually bragging about this giant leap forward in which today's cafeteria kitchen staff makes nothing out of something. But that can't be all bad, can it? If school food is healthy, it's got to be good, right? Not so says a Greer policeman stumbling back to the station from a local school the other day. "I had forgotten how bad school food is until I ate lunch in a school cafeteria today," the officer grumbled while phoning in an order for a pizza.

Now, Greenville County District school lunches have been planned by a committee that created a master menu for the entire year. No matter what school you attend, you will be served the same food as a kid attending another school 30 miles away. There are a few bugs to be ironed out, like which days every school runs out of ice cream at the same time.

When I was in school, the same lunches were served on the same days. This had advantages. Greer High actually won the state football championship in 1956 because hot dogs were served on Fridays. Those were the best hot dogs I ever ate. Today, they would be banned by DHEC for being overloaded with fat, sodium, salt, etc. The chili was floating in so much grease that it was a chore to keep the wiener from squirting out of the bun. But those hot dogs left you with a case of heartburn that would keep you warm on the coldest winter's night at a football game. Football players got an extra hot dog—loaded with onions. They literally blew the opposition away. So much for training table theories.

Today, students have choices. They can even opt for a salad bar at some schools. Their menus often include pizza, chicken nuggets, corn dogs, and tater tots—none of which had been invented in my day. All of this for $1 and change is a bargain.

And yet, students just as often buy snacks from vending machines instead of lunch. We didn't have vending machines either. But they are big money makers at some schools, even outstripping football gate receipts.

Parents and grandparents are invited to eat lunch at public schools next week. It will be, they claim, the best $2 meal in town. While you are checking out this claim, pass the Butterfingers please.

Chicken Michelin - Dec. 2, 1987

Most people don't know much about the Chamber of Commerce and even fewer know that the primary function of a Chamber director is to eat lunch a couple of times a month during board meetings. In order to serve, a Chamber director must have a cast iron stomach or figure out a way to beat the lunch system.

During my four years as a Chamber director, I succeeded in winning only a couple of times. That was when I managed to con Kay Moseley, who had been assigned to plan these lunches, into slipping me an advance warning about the Chamber menu so I could arrange to attend a conflicting meeting. But Moseley soon caught on to my tactics and appointed me to be the Chamber's official food critic—not because I know anything about food, but because I know how to criticize.

As one might expect, I don't hand out many compliments when broccoli soup and/or tuna fish sandwiches are served at board meetings.

As the food critic, I have come to compare Moseley with a baseball player. Sometimes she strikes out, as with the tuna fish sandwich lunch. Other times, Moseley hits a home run, like the time she carried the entire Chamber Board to the Forest House for lunch. It was the highlight of the year, marred only by the Chamber's Executive Director who was so excited that he kept knocking over his glass of tea and soaking the linen tablecloth.

Most recently, however, Moseley hit a fowl ball. Yes, fowl. The other day, she produced a dish that I call Chicken Michelin. The entire meal consisted of what appeared to be a slice of a hapless chicken that had been flattened by a steel-belted radial tire. The goo was full of green specks that were diagnosed as broccoli bits. In my book, chicken with broccoli is a deadly combination, so I advised Kay to notify the Surgeon General about the hazards of eating lunch at the Chamber.

For once I thought I had finally gotten the best of Moseley. Boy, was I surprised! Not only did Moseley charge me two cents for the Chicken Michelin, even though I refused to eat a single bite, she also retaliated by serving me a peanut butter and jelly sandwich at the next meeting. Don't even ask what I think of peanut butter sandwiches.

War on the Home Front - Mar. 26, 2003

War on the home front was declared last week. The Battle of the Bulge has nothing to do with ousting Saddam from Iraq. It has everything to do with whittling down to squeeze into the outfits we wore last spring.

"From now on, I can't have any sugar," my wife announced.

"I guess that means you won't be able to have anything to do with me," I replied.

Although I am not into the 'No Sugar Diet', I have been trying to avoid meals of mast waistline destruction, such as Big Macs with Super Sized French fries. But when I refused to plunk down $20 for the newest Atkins diet book, I wound up gaining another five pounds from grazing salad bars. So I decided to ask three of my dearest friends for advice.

Mrs. Kate Gaston knows a thing or two about dieting, having just reached the age of 92. "Last Sunday, the preacher announced from the pulpit that I am 93, but I didn't mind because I'm going on 93," she said.

Mrs. Gaston is going far beyond 93 if her new diet is successful. After nine decades, Mrs. Gaston is putting aside biscuits, country ham, mashed potatoes and gravy, in favor of a diet of shock and awe: cabbage, broccoli and Brussels sprouts.

"The worse food tastes, the better it is for you," Mrs. Gaston explained. "I wish I had learned this many years ago."

Even President George W. Bush won't touch broccoli. I think he should pass a law requiring a nutrition label, which spells out all of the calories, cholesterol and other bad stuff in food products, to be glued on every stalk of broccoli before it can be sold.

Mrs. Gaston claims cabbage broth is especially beneficial.

John Williams would agree. He single-handedly turned the Blue Ridge Water Co. inside out after going on the cabbage soup diet. He was like the cartoon character Popeye springing into action after downing a can of spinach.

Mrs. Gaston's favorite saying is "you are what you eat." If that's true, it's a relief. Instead of a turkey, I will be mistaken for the Chick-fil-A cow that is constantly harping about "eating more chicken."

When Mrs., Gaston went on to declare that "ice cream and cake are from the Devil," I was forced to seek a second opinion. I asked the baker of the world's best cakes, Leah Lurey, who said "it's not the quantity of life, it's the quality." Mrs. Lurey was talking my language. Living to age 125 won't be any fun without ice cream and cake.

Mrs. Lurey doesn't believe in prescription medications for arthritis, high blood pressure and other ailments that are likely caused from eating high on the hog. "I get plenty of calcium and vitamins from orange juice and milk," she says.

Merle Mullins, who has survived being hit by a car and more harrowing spills than an NFL running back, has other ideas. She has done amazingly well on the "world's best" dishes of her own, especially macaroni pies and mouth watering chicken salads.

"I also take something to build up my bones, but that's because the doctor wants me to," Mrs. Mullins said.

What I gathered from these conflicting opinions is that you can become another Strom Thurmond and live to be 100 by sticking to a diet of ice cream, cake, orange juice, milk, macaroni pie and chicken salad—provided that you first consume a plate full of cabbage or broccoli.

Dining Out in Greer

I Draw the Line at Sushi - Nov. 6, 2002

Greer resident Gloria Swangler once told me the story of how she met her husband at Lewis' Drive-In shortly after World War II.

Lewis' Drive-In is only a fond memory today, as are downtown Greer's mid-Twentieth Century "upscale" destinations for dining out—the Poinsett Restaurant and the Wayside Inn Hotel. How times have changed 50 years later!

With the opening of the New China Buffet, Greer became the home of four Chinese restaurants. That is just one less than the number of local Mexican eateries. Amazing! Greer has either become a truly international community or real hamburgers are a species that is vanishing faster than the bald eagle.

The New China moved into a former Shoney's Restaurant. That reminded me of the first Shoney's I had ever encountered. Passing through Brunswick, Ga. in 1961, the car radio aired a commercial for Shoney's, which was advertising the "Big Boy," a huge old-fashioned hamburger, with French fries and onion rings along the lines of Spartanburg's famed Beacon Drive-In plates "a-plenty." So we stopped and had our oil changed at Shoney's. It was several days before we had to eat again.

Then there is Oriental Cooking, which is a mystery to me. When I was growing up, the only Orientals I had ever seen were on the screen in Movietone "news of the week" reels that preceded the feature film at the Grand Theatre. America was at war with Japan, and I recall seeing an American prisoner of war being interrogated. The Japanese threatened to kill the soldier unless he revealed the true identity of the name of a secret agent found printed on a slip of paper in his pocket. The name on the paper was "Juicy Fruit."

Although I refuse to cross the line into Japanese sushi, I have helped to further international relations by patronizing Chinese restaurants. And I made new discoveries, like Chinese aren't into serving low calorie entrees. They also have even more recipes for chicken than the Clemson Extension office.

No matter what's on the menu, the best part of a Chinese meal is the fortune cookie for dessert. Sometimes, the fortune is easier to swallow than the cookie. A recent fortune that came my way stated "You are your wisest counselor." I had it framed and mounted on our refrigerator to settle all family disagreements.

My favorite Chinese restaurant is the Grand China because a treat comes with every meal—the opportunity to chat with the friendly owner, Paul Chan. You can't find the manager at most restaurants, let alone the owner. But there is evidence of Paul Chan everywhere in the Grand China. He has done dozens of paintings that decorate the walls of the restaurant.

Chan, a former school teacher, has taken such an interest in Greer that he spends most of his free time painting local landmarks, from grist mills to churches. Chan has even printed and boxed sets of note cards featuring some of his paintings.

Chan is happy to explain his paintings, which he describes only as "time consuming." One notable work is a collage of the business firms along Wade Hampton Blvd., compacted onto a 12-inch-wide canvas. It makes the Greenville Motor Mile look like a ghost town. Chan said the painting is making a statement. "I'm showing how much business there is in Greer."

One of his recently completed efforts features the new Greer Station clock that stands at the corner of Main and Poinsett with the City Hall in the background. It is realistic and highly detailed. Chan's flourishing touch to this painting is a pine forest background, which is entirely in character, for the earliest photographs of Greer (around 1900) reveal a pine forest standing where City Hall sits today.

Health Care in Greer

The Chair - April 1, 1987

I have yet to be sentenced to the electric chair, but I know how it must feel to make that long walk from death row, facing the worst.

I got that feeling again while waiting in the dentist's office for a recent appointment. As I was trying to read a magazine to take my mind off the looming ordeal, a fellow patient piped up and exclaimed "I sure do hate to go to the dentist."

With that remark, the man proceeded to pour out all of his dental problems to the room full of people. Another patient jumped in with the comment, "I wish I hadn't had all my teeth pulled. My new ones don't fit so good."

Before I could relate my old memories of growing up and visiting the family dentist, the late Dr. J. Roy Jackson, my turn came for the chair. So I've had to wait until now to share these nightmares.

I felt that climbing up the long stairway to Dr. Jackson's second floor offices in the old Victoria Street Building must be like hiking to the electric chair. Even worse was the air, heavy with the odor of clove and other dental medications.

Once you sat down in the dentist's chair, there was no turning back. Dr. Jackson, with one arm wrapped around your head, which was drawn securely into his ample belly, would command "open right wide, sweet boy," and the drilling would commence.

Dr. Jackson took such good care of me that I still have the originals, even though I distinctly recall that he predicted my teeth would not last until I was 40 years old.

There are times, however, when I wish I didn't have some of these aging teeth, like a few weeks ago when I suffered through another dental crisis. I rushed to the dentist at five o'clock on a Saturday afternoon. "Which one hurts?" he inquired.

"I don't know." I responded. "I have sympathetic teeth. When one aches, they all ache."

"Well, we can't have our newspaper editor with a toothache," the dentist remarked as he fumbled around until he found a tooth that was committing suicide. "This one's strangling to death," the dentist explained while reading a set of x-rays.

The situation called for an RC (root canal, not be confused with an RC cola and moon pie that likely helped get me to the dentist's office in the first place).

I hate to bore anyone with gruesome details of a root canal except to report that a great deal of excavation is required, accompanied by several gallons of Novocain that I have grown to especially appreciate. After numerous office visits, the dentist has yet to strike oil, but he has acquired the habit of saying, repeatedly, "open right wide"—just like Dr. Jackson.

Allen Bennett Hospital Remembered

– Jan. 18, 2011

Sometimes I wake up in the middle of the night haunted by the memories of Allen Bennett Memorial Hospital. It is constantly on my subconscious because the old hospital is a gift that keeps on giving—especially to the news media.

Allen Bennett has been in the headlines off and on for several years, most recently when an exterior storage building was burglarized. The building contained cardboard boxes full of old billing records. I'm sure those records reveal how the hospital managed to draw blood from a turnip—me.

The break-in occurred right after the hospital had dumped a few thousand gallons of heating oil into Frohawk Creek. That incident was most notable for inflating the value of the creek. Fortunately, a cadre of beavers had built a log dam that prevented the oil spill from reaching historic Apalache Lake. Otherwise, the load might have been too much for the world's oldest stone dam that seismologists claim is an imminent threat to collapse and send water gushing uphill into downtown Greer.

A forest of pines would be required to produce enough paper to record the memories made at Allen Bennett. The hospital was good for Greer and ahead of its time in some aspects. There were no nursing homes when Allen Bennett opened its doors in 1952. But it soon became a nursing home for Dr. Johnny Walker, a retired pharmacist who spent the final years of his life there in a private room where he took meals and smoked cigars.

Yes, smoking was permitted in Allen Bennett. It once had a cigarette vending machine in the lobby. During the birth of my first kidney stone, I paced the hospital halls puffing one cigarette after another.

Other Allen Bennett memories I'd like to erase include my first colonoscopy and the time my appendix exploded, causing me to miss my first Greer High football game in 25 years.

I really appreciated Allen Bennett's convenient location, especially because we didn't have far to drive when our first child arrived in the world some 15 minutes after we made it to the hospital.

The late Dr. Lewis M. Davis was on call 24-7 for emergencies. Dr. Davis could drive from his home to the emergency room in two minutes flat, shifting gears 13 times along the way, so he said. For the same number of decades, Susan Hawkins made sure the nursing staff was on its toes.

Allen Bennett was on a par with other hospitals when it came to food. Its fare was as bland as all the rest, but folks went there for Sunday dinner anyway, carrying their own salt shakers.

My favorite Allen Bennett story is from the 1970s when the late Rep. Lewis Phillips underwent major surgery. After Phillips was wheeled back to his room—there was no ICU in those days—he regained consciousness and moaned, "I see the golden arches." Alarmed family members at the bedside thought he was referring to the Pearly Gates. Actually, Phillips explained later, he was looking at McDonald's across Wade Hampton Blvd.

The late (former police chief) Dan Stepp doubled as Allen Bennett's night security officer in the early days. His primary responsibly was to shoo relatives and friends out of patients' rooms when visiting hours were over. Hospitals are not the social gathering places that they once were.

The new Greer Memorial, which outshines everything in Greenville, made Allen Bennett expendable. That was right after the Greenville Hospital System (GHS) had spent $5 million to expand and enlarge the primary care facility, aka the Emergency Room, for everyone whose health insurance had disappeared.

Since Allen Bennett was the largest Commission of Public Works utility customer, GHS wanted to get rid of it in the worst way. But the Bennett family refused to take it back. GHS offered to give it to the federal government for a veterans' hospital. But the feds refused claiming veterans need the exercise of traveling to Columbia for hospital care.

After first failing to palm the hospital off on Greer for a new City Hall, GHS finally got the city to accept it anyway. Since then, Allen Bennett has become a Cinderella. The unwanted stepsister was recently snapped up by a handsome suitor from the "Nawth" with plans to make the old hospital the Queen of assisted living. And a call center will go into the adjoining Roger Huntington Nursing Center. I just hope they don't phone a doctor and expect a real person to answer.

An early Family Festival afternoon concert attracted a large crowd.

Family Festival Tales

Flattened by the Festival – Aug 12, 1987

Although tired and broke after my annual vacation, I returned to plunge into the annual Greer Family Festival and self destructed with a bang.

As far as I could tell, it was a great festival. At least that's what witnesses said. After I had been run over, I didn't see a thing.

My first mistake was volunteering for a six-hour stretch working Friday night in the Lions Club concession stand at the Beach Bash. I wound up on the receiving end of the bash.

I should have been forewarned when Jack Coggins was assigned to the popcorn popper. His fiery furnace had raised the temperature inside the concession booth to 110 degrees by the time the concert started. But that didn't slow Coggins. He fed 50 pounds of popcorn kernels into that infernal machine and even sent out for more.

By 10 p.m., Coggins had popped enough corn to feed every resident of Greer. Coggins had boxes of popcorn stacked from the floor to the ceiling. Then someone sneezed, and the mountain of popcorn came tumbling down, pelting us roaring Lions with boxes as we scattered to avoid the landslide. Even after shoveling much of Coggins' handiwork out the door, I counted 118 boxes of popcorn on the shelves when we finally closed the concession stand at 1:30 a.m.

Barely able to move after having paced up and down on the concrete floor, I somehow made it to the Greer County Club by 8 a.m. Saturday for the festival golf tournament.

I kept telling myself that this was for a good cause. Until, that is, just minutes after the tournament started and my back went one way and I went the other. It was the same back that I had yanked out of whack during our vacation.

Fortunately, I was playing golf with noted Greer optometrist Dr. Jim DuBose. Unable to move after having bent over to retrieve my ball from the cup, I groaned, "Doc, can you help me?"

"What's wrong? Can't you see the ball?" the eye doctor questioned.

"Sure, I can see it fine. I just can't stand up," I replied.

"In that case, I can't do much for you. I don't even have an aspirin," he said.

It took DuBose six hours to finish the round because every time he hit the ball, he had to stop and drag me along.

If finishing last wasn't embarrassing enough, a little old lady spotted me the next day when I was trying to get a bite to eat in a restaurant. "Aren't you the fellow who works at the newspaper?" she asked.

"Yes," I croaked in reply, unable to turn around to face my accuser.

"Ah ha! I thought so," she exclaimed. "I could tell by the way you are bent out of shape."

The Chamber

The Chamber in Retreat - Feb. 11, 2004

Many? readers have inquired why I went on a sea cruise. The answer is, when you reach my age you start doing all the things you have never gotten around to because time is running out. That's why, I keep telling myself I signed up to participate in the Greer Chamber of Commerce retreat last weekend.

Having never retreated (I always thought retreats were reserved for folks like General Custer), I was curious. Perhaps at long last I would discover the true meaning of the Chamber. I had only a couple of clues, having once used a chamber pot as a small boy when I spent the night at my great aunt's home that had no indoor plumbing. More recently, I learned about chamber maids, females of antiquity, when one was revealed to be the mother of Strom Thurmond's firstborn.

I soon figured out that the retreat took us across the state line so that no one would suspect we are from Greer when we started "networking," whatever that means. The only network that I am familiar with is the Greer Yellow Jackets network, which consists of just one radio station. "Maybe I can simply sit by the roaring fire and be a one-person network," I thought hopefully after arriving at the mountain resort.

117

Wrong! The participants were snapped to attention in short order by Sue Priester, the new Chamber Chairman, as efficiently as my high school English class was whipped into shape by Fronda Rice.

Priester assigned us to committees, including one for Gathering Intelligence, which is the top priority because of the great lack thereof. This handicap became quite evident during a brainstorming session when not enough wind was generated to blow out a candle. Priester eventually resorted to bribery, offering $1 for each new idea that was put forth. When an idea finally surfaced, which was to begin the cocktail hour three hours ahead of schedule, the two Davids, Swenson and Langley, both tried to claim the hard earned greenback.

I was appointed to a panel to seek out Weapons of Mass Destruction, and soon discovered one in our very midst: the reams of paper that nailed us to our chairs when they were dropped into our laps. Standing committees were instantly converted into sitting committees.

Wading through 500 pages of the proposed 2004 Program of Work was our mission for the weekend. As the minutes slogged past like hours, I secretly hoped that a member of the Intelligence Committee would discover that spending money on copy paper is the reason Chamber stays broke.

Not to worry. Later in the day, I was heartened to hear Larry Wilson proclaim, "We can't continue to do things the same way, year after year, and expect to have better results!"

Eventually, an entire division was assigned to investigate why the average length of time a visitor stays in Greer is only 23.5 minutes. This group will also try to determine if the "after hours" part is what really killed "Business After Hours."

Another division was directed to post useful information on the Chamber's website including links to such local attractions as Sugar Tit, Froggy Bottom, the Dark Corner and time shares at Pelham Beach.

A third division, Greer Events, was assigned to launch a new downtown festival to be known as "A Taste of Greer." It will feature samples of grits, collards, and Vienna sausage for throngs expected to flock to the celebration. This committee will also work on a long-range project, a Greer black tie ball at Thornblade, tentatively named "Strangers in a Strange Land."

The Communications Division will add Confederate flag license plates, Willie Nelson T-shirts with cut-out sleeves, and Greer logo shot glasses to its fledgling line of merchandise. These sales will hopefully enhance non-dues revenues, to make up for those members who don't pay their dues, so that a contractor can be hired to plug the leak in the wall of the Chamber building back home.

"What next?" I wondered on the long trip home. Perhaps I'll spend this weekend at The Tooter Town Elder hostel.

The Chamber in Retreat – Again - Oct. 4, 2006

One of the benefits(?) of my job is keeping tabs on everything. So, when it came time for the Greer Chamber of Commerce board's annual planning retreat last week, I made the trek to a distant mountaintop in North Carolina to join the directors sitting around a huge round table and ruminating.

As a tax write-off, I kept a diary to inform readers what Greer residents do when away from home and to explain why the innkeeper breathed a sigh of relief at seeing our taillights disappearing out the driveway.

Thursday morning:

9:55 a.m. - Nametags are ready. Translation: we must remember who we are when the meeting starts.

10 a.m. – Meeting starts with three people present, all having made the trip the night before.

10:05 a.m. - Those who stopped to ask for directions begin arriving.

10:29 a.m. – Hard core computer addicts relying on MapQuest begin arriving, one by one.

10:30: a.m. - A special guest, a female heroine of the *Survivor* reality TV series, gives inspirational testimonial "to get us thinking." My thought: "Why am I here?"

10:35 a.m. - Break to gulp down glasses of water after watching video of the Survivor woman trudge across 50 miles of red-hot sand dunes in Sahara Desert.

10:40 - Tray of donuts and sweet rolls arrives with several pots of coffee. A ten-minute recess declared.

10:50 – Meeting resumes with a period of bonding. Everyone stands in a circle and plays Gotcha! by trying to grab neighbor's pinky. (That's your little finger for those with dirty minds)

10:55 – Ten minute break to use restrooms. High-test coffee is working faster than anticipated.

11 a.m. – New research proves contention that Greer is bigger and better than Greenville and Spartanburg. "Unfortunately, this doesn't qualify for All America City status," announces Larry "Big Poppy" Wilson, bringing the group back to reality.

11:05 – Bar graph slide presentation inspires everyone to get up and head for the bar.

11:10 a.m. – Meeting resumes after Chairman-elect Phil Feisal invokes hotel manager to shut down the bar.

11:12 a.m. - Development guru David Swenson reports Greer's Economic Engine hitting on one cylinder. Members approve an oil change.

11:17 a.m. - Directors give green light for a Greer Day in Spartanburg excursion to investigate mental state of county council members.

11:18 a.m. - Marvin Robinson is recalled as the Chamber Ambassador following presentation of in-depth survey showing that 98.9% of the membership never want to see an ambassador. Ever. (70% somehow completed the Email survey even though they don't have Email).

11:20 a.m. - Break for lunch

12 noon - Meeting resumes. Board rubber stamps proposal to extend three-year Program of Work, meaning nothing else needs to be done before 2008.

12:05 p.m. – Mandatory lesson in etiquette presented by Chairman Bunny Richardson—in the event that Greer ever gets a "seat at the table" with Greenville and Spartanburg. Otherwise, we must continue to scramble for crumbs on the floor.

12:10 p.m. – Tray of fresh brownies arrives. Break for dessert.

12:15 p.m. – Clemson Extension agent gives update on Chamber's grass roots project. Diagnosis: we're full of fertilizer.

12:20 p.m. – Chamber endorses city's ambitious quest to annex Woodruff following presentation of battle plan by Ed Driggers.

12:25 p.m. – Another round of bonding requires us to divide into groups and come up with 26 items, starting with letters A-to-Z, on our persons. My group is leading the race until we reach the letter U – for underwear. None of us is wearing any. Feisal wins with a pair of yellow boxers (so he says; no one asks to see proof).

12:30 p.m. – Financial whiz Dennis Trout gives treasury update, reporting a record amount of non-dues income since pay toilets were installed in the Chamber building.

12:35 – 1 p.m. - Board okays Tiered Dues Structure proposal. Translation: members will be in tears after their bills arrive.

12:55 p.m. - During lengthy discussion, cigarette tax legislative proposal goes up in smoke while date expires on the 64-oz. Diet Cokes on refreshment table.

1:05 p.m. – New business items introduced: Big Poppy urges Chamber to get reaccredited, i.e. our rubber stamp is worn out.

1:08 p.m. - Cold front blows through the resort. We grab cups of hot coffee to keep warm since "rustic" inn that has no heat or air conditioning. (Adverse side effect: we are now wide awake)

1:19 p.m. - News flash from Webmaster Miles Nason: Google search fails to unearth any trace of the Greer Chamber.

1:20 p.m. – Directors set top goal for 2007: Expand the Chamber's footprint. Translation: a free membership for Big Foot.

1:26 p.m. – Closing discussion to rate success of the retreat. "I think it was a good three-day retreat," Amanda Somers declares. "Actually it just seemed like three days."

1:30 p.m. - Ringing down the gavel, Richardson concludes: "I like to debate. At the same time, however, we need to shut up."

1:31 p.m. – Adjourn for networking. Translation: Tee time approaching for round of golf.

3:35 p.m. - Sudden thunderstorm drenches everyone on the golf course. Those out shopping in upscale boutiques get soaked elsewhere.

4:00 p.m. – Happy hour begins an hour early.

Not until I was safely home did I realize that we never investigated the great mystery: What does the name Chamber mean? Does Chamber Pot or Chamber Maid fit somewhere? I guess I will never know.

The Presbyterian Church

Communion Must Be Perfect – April 5, 2000

Some say that preparing a Communion service at the First Presbyterian Church ranks among life's least pleasant and inescapable tasks. It has been compared with getting a root canal, filing an income tax return and even a prostate exam. I must agree, speaking from experience after it fell my lot to prepare Communion last weekend.

One would think this is a simple task. Not so. Every detail must meet long-established standards that exceed the finery of the Biltmore Estate. Nothing less will do. And to make sure, the church has compiled a book with explicit instructions for the preparation of Communion. The Bible devotes less space to describing construction of Noah's Ark. Our Communion guidelines were developed over a half century by the world's most prim and proper ladies: Esther Smith, Josephine McMurray, Margaret Patrick, etc.

It was Thursday night before I began wading into the Communion schedule that is longer than the checklist required of a pilot before taking off in a 747-jet airliner. First, I ventured to the bakery to purchase a perfectly round loaf of bread for the minister to break ceremonially to begin the service. "Do you have and old round loaf?" I inquired of the clerk behind the counter. "No." she replied. "All of our bread is fresh." A really old loaf would be so dry and brittle that it would explode in the pastor's hands, showering everyone nearby with crumbs. That would be quite a show. But I settled for a freshly baked loaf, resolving to start earlier next time.

Next was the grape juice: it must be Welch's red, not purple. I also had to get a loaf of sliced bread: it must be the Sunbeam brand because it is the only bread with no holes. Then the bread must be frozen so that it can easily be cut into one-half-inch square cubes. The cubes cannot be thawed until an hour before the service. The bread must be served on silver plates, each bearing 75 cubes and covered with linen cloths folded in 90-degree angles at the corners.

And that was the easy part.

For the rest, I was assigned two helpers, Dr. Bill Byars and attorney Ronnie Bruce. Under normal circumstances, I couldn't afford the fee to spend an hour with either man. But preparing Communion is not a normal activity. It is a duty required of all Elders.

It took exactly an hour for the three of us using eyedroppers to fill 300 thimble-size glass cups with grape juice. All the while, I had to listen to conversations about how difficult it is for Gamecocks to learn their own fight song and the growing epidemic of gall bladder problems.

"Maybe the people will just grab the cups and gulp down the juice so quickly that they won't notice these streaks down the sides of the glass." Bruce suggested of our hit and miss approach to filling them.

Byars set out for the catacombs in search of the ceremonial silver cup and pitcher that are locked away under tighter security than the Holy Grail.

Meanwhile, Bruce and I attempted to stack the Communion trays four high. This is not easy because the trays do not fit evenly, one on top of another. The trays vary slightly in size, having been obtained one-at-a-time over a period of many years. Because Presbyterians are thrifty and all of the other adjectives that you can imagine to describe people who pinch pennies, the church would only purchase an additional tray when enough new members had joined to justify serving more cups. The oldest tray, dating from around 1840, was made by Paul Revere. The newest is inscribed on the bottom "Always Low Prices, Always."

The bottom of each tray is labeled with several sets of numbers, but using them as a guide for stacking was like trying to figure out the combination to a bank vault. "We could be sued if these trays fall over on someone," fretted Bruce the attorney.

Early Sunday, we covered the Communion table with starched linen cloths and then set out the elements according to the diagram in the handbook. When the top cloth was put into place, the embroidered "FPC" monogram was askew because the stacks of trays underneath were leaning like the Tower of Pisa.

"This doesn't look right. What if someone complains?" I worried.

"If they do, tell them we are still learning," Byars suggested.

The minister had so much difficulty restacking the trays after the service that his struggles set off ripples of titters across the sanctuary. "That does it!" exclaimed the chairwoman of the Worship Committee. "Either we are going to buy new trays or else men will never again be allowed to prepare Communion." I seconded her motion on the spot.

A Routine Three-hour Meeting - Oct. 22, 2003

Presbyterians do everything by committee. As a result, I've attended more committee meetings than I can count over the years.

And one thing never changes: no matter what the agenda, a committee meeting always lasts a minimum of one hour. This unwritten law also applies to committee meetings of civic clubs, charities, and such secular organizations as the Chamber of Commerce. Anyone who has ever served on a committee habitually plops down in a chair and does not budge for at least 60 minutes even though the business may have been transacted in five minutes.

The granddaddy of all committees in the Presbyterian Church is The Session. This body consists of Elders who are old people like me. We are supposed to be all-knowing but hopefully haven't reached the stage in life when we have forgotten everything.

Once a month, The Session gathers around a large table in a special room near the catacombs to tackle the church's business. These meetings always take at least two hours or more because having reached an advanced age, everyone has lost their inhibition about speaking up and feels the urge to sound off (sometimes repeatedly) since it might be our last chance to be heard. And so every new proposal is hung up like a piñata for everyone to take a crack at. The end result is often unrecognizable from its original form.

The Elder with the most clout sits underneath the thermostat and controls the temperature, thus determining whether the crowd dozes off or remains painfully wide awake. Carlton Greene is customarily at those controls, so the female members instinctively reach for their coats and bundle up for a long winter's evening, as was the case last Sunday.

The proposed 2004 budget was the only item up for discussion, and since it was the combined work of many committees, the time limit for the meeting had been extended to three hours.

The budget had barely hit the table before a 60-minute "chicken-or-egg" type of debate erupted over whether it is best to draw up the budget after members of the congregation have made pledges, or to make the budget a target beforehand in hopes that the pledges come in. If the money falls short, another three hour meeting will be required to revamp the budget in December.

The first hour having evaporated, Elizabeth Clayton reached boldly for the thermostat and turned on the heat. Ten minutes later, the women were coming out of their coats. Another ten minutes passed, and the men were converting reams of budget documents into paper fans. At that point, Greene readjusted the thermostat, returning the room to the climate of a meat locker.

Observing the layers of scrambled papers piled high across the table, like a giant version of "52 pickup," Sam Clayton suggested that too many committees have unnecessarily complicated the budgeting process.

"What we need is a bold leader to become our champion—get this budget in order for next year, at least by June because it's too late for this year," injected Hugh Earnest.

Naturally, I had the perfect solution. By next spring, Arnold Schwarzenegger will be unemployed, having been recalled as Governor of California, so I made a motion that we hire him to become our Budgetnator.

Before the motion could get a second, however, the preacher's wife popped in with homemade apple pie and cake. While we were stuffing our faces, Elizabeth Clayton turned up the heat.

Now two hours into the meeting, a side discussion arose as to whether or not we should throw a church wide dinner to celebrate reaching the budget Target (not to be confused with a shopping opportunity). Without knowing what the pledge drive will produce, we couldn't decide between Burger King and Gerard's to cater the meal.

At that point, Dr. Kyle offered up a prayer, "Lord, give us patience, and give it to us now!"

While everyone's eyes were closed during the prayer, Greene returned the thermostat to the subzero setting.

When it came my turn to speak, I suggested that some bold new approaches be implemented to separate the congregation of Scottish descendants from their moldy dollars. "We could equip the deacons with battery-powered vacuum cleaners for sucking money out of their pockets. Or lock the doors on Sunday mornings and continue to pass the offering plates until there is enough money to meet the budget. If all else fails, we could offer a ten percent discount on tithes as an introductory rate for new (contributing) members."

Before my motion could get a second, the meeting was adjourned. We had exceeded the three-hour time limit.

Except Presbyterians – April 3, 1991

Greer's new police chief had hoped to get off on the right foot. Alas, he has suffered a stroke of bad luck that could ultimately overshadow even many of South Carolina's disastrous blunders that have made national headlines.

Not only that, State Senator J. Verne Smith reacted by introducing legislation to do away with law enforcement in South Carolina.

You can't say Chief Dean Crisp wasn't warned. On his first day on the job, I advised Crisp not to write any parking tickets, at least not until he had been in town for a good ten years.

You see, parking customs are strange in Greer. For example, business owners park in front of their stores so customers can't get near the places. People who are perfectly healthy park in the handicapped spaces. Handicapped people just drive through the front doors.

What happened Sunday topped everything.

Chief Crisp was taking his Sunday morning stroll on Lake Cunningham when his emergency pager sounded. An incident of global proportions had just occurred on South Main Street.

It seems that a rookie officer, apparently anxious to make a good impression on the new boss, was writing traffic tickets. These weren't ordinary citations for routine offenses, however. The new officer was ticketing members of the First Presbyterian Church who were parked along the yellow curb.

The last time a Presbyterian got a ticket on a Sunday was during the reign of Chief James Beason. No one knows what happened to Chief Beason after that, but he has not been heard from in years.

So it is understandable that Chief Crisp rushed back to town with lights flashing and siren blaring.

He was immediately confronted by Mrs. Wardlaw (Lib) Smith, who was clutching a blue citation. Church organist for years and a member in good standing of the Lidie Shanklin Sunday School Class,

Smith was indignant. "I come to church 30 minutes early every Sunday just so I can park under this sign!" Smith exclaimed, resting her case.

The red-lettered sign states: "No Parking Any Time." There is not enough room at the bottom of the sign for the remainder of the warning: "Except Presbyterians."

Everyone but the rookie cop knows that sign is only half done. It seems the city ran short of metal when making it up.

Not only that, the Smith family's Presbyterian ancestors began parking on that very spot when the church was established. South Main Street was a wagon trail back in 1841. Only in modern times has the street been paved and a yellow curb installed.

What's more, this is the church that founded the First Presbyterian Church of Greenville. So Greer Presbyterians have never taken much guff from local authorities.

Fortunately, the rookie cop did not write fast enough to give tickets to every Presbyterian in the no parking zone. But he struck a raw nerve when he picked on Lib Smith. She was already put out with the men in blue. Just a few weeks earlier, her son, Bill, had his car stolen. A police officer found the car before the younger Smith discovered that it was missing. Instead of informing Smith about the theft, the officer had the car towed away.

With no way to get to work, the younger Smith rented a car. He discovered that his car had been found several days later when he read an account of the theft in this newspaper.

The jury is still out on the rookie cop. As for Chief Crisp, he will not be allowed to lead another Christmas Parade until he has "Except Presbyterians" added to the South Main signs.

Melting the 'Frozen Chosen' – Jan. 16, 2002

Our new associate pastor has quit preaching and gone to meddling. I'm sure Rev. Wayne Cole had the best of intentions when he decided to organize a church-wide retreat without having to ship the congregation off to the mountains. Having reached the advanced age when my recliner is the most appealing object in life, Cole's promise of big adventure without leaving town sounded just like the type of activity I could go for.

The retreat was set for the weekly gathering known as "Wonderful Wednesday." Church members gathered around tables in the social hall and feasted on garden salad and soup-like stew in keeping with our New Year's weight loss resolutions.

Cole had persuaded his old college roommate, Steve Price, to lead the retreat. I felt especially warm and fuzzy when Price revealed that he is a native of Cowpens, but my comfort level soon ratcheted up to the stress level of a visit to the dentist. Cole apparently had directed Price to devote the entire hour to putting us through a seemingly unending series of activities known as "ice-breakers." Cole's objective obviously was to melt the "Frozen Chosen," as Presbyterians are universally described.

The first exercise was to introduce ourselves, as if we didn't know each other already. What was unique about this particular activity, however, was that we were instructed to back up until we bumped into another person's backside. And then we had to guess the identity of that individual. The person I was greeting thought I was Casper the Ghost since we collided with the impact of a hummingbird alighting on a daylily. I have no posterior to extend, having had it chewed away by countless readers who took issue with items printed in the newspaper.

Next we were instructed to follow the leader in one of those exercises that reduces everyone to silly putty. We were told to grab our left ear with our right hand while touching our nose with our left elbow. If I had been wearing yellow, I could have passed for Big Bird.

Price then sent us into a time of sharing--that is we were ordered to confess something unique about ourselves to others seated around the table. Grasping at straws, there was only one dark secret that I could share without going to jail: most of my clothes no longer fit me.

"What was the best Christmas gift you received?" was the next question we had to answer. "The one I took to Belk's and got a refund," was my reply.

"What was the best Christmas gift you gave?" I answered, "The sweater I hated last Christmas. All I had to do was wrap it up and replace the gift card."

Then the group plunged into a bonding activity that had me on the verge of a panic attack. We were instructed to hold hands and sing. As the only member of the congregation who has been asked not to join the choir, I cannot make a sound that might even be considered a "joyful noise."

Still, it might not have been so bad had I not been seated between Ken Shaffer and Ed Driggers. I could only think, "What if word gets out that I was holding hands with these two guys, in church no less, and while our denomination is in the midst of a highly publicized battle to the death over whether or not gay people should be ordained. Besides, Driggers the City Administrator did not appear to be thrilled to be seated next to me, considering how some of the city's escapades that get into print do not always fall in the category of "good publicity."

When the program finally came to a welcome conclusion, I was supposed to have become such a free spirit that I could share with everyone how I really felt. Which was far from joyful, especially when Missy Nicholson flitted over and exclaimed, "I really had a lot of laughs tonight!"

"You did?" was my incredulous reply.

"Yes." she said. "We have been watching you the entire time."

With that I retreated all right, straight into my shell where I concluded there is much to be said for being a "Frozen Chosen."

The "Frozen Chosen" never volunteer for anything. It takes years for us to summon up the courage to even consider making a change. We are the last to adopt the latest fad, like the I-Phone. We just want to be left alone to do our own thing. That's why we scramble for the back row seats where we can take a nap if uninspired by the sermon.

And when the "Frozen Chosen" get to Heaven, I am sure we will be continuing our community service in such capacities as lampposts and park benches.

(Unofficial) History of Greer

Intro to Greer History

(My selective memories of Greer history)

This could be the story of every small town. But it isn't. This is the story of Greer, South Carolina, the place with a split personality.

Greer can come across as having an exaggerated sense of self worth since many inhabitants proclaim it to be the center of the universe and therefore a cut above all other small towns.

My earliest recollection of living in Greer is the air raid drills during World War II. These were somewhat like a school fire drill. Sirens would sound a warning, followed by action: residents were required to turn off all lights in their homes. My mother hung blankets over the windows in our house in the event that the Germans flew over they couldn't see any lights to guide them in dropping bombs. How's that for feeling that you are the nation's most important target? We knew Greer was the center of the universe. But the Germans did not discover Greer until 1992 when they decided this was just the place for a BMW automobile assembly plant.

Before then, the only way Greer could get anyone's attention was by beating them silly with the high school football team that was the winningest in the region and a big part of our history.

Otherwise, Greer was like a red headed stepchild at a family reunion, shunned by our neighboring cities, Greenville and Spartanburg. This gave Greerites a sense of smallness that was expressed by Dr. Pete Smith in 1975 when he was on a mission to invite future President Ronald Reagan to speak at the Greer Chamber of Commerce annual meeting. Instead of contacting Reagan, Smith was intercepted and grilled by Republican Party bigwigs. He quickly confessed, "We're not anybody. We're from Greer."

I was blessed to observe much Greer history from a close-up perspective, and to report on it in the newspaper for anyone who cared to read – and many did. During my career as editor of *The Greer Citizen*, I found humor in much that happened in Greer. I did not consider every issue to be a matter of life or death—just football.

Textiles drove economy

Textiles drove Greer's economy throughout most of the Twentieth Century. There were four textile mills in Greer, none of them within the city limits for tax purposes. Each mill was surrounded by villages that the mill owners had built for employees in the early 1900s. Most mill villages had a company store that catered to employees. Victor Mill was the largest, and at one time employed 3,000 people. The others were Apalache, Greer and Franklin. Today only the Greer Mill and Apalache Mill buildings are still standing.

Three historic downtown churches, First Baptist, Memorial United Methodist and First Presbyterian, all over 150 years old, can trace their roots to the time of the community's first settlers. First Presbyterian was quite influential in the upstate, having established the First Presbyterian Church of Greenville. Churches in each mill village are over 100 years old—Victor Baptist, Victor Methodist, Apalache Baptist and Apalache Methodist (that closed in 2010), Concord Methodist and El Bethel Baptist in Greer Mill.

Passenger trains came through Greer on a regular basis. We went down to the Southern Railway Depot when I was six years old to see President Franklin D. Roosevelt's funeral train come through from Warm Springs, Ga., en route to Washington, D.C. Many people rode the P&N Railway train, some daily to work, to Greenville or Spartanburg,

If we went to Greenville for any reason, it was a big deal. In the late 1940s, Wade Hampton Blvd. was widened to four lanes from Greer to Greenville. After that, it was known as the "Super Highway." It was a good many years before the highway was made four lanes to the east, to Spartanburg.

In the 1950s, the Greer City Hall was on the first floor of a Trade Street building that now houses the Chamber of Commerce. The Commission of Public Works was located on the second floor of that building. Claude B. Cannon, City Clerk, was the only City Hall employee.

Schools important

Public schools have always been important in Greer. An elementary school served each mill village: Victor, Apalache and Duke Street (which served both the Franklin and Greer Mill areas). Kids who lived in the center of town attended Central Elementary School on School Street.

Built in 1905, Central originally included Greer High School, which dates back to at least 1895 (the earliest year noted on state records). Prior to that, Greer had a one-room school that operated in various downtown houses dating back to the early 1870's. The first school building was built in 1880 on South Main Street, and later two large wings were added. The catalog of Greer High School in 1897 lists eight grades.

A $50,000 gift from the Davenport family was used to build Davenport High (technically Greer High) on Church Street in 1925. When that occurred, the 1905 building became Central Elementary.

Greer schools were segregated until 1968. Before integration, Black students attended Dunbar Elementary (now East Greer) and Lincoln High School on St. Mark Rd.

Greer High established a football team in 1921, and games were played at Victor Park. The school's first basketball team played games on an outdoor court at Central School in 1922-23.

In 1952, a new Greer High School was built on North Main Street. At the time, Greer City Schools was a school district unto itself, one of 87 districts within the county. The Greer City Schools Board met in a continuous session for several days in order to award contracts to build the new building for fear that it would not happen under consolidation that had been approved by the legislative delegation. In fact, when consolidation occurred, the Greenville County School District eliminated the auditorium from the new Greer High building. The first two classes to graduate from the new building held commencement exercises at the football stadium (which still exists, built in 1938 by the City of Greer.) The auditorium was added in 1955. That facility became the Bonds Career Center after a new Greer High School campus was built on Gap Creek Road.

Blue Ridge High is the 1954 consolidation of Mt. View and Jordan High. Riverside High was built in 1972.

Saturday shopping

People came from miles around to shop in downtown Greer on Saturdays in the 1940s and 1950s. None of the stores were open on Sundays—not even the drug stores unless you needed an emergency prescription filled. The sidewalks were crowded with folks who shopped at McClellan's and Harper's, variety stores known as five and dime stores. Four stores specialized in men's wear: Stanley's, Lurey's, Tillotson Brothers and Smith & James. Harrill's sold both men's and women's clothing. There were four department stores, Graham Cash, Peebles-Kimbrell, Bailes-Collins and The Leader, which had an entire second floor devoted to endless bolts of cloth, thread and racks of dress patterns.

The downtown had three drug stores that were destinations: McLeskey-Todd, Frierson's and the Greer Drug Co. (Rexall); two hardware stores: Miller Cook Co. and Sullivan's; several barber shops including the Palace and McCarter's; several restaurants and cafes including the Carolina Lunch, Sanitary, Poinsett, and the Wayside Inn, which was in Greer's only hotel. Greer also had a downtown drive-in restaurant, Lewis' on East Poinsett St., a favorite hangout for teens.

Greer had only one bank for many years after the Great Depression when all local banks had failed. That was the Bank of Greer, which had been founded in Duncan and moved to Greer. The Bank of Greer eventually merged with United Carolina Bank that later became part of BB&T. The First National Bank was established around 1960, and became part of Bank America after numerous mergers.

Automobile styles changed every year, sometimes dramatically, in the 1950s, and the annual unveilings of new models were a big deal that attracted large crowds to the showrooms. Automobile dealers in the 1950s were D&D Motors (on East Poinsett), which continues to operate the Ford franchise; C&D Chevrolet (on West Poinsett), which later became Paget Chevrolet: Duncan Pontiac (North Main St.); Vincent Duncan Motors (on Randall St.) which sold Dodge and Plymouth; Cloninger Buick (West Wade Hampton) and Minyard Olds (West Poinsett St.)

Greer had no DMV office. Drivers' licenses were issued by a Highway Patrolman who had a desk in D&D Motors (the building is still there, on East Poinsett Street). The officer came to town once or twice a week and gave driving tests.

Greer's industry began to diversify around 1960 when Bowers Battery (later Exide) and then Homelite built manufacturing plants on Buncombe Rd.

Greer supermarkets of the Fifties were Community Cash (forerunner of Quality Foods) on the corner of Main and Poinsett where the Police/Municipal Court building stands; Dixie Home (forerunner of Winn-Dixie) was on Cannon St. and later relocated to North Main where McLeskey-Todd Drug Store is now. Clement Brothers was located on South Main St. and would deliver groceries to your house as well as offering charge accounts. Many people paid their grocery bills once a month.

Movie theatres

Ponders, located on East Poinsett, was famous for its ice cream and orange ice. Greer had an ice plant that sold blocks of ice for home refrigerators (ice boxes) just across the Southern Railroad Tracks on Trade Street.

Greer had two downtown movie theatres in the early 1950s, the Grand and Rialto. My earliest recollection is that admission for kids was 8 cents, and then it took a huge jump to 12 cents. On Saturdays, kids would spend 4-5 hours seeing a double header (two westerns, cartoon, newsreel, and serial) and enjoy a Coke and popcorn, all for a grand total of 25 cents.

Movies and the radio provided our only entertainment back in the days before television. It was a big deal when The Greer Theatre opened on North Main (next to the Tire Exchange) and the Rialto Theatre closed in 1952.

Theatres were the only two buildings in town with air conditioning. On hot summer nights, people would go to the movies just to cool off because no one had an air conditioned house, and there was no air conditioning in cars until about 1955. Greer also had two drive-in theatres – the Greer and the King Cotton, which were good places to cool off and to date.

We listened to music on 45-rpm records with single songs on the front and back. A 33-rpm record contained an entire album. I am fortunate to have come in on the wave of great Rock 'n Roll hits by Fats Domino and Elvis Pressley.

When I was a student at Greer High School, the Teen Canteen opened on second floor of C&D Chevrolet (now Gregory's Boutique) on West Poinsett Street. Once a week, we had dances—the shag, bunny hop and more.

Greer had a public swimming pool, Suttle's, that was located on West Wade Hampton where the Comfort Inn is today. We also would swim in Chick Springs Lake at Taylors.

How Did We Get This Way? – May 26, 1999

Greer's image was one of the burning issues arising out of the recent Partnership for Tomorrow forum. It was said that newcomers, who have a Greer telephone number and mailing address, are reluctant to claim the place as home—especially if they once had an address north of the Mason Dixon Line, in a place like Chicago, Newark or Toledo.

Since the Chamber of Commerce offered a reward leading for information that would explain why Greer is disrespected, I put our investigative attorney Errik Bridwell on the case. But he left town immediately. So I went to the Greer Heritage Museum looking for answers, but it was closed.

Finally I interviewed LeRoy Jones, Harley Bonds and several other old timers who were around (well, almost) "in the beginning" in an effort to discover where Greer's troubles started. Everyone said that Greer was not getting respect many years before comedian Rodney Dangerfield made it fashionable to get snubbed.

They said Greer was just minding its own business in 1865 when General Sherman marched from Atlanta to Columbia during the final days of the Civil War. Sherman did not bother stopping to burn Greer. There wasn't anything in Greer worth the price of a match.

From then on, Greerites have been resigned to being ignored or being witnesses to colossal flops. It's a fact of life. Peeping Toms don't even look in our windows. All Greer banks failed in the big crash of 1929. The only downtown streetscape revitalization that ever came off the drawing board was mistaken for a skateboard park when it was completed in 1989.

But no one puts up much fuss because being ignored has become comfortable. Who would want Greer to be seen live on the CNN fishbowl after having been hit by a tornado, or because some unwed local mother on fertility pills gave birth to a litter of ten babies?

Whenever a gold nugget has turned up in Greer's path through history, it has been snatched away. There are many examples of Greer being ripped off, and I will cite a few. In the 1970s, cheap imports from the Far East shut down our textile mills. That was after television had closed all three of our movie theatres, and just before the advent of malls in Greenville and Spartanburg that wiped out the once-prosperous downtown Greer business community.

When Greer landed the prestigious BMW Manufacturing assembly plant, Spartanburg claimed it.

That was 40 years after the Greenville County School District swallowed up the Greer City Schools, a system that was a cut above most.

Then there was the S.C. Peach Festival. Gaffney stole the festival in the early 1960s when the organizers took a year off to catch their breath.

More recently, Bell South canned Greer's own telephone directory, and then added insult to injury by putting Greer numbers in the back of the new consolidated phone book that is being used in body-building gyms everywhere.

Why is all of this important, you ask? For one thing, we can't find a solution to the problem unless we know the cause. Furthermore, many Greer people are seeking justification for continuing to use medication.

On the Hysterical Register - July 30, 1997

Yes, Virginia, there is something happening in Greer. Another controversy! This one is over serving alcoholic beverages on Trade Street on Saturday nights. Is it right or wrong?

I am not taking sides here. I would merely point out that downtown Greer seems headed toward becoming a hysterical district instead of the hallowed National Historical Register.

Hysterical may be a more accurate designation anyway. One of the things that adds spice to life in the Center of the Universe is constant controversy. At this very moment, Greer is doubly blessed to be battling in court over fire protection and arguing in churches about downtown drinking. At least the subject has changed. We haven't heard a peep out of the drag strip lately.

The first Greer controversy I can recall involved downtown. It was about too many teenagers congregating on the sidewalk in front of the McLeskey-Todd Drug Store (located on East Poinsett Street then) in 1953.

Someone eventually found a cure for downtown crowds—parking meters. Then the meters themselves became controversial until city administrators grabbed the spotlight.

That was when the marijuana plant incident put Greer on the map. The Public Safety Director was accused of removing one of the illegal weeds in a paper cup from the police evidence locker. That was in 1976, and a Citizens Committee was appointed to investigate the administrator who hired the executive.

Years later, City Councilman Singleton Gilmore got rid of another administrator. In the process, the police department was burglarized, and everyone feared the phone lines were bugged at city hall.

Your history lesson would be incomplete without the fables of how Greer tried to capture BMW and then the GSP Airport. Those were molehills compared to the flap that pitted the City Council against the Commission of Public Works. That struggle raged for two years before running out of steam back in February.

But nothing lasts forever, not even peace and quiet. And so, six months have passed and someone decided Greer needed renewed attention, even if it did mean waiting until midnight to roll up the sidewalks. Jazz and Candlelight events have drawn the largest crowds to downtown Greer since Mike Bullock took a week's vacation and there were 200 men waiting outside the barbershop for a haircut the following Monday morning.

I trust the City Council to come up with a Solomon-like decision that will please everyone. Could we take a sword to downtown Greer?

At least one city council member has refused to visit downtown on Saturday nights to take part in the research. Gave the excuse of not wanting to be near "alkehaul." This elected official has resorted to buying groceries through the QVC Shopping Network to avoid supermarkets that sell beer.

Another council member wants to keep the Jazz and Candlelight parties going to help build police revenue—said a staggering drunk in the hand is worth three speeding tickets in the bush.

There is an out for people who want to drink and not be seen. They can hide among the branches of the Trade Street Bradford Pear trees that are growing faster than kudzu.

While awaiting the outcome of this latest controversy, I will put forth my own win-win solution: simply contract with the Department of Motor Vehicles (they run the highway office in Greer) to oversee the selling of alcoholic beverages. People would still flock downtown, knowing that ice-cold beer was on tap on a hot August night. But, by the time they finally made it to the head of the serving line, the midnight curfew would have arrived and the party would be over.

Old Greer vs. New Greer – Jan. 19, 2000

All Greer residents fall into two basic categories: Old Greer and New Greer. Like the Biblical warning against pouring new wine into old wineskins, Old Greer and New Greer do not easily mix. No one is automatically considered to be Old Greer unless they were born in Greer and have one of the following surnames: Bailey, Davenport, Dillard, Dobson, Duncan, Gibson, Green, Hawkins, Hill, Hughes, James, Smith, Taylor, Waters, Williams or Wood.

After I moved to Greer at the age of two, it took 50 years for me to become accepted as Old Greer. I have felt like an outsider most of my life. It is humbling to realize that McGee is considered Old Greer and almost everyone else is New Greer.

An uneasy truce exists between Old and New Greer because neither camp understands the other. For example, Old Greer people don't understand why Larry Wilson built an outdoor overcoat rack at the State Auto building when there are very few days of the year that the temperature dips so low that winter top coats are necessary.

Numerous other obvious differences distinguish the two Greers. Old Greer knows that The Fork is a restaurant. New Greer thinks The Fork is an eating utensil.

An Old Greer resident would remember seeing a crowd downtown in the 1940s or 50s. But the New Greer newcomers do not even realize that they reside in Greer, despite having a Greer mailing address and telephone number. They think that Wade Hampton Blvd. is the center of town.

Old Greer folks remember feeding parking meters on Trade Street. New Greer folks look for a payoff any time they put coins into a machine.

Old Greer culture considers chasing the Blue Light specials at Kmart to be a night out on the town; the New Greer clan prefers staking out Wal-Mart aisles to catch an associate actually rolling back the prices.

Old Greerites are poor but proud; New Greerites are merely proud.

Football is the game of choice of Old Greer sports fans; New Greer spectators prefer soccer.

Burgiss Hill is the preferred neighborhood for Old Greer homeowners; Thornblade is the coveted address for New Greer.

You can distinguish Old Greer neighbors by their accents and conversation style: they start every sentence with the word "well." By contrast, New Greer neighbors launch every utterance with the term "you know."

Chili cheeseburgers are the favorite food of Old Greer people. New Greer residents have opted for quiche.

The Old Greer's favored mode of transportation is the F-150 pickup truck; New Greer prefers a BMW.

The Old Greer crowd would never do anything flashy like hopping aboard a jet airliner for a weekend in Cancun. Instead, Old Greer citizens are saving aluminum cans for a rainy day.

New Greer arrivals have never set their feet under a table at the New Dixie restaurant while Old Greer people are as scarce as snowflakes in July at Applebee's.

The New Greer crowd has no idea where the Greer Dragway is located or the difference between New Woodruff Rd., Old Woodruff Rd., South Line Street and Highway 101 South.

Old Greer society considered the Miss LeFlambeau Pageant to be the social event of the year; for New Greer residents it is the Thornblade Classic.

Over time, it has become easier to fit into the community, although there can be setbacks along the way. Old timers have maintained what amounts to ice hockey's penalty box—make a mistake, and it will set you back for a while. That's what happened to Wilson.

Arriving from Ohio nearly 20 years ago, Wilson promptly bought a house in Sugar Creek and then wondered why he wasn't welcomed with open arms. The reason was that Sugar Creek people, back then at least, considered themselves to be residents of Greenville. And old timers were put off because the Sugar Creekers never came downtown to shop on Trade Street.

Wilson finally overcame that handicap by becoming Chairman of the Chamber of Commerce. Just when he was fitting in, however, Wilson erected the world's largest outdoor coat rack, stretching two stories high, on the grounds of State Auto Insurance. Old timers considered that to be "strange," and Wilson was remanded to the penalty box.

Then Wilson atoned by leading the original Partnership for Tomorrow drive. He was quickly accepted again only to move out of Sugar Creek and into Mountain Meadows. Old timers decided Wilson didn't know where Greer is after all, and back he went to the penalty box.

Despite all of the above, Wilson cannot understand why he is branded as New Greer, even though he has been in town for 15 years. I patiently explained to Wilson that even people like Bill Jordan, who were born in Greer, moved away, and then returned 40 years later, have to start over just like any transplanted Yankee. This means that even though Jordan and Ronnie Bruce are senior citizens, they are still assigned to the New Greer Camp, and their status must be declared on applications for admission to the nursing home.

I did suggest to Wilson that there are two ways he can greatly speed his quest for Old Greer status: (1) by becoming famous or (2) with a great achievement, such as annexing Mountain Meadows into the Greer City Limits.

Meanwhile, the growth that has followed BMW Manufacturing is also forcing old timers to change their habits to coexist with the newcomers. Among them are dining out at Gerard's instead of Hardee's;

discovering soccer; no longer driving the center lanes of West Poinsett Street because the outside lanes are bumpy; doing volunteer service at wine and cheese benefits for the Red Cross instead of working in the Soup Kitchen; and driving such automobiles as Saab, Lexus, Volvo that 20 years ago no one knew existed.

National Geographic needs Greer map
– Nov. 19, 1997

National Geographic magazine might as well go ahead and publish one of those huge fold-out maps of Greer. You know, the kind of map that falls out of the magazine and you can't ever fold it back correctly after having opened it up.

For one thing, such a map would save 35th century archeologists a lot of trouble looking for places to dig for things in (then) prehistoric Greer. The old landscape is disappearing right before our eyes. New things are going up everywhere, and I mean up—on top of something that was here first but soon forgotten. For instance, not many more years will pass before no one is left who remembers that a motel sits on top of one of Greer's most famous landmarks, Suttle's Swimming Pool.

Did you know that Greer has three Post Office buildings, and it is difficult to buy a stamp at any of them?

As we speak, hundreds of families in the city's second most up-scale mobile home park are being uprooted in the name of progress— a new Wal-Mart is going up, which raises the question, can Sam's be far behind? If so, Greer may need more chiropractors to treat people with backs ailing from lugging around cards—shopping membership cards, club cards, bonus cards, discount cards, credit and debit cards, etc.

Political blood was shed to establish a new industrial park that opened in fine fashion on Highway 101 South. The reason for designating it as an industrial park was to prevent anyone from locating a mobile home on the place. Before it was a park, the land was used for growing peaches, which were Greer's claim to fame before BMW. That is another reason a map would be useful—some disoriented Germans continue to insist that the BMW plant is in Spartanburg.

"What next?" you may ask. Well, we have just been introduced to the Greer Chamber of Commerce's 57th annual long-range plan. It calls for a new city hall to occupy the semi-hallowed ground where the famed Lewis' Drive-in once stood.

As you can see, space is at a premium in Greer. A new motel has just been built in the back yard of a fast food restaurant on West Wade Hampton Blvd. I remember people talking for years about wanting a motel—how wonderful it would be to have a place to send out-of-town relatives who are camping in your spare bedroom. Sometimes our dreams come true.

Speaking of mysterious events, Greer was featured recently in an ETV special "Steven Hawking's Universe." Scientists theorized that a black hole exists in Greer. How else could you account for the disappearance of the new Rite Aid Drug Store that was built next to Shoney's or the vanishing of the Strategic Planning Committee?

According to the ETV special, the center of the universe is Bullock's Barbershop on Trade Street. The proprietor Mike Bullock, opted out of being part of the historical district, not out of disrespect for such long gone landmarks as Ponder's and the Wayside Inn Hotel, but more importantly because there is not enough wall space on a National Register plaque for his football posters.

Next door on Trade Street, Citizens Building and Loan sits on top of the original Frierson's Drug Store. Down the street, the once-famous Sanitary Café is now a parking lot.

Across the street from Bullock's, the Greer Heritage Museum is bursting at the seams with things that have been displaced. The downtown trees have also outgrown their bounds, causing a major dilemma. The city will have to trim the trees to wrap the strands of Christmas lights on them or else purchase more lights.

The moral of this story is you can't live in Greer as cheaply as you once could. You can't even find your way around without a map.

Greer has Fewer Banks - Nov. 13, 1996

If you take a long nap in Greer, you might not recognize the place when you wake up.

That fact was brought home last week when United Carolina Bank (UCB) was sold to Southern National. UCB will soon join the growing list of banks that have disappeared. I expect the new Greer Heritage Museum will devote an entire section to our extinct banks. Do you remember First National, People's National, Greer Federal S&L, Fidelity Federal, C&S, NCNB, and SCN, just to name a few that have come and gone since the fifties?

Then there was the Bank of Greer, which was swallowed up by UCB in 1986 after having fought off several other suitors. Lawrence Dobson recently recalled that his father, the late R.A. Dobson, and several other prominent Greer residents bought controlling interest in the Bank of Duncan. They moved that bank to Greer in 1933, on a Saturday afternoon on the back of a flatbed truck, no less. That was after all the Greer banks had failed during the Great Depression.

One week, it was the Bank of Duncan, and the next it was the Bank of Greer. No wonder Duncan residents don't trust Greer folks. But it proves that in the world of banking, the more things change, the more they stay the same. And, by the way, this probably set the precedent for Greer's attempt to annex BMW Manufacturing.

I admire those old timers who bought stock in the old Bank of Greer and held it through thick and thin when the price didn't budge for years. Now that their investment has skyrocketed, their descendants will enjoy spending the windfall.

One reason I have been designated an official artifact of the Greer Museum is that I remember things like the old Bank of Greer. You could hear a pin drop in the lobby of the Trade Street bank. It was quieter than a funeral home.

The late B.A. Bennett was president of the Bank of Greer in the 1940s, and was widely regarded as the leading citizen in the community. A very reserved, slightly built man, Bennett did not have time for small talk and glad-handing. His wife, Lula Belle, was just the opposite and probably would have been mayor if she had come along a generation later.

Paul Brannon, who succeeded Bennett, was one of the friendliest, most approachable bankers Greer has ever had. He ran a tight ship with the help of Sheaffer McClimon who was in charge of making loans. The word on the street was that if you needed money, it was almost impossible to get a loan at the Bank of Greer. But if you didn't really need it, McClimon would loan you the money.

No matter what the name is on the exterior, the old Bank of Greer building should be preserved. It was the center of commerce in downtown Greer for over half a century.

I opened my first bank account at First National, a new bank that popped up across Trade Street from the Bank of Greer in the late 1950s. That was the first of several banks that have vanished with me on board. But First National did not sink into the ground under the weight of my money in the vault.

Great Events in Greer History

Greer's First 15 Minutes of Fame - Feb. 9, 2000

Like a modern day gold rush, former President Ronald Reagan's visit brought Greer a long overdue 15 minutes of fame when dozens of national TV camera crews, newspaper photographers, and reporters descended upon the event. Reagan spoke at the annual meeting of the Greer Chamber of Commerce on his 69th birthday—and fell into a flaming cake. That was Feb. 6, 1980.

Until then, the most noteworthy event that has ever happened in Greer was the appearance of Miss America in the 1957 Peach Festival Parade. Which barely topped a bullwhip exhibition given by Hollywood western movie star Lash LaRue on the stage of The Greer Theatre in 1953.

How Reagan wound up in Greer is the best part of the story. It began six months earlier when Dan Fishner decided that something must be done to improve Greer's backwoods image. Having a famous person speak at the Chamber's annual meeting would be just the thing to put Greer in the limelight. Reagan was at the top of Fishner's list. He was already famous as the host of a long-running television series and had gone on to become Governor of California. Fishner was convinced that Carroll Campbell (then a Congressman) could persuade Reagan to visit Greer. Fishner had thrown a campaign barbecue for Campbell and was calling in the chip.

Fishner devised a plan to snare Reagan when he came to Columbia to seek the blessing of the state's Republican Party big wigs before launching a bid for the Presidency. Fishner persuaded Chamber President Pete Smith, President-elect Stan Grist, and me to accompany him to Columbia to put the rush on Reagan. I went along because Fishner was certain that I would get an exclusive interview with the great man. I doubted that Reagan had ever heard of Greer, much less would dispense any gems of wisdom for our newspaper readers, yet it seemed like a good idea. After all, Fishner was a persuasive, fast talking newcomer with an accent—a rare bird in the days before BMW.

Fishner had everything mapped out. When Rep. Campbell arrived from Washington, D.C., he would usher us in to meet Reagan, and the candidate would be unable to refuse Fishner's pitch (nobody else had).

As luck would have it, however, the date was Nov. 13th, and we should have heeded that omen. But Fishner was bubbling over with enthusiasm as usual, regaling us with how we were going to meet Reagan and enjoy a big banquet. Against my better judgment, I put aside all thoughts of jumping out of the car and walking home.

Soon after arriving at the Sheraton in Columbia in the early afternoon, we began to realize that this wasn't our day. Although Fishner had the big picture, he was short on details—like we had no credentials or tickets for the dinner and rally to follow Reagan's high-level strategy session.

But Fishner assured us, saying "no problem." He promised that a man named "Sam" would take care of everything.

Although we asked dozens of people, including bellhops and security guards, no one had ever heard of Sam. Even worse, Campbell's flight from Washington had been delayed by bad weather, so he could not intervene on our behalf.

Eventually we set out on our own to find the conference room and were soon confronted by a small army of Secret Service Agents.

Fishner informed one agent "We're from Greer, and we are to meet a man named Sam who said we could get in see Governor Reagan." The agent said, "I don't know you or anybody named Sam. You can't go in."

So we stood outside in the hall, and two hours later to our amazement out walked Governor Reagan. We were so dumfounded that none of us could open our mouths to say anything. As we watched Reagan depart, one of his cadre of agents turned and asked "are you with the Reagan party?"

With that, Smith blurted out his all time infamous response: "we aren't anybody, we're from Greer."

We hung around another couple of hours, emptying the vending machines of crackers and soft drinks, and eventually Campbell dashed into the lobby. We stopped him long enough to learn that he was overdue for a private dinner with Reagan upstairs. Fishner made amends by taking us out to dinner – at McDonalds. And Campbell went to great lengths to make amends by persuading Reagan to speak at the Chamber banquet.

For the record, Fishner doubled the price of admission to the banquet and moved the venue to the Greenville City Club. Greer's "po but proud" old guard said it would be a disaster, but all 450 tickets were snapped up the day they went on sale.

It came to pass that one snowy February night, the future President was presented a Greer firemen's helmet from Chief Mack Bailey and then splattered his brown suit with white icing while blowing out the candles on his birthday cake.

Time Capsule Missing Key Items – May 8, 2002

The big news in Greer last week was the celebration of the 50th anniversary of Allen Bennett Memorial Hospital. The original hospital may be gone, but old timers remember what it looked like and the miracles that occurred there.

There were things about the hospital that fascinated me way back when it opened in 1952. The late Dr. Johnny Walker, an owner of the Greer Rexall Drug Store, took a room at the hospital in the Fifties and lived there a very long time. He was a pioneer of the nursing home concept, which was unheard of at the time. I imagine Dr. Walker holds the record for the number of days that an individual spent in Allen Bennett.

I remember Dr. Jack Packard who drenched himself with the world's most powerful after-shave lotion. That lotion was better than a pager—everyone knew where Dr. Packard could be found because his scent could be tracked, even by folks with clogged sinuses. Dr. Packard ran the X-Ray Department and worked around the clock for years. An injury that Dr. Packard suffered in a pick-up basketball game, on a rare day when he took a couple of hours off, short-circuited his career.

I remember when former Police Chief Dan Stepp was a rookie cop and worked nights at the hospital. His job was to run visitors out at 8 p.m. sharp. This took some doing because no one wanted to leave—except the patients who could not go anywhere.

None of my memories went into the time capsule that was buried during the 50th anniversary celebration. There wasn't even a copy of the hospital cafeteria cookbook containing 1,000 no-salt recipes.

A great many other things were also overlooked—simply because no one requested a contribution from my assortment of health care memorabilia that I have been collecting over the years. I was offended because I have been saving a couple of kidney stones for 25 years, just waiting to donate them for such a special occasion. I also would have parted with the living color video of my colonoscopy, a set of X-rays of my head that show nothing, and the silver foil hat that I wore into the operating room when my appendix exploded.

The time capsule should have contained the truly important artifacts of present day medicine that I hope can be improved upon before it is unearthed at the hospital's 100th birthday celebration. Surely by 2052, someone will have improved the world's most embarrassing garment—the hospital gown. Ditto for the bedpan, at least one that is not as cold as an icicle-draped signpost in the dead of winter.

Perhaps the rubber glove will also become a thing of the past. The time capsule could have used a pair along with instructions for their many uses, including serving as water balloons.

Not a single aspirin, the wonder drug that is rediscovered every half-century, went into the capsule. It also lacked a tongue depressor and a Band-Aid. Most noticeably absent was the glass of white chalk that must be choked down for a "GI Series" and that age-old therapeutic device, the enema.

The greatest omission was a time-stamped ticket stub confirming that the wait in the emergency room is even longer than at the DMV office.

Most of all, I find it interesting that the hospital buried a time capsule, confirming the widely held journalistic theory that doctors bury their mistakes but editors print their errors for all the world to see and criticize.

Fire Truck Brings Back Memories – Sept. 4, 2002

I am surrounded with reminders of having reached an age older than classic cars. The latest such memory-jogger occurred Friday when I was summoned to City Hall to see Greer's old Engine Number 3 off to the Fire Department in the Sky. Actually, the engine is going to a firefighting museum, which is an intermediate move like checking into a nursing home en route to the graveyard.

The 1964 Howe truck is older than every fireman who turned out to give it a proper sendoff. The truck still carries the plaque with the names of the mayor and city council members of that day. Only one of them, Broadus B. Dobson, is still with us.

But to gather more details, I had to dig out a mirror. I realized that I am one of the few people who remember the day that Engine 3 arrived in Greer, fresh from the factory. I've never seen anyone, even my kids on Christmas morning, any more excited than the late Fire Chief R.B. Colvin was that day. Grinning from ear to ear, Chief Colvin pulled up in front of the newspaper office, having driven the truck straight from the factory in another state. He sounded the siren, causing us to rush to the door.

Talking faster than his customary 498 words a minute, Colvin began to spiel off the features of the truck with its Chevy engine—how it could carry 250 gallons of water, enough to extinguish a small fire; how it had a deluge gun mounted on top, meaning that it could match a hurricane when it came to spraying water. In its prime, the truck could pump 750 gallons of water per minute from a fire hydrant. But if a hydrant wasn't capable of delivering that much water, I've seen the truck literally suck the hydrant out of the ground.

Old Engine 3 led many a Christmas parade through downtown Greer. It also sat patiently during countless tours while kids scrambled through its cab and swung off the ladders on the sides.

Greer's Engine 3 battled some historic blazes. The most memorable was when the old Davenport High School burned to the ground. I also observed the engine hurling untold thousands of gallons of water onto the huge blazes that seemingly could not be extinguished at the (then vacant) old Central Elementary School and Franklin Mill.

On its' 38th birthday, Engine 3 has only 28,930 miles on the odometer. Any used car salesman will tell you that low mileage means a vehicle is a real cream puff. And yes, it runs just like new—if only the water tank did not leak….

Back in 1964, Engine 3 was a big improvement in the city's fire fighting hardware. It was 12 years newer than the 1951 Ford that had been the department's work horse alongside a 1941 Chevy Howe with an open cab that gave it the resemblance of a convertible.

My first close encounter with a real fire truck was part of my education at Wofford College. My fraternity decided to obtain a fire engine and decorate it so we could keep up with another frat that had just acquired a fire truck. One of our fraternity brothers found a fire engine for sale in south Georgia. It was a 1930s-something Seagraves model going for $600. We plunked down a sizeable chunk of dues revenues to buy the truck, although none of the fire fighting apparatus was in working order, and the motor was as out of sorts as a mule in a nest of fire ants.

In spite of several breakdowns along the way, we eventually got the truck back to Spartanburg and had it lettered ΠΚΑ in gold. Just in time for the college's annual Homecoming Parade prior to the football game with Presbyterian College.

Not to be outdone, the Delta Sigs topped us by adding an attraction to their frat's fire engine. One of their members was ensconced atop a white porcelain commode on the back of the truck. Their parade entry carried a huge banner that proclaimed, "Wofford flushes P.C." (with the added insinuation that P.C. was an abbreviation for "Public Commode.")

When the parade passed by the faculty's reviewing stand, the Dean of Students blew his top. He gave the offending fraternity six months probation and ordered them to get rid of the fire truck.

Our IIKA ladder truck proved to be a burden. Not only did the insurance cost more than the truck itself, none of us had enough mechanical know-how to keep it running. But if the fire-fighting museum ever decides to get rid of old Engine 3, I'll bet a college fraternity will be waiting to snap it up.

Loony for Clooney – Jan 31, 2007

Do you remember where you were and what you were doing when terrorists hijacked jetliners slammed into the twin towers in New York City? Or, if you're age 50 or older, the day that President John F. Kennedy was shot? Well, here is a new benchmark: what's your memory of the day that George Clooney came to Greer?

Greer has gone loony over Clooney! After all, he is the first movie star to hit town since Lash LaRue appeared on stage at The Greer Theatre in 1953. That was even before the Clampetts headed to California. A half century later, Beverly Hills has repaid the favor by coming to Greer.

I was at my computer typing away at 4:05 p.m. on the afternoon of Jan. 12, 2007, when there arose such a clatter that I jumped from my chair to see what was the matter. All the women in our office were trying to squeeze through the front door at once, shrieking in unison "George is here! George Clooney is here!"

The women raced down the street as if chasing the blue light at K-Mart. They were caught up in the largest crowd in years on Trade Street, other than the daily gatherings in Bullock's Barbershop.

This curmudgeon didn't budge, however. I had rather see George Davenport than George Clooney. I wouldn't try to get a movie star's autograph unless it is on a check.

Clooney was scouting out downtown Greer as a location for shooting scenes for his next movie, "Leatherheads," a 1920s era tale about football players who wore leather helmets. That's when downtown Greer was built and nothing much has changed, except the streetscape that converted our sidewalks into a skateboarder's paradise.

Greer has many other assets for the Clooney movie. The old city stadium was under consideration for football game scenes until it was discovered that our Olympic cow-chip throwing team has it booked for practice every afternoon.

We have many available "extras" for crowd scene shots. Unfortunately, we are twice the size of people who walked the downtown streets in the Twenties, so wide-angle lenses will be required for the movie cameras.

Another downer is that no former Greer High football players who wore leather helmets are still vertical. But we have many plastic heads available for game scenes as well as Pat Sudduth who did not need a helmet. Then there's Darrell Leonhardt who played football in his bare feet, so the sequel, Leatherfeet, could have been filmed in Greer had not Willie Rowe shut down the Dixie Shoe Shop.

Ronnie Bruce is waiting in the wings for a call back as a supporting actor in Leatherlungs, which will complete the trilogy. It will be a World War II story about the bombing of London—filmed on the site of the demolished old Victor Mill.

I wonder if anyone has considered the consequences of using Trade Street for movie making. For one, the wait in traffic will double from two to four light changes at the intersection of Main and Poinsett. The Cliffs dwellers may actually drive past Gerard's without stopping in order to get a look behind the scenes. Such a situation could spiral out of control into a social demolition derby.

The timing could not be worse since the filming will disrupt the annual downtown Possum Cook-off in March. Tow trucks will be summoned to remove turnip wagons parked in the Trade Street tow-away zones to make room for film crews. The interiors of some downtown buildings will have to be redecorated, meaning the paintings of Elvis on black velvet will have to come down.

Obviously Clooney has failed to consider that no nighttime scenes can be filmed here since it never gets dark because of the glow from thousands of red necks.

But Clooney is a good guy, according to Bernard Price, who said "He puts his pants on one leg at a time." If Smith & James puts 1920s prices on those pants for movie scenes in the store, Clooney will be jumping into them both legs at one time.

Does Greer, the Center of the Cosmos and already bigger and better than Greenville or Spartanburg, really need the added fame of silver screen? We already have the home place of the American Idle at The Poinsett Grocery. The only good that can come of this is for Greer to push Ware Shoals off the 10 o'clock Firefox news—what happens in the Las Vegas of the east coast should stay here.

BMW

Actually, Greer Got Wrong Car Company
- Aug. 23, 1995

A team from Vance, Ala., is planning to visit Greer to learn what effect BMW has had on our town. It seems Mercedes is building a plant near Vance, and they don't know what to expect.

The price of this edition (50 cents) will save them thousands of dollars in travel expenses. I am revealing everything they need to know about what has happened to Greer.

First, a little bit of history: Greer got the wrong car company. Henny Penny actually dispatched development guru Peter McCord to Europe to recruit a Yugo factory. I must agree that Yugo would have been a perfect fit. Most people can afford a Yugo. Also, we are prone to fight among ourselves, just like the Yugo inventors in Bosnia.

The date was January 13, 1991. McCord boarded a crash-proof U.S. Air jet to Yugoslavia. In mid-air, McCord was taken hostage by terrorists and the flight was diverted to Germany. The efficient German police captured the hijackers and promised the offended McCord a BMW factory to prevent an international incident.

That's when it became obvious Greer is endowed with a mutation of the Midas Touch: Everything Greer touches turns to substance similar to the stuff found on barnyard floors.

169

Greer immediately established a Strategic Planning Committee to usher in the BMW era. That was three years ago, and there is no plan.

As a result of BMW buying land, several farmers became instant millionaires. They are the only ones who can afford to buy a car made in Greer.

In less than a year, Mayor Don Wall attempted to annex BMW. During a showdown with Governor Carroll Campbell, however, Wall sprouted leg feathers and settled for a road instead. The traffic has arrived, but the road is nowhere in sight.

The Mayor also irritated Spartanburg County Council, which had spent a huge amount of money on BMW. They retaliated by curtailing the only nightlife in town: the Greer Dragway.

Many other things have happened, including:

The line of people waiting in the Post Office lobby now extends into the street.

In an Avant-garde move, the Community Cash store was completely rearranged, leaving grocery shoppers totally confused.

Ma Bell discontinued the Greer telephone book.

The present economic boom is about to spawn a second Waffle House.

Some of our most famous residents have been refused exit visas. Our police chief, who attempted to move to Florida, and our football coach, who attempted to leave for Greenwood, are under house arrest.

The city council passed a Highway 101 beautification ordinance requiring that refrigerators on front porches be painted in decorator colors.

An estimated 17 people have converted to GARP.

The school board refuses to build a new Greer High School, although the plans were announced back when the present seniors were in the third grade.

And so, my advice to the good people of Vance is to swap Mercedes for a moped factory. If that's not possible, then move to Mississippi.

I Wish They Would Quit Picking on BMW
– Feb. 25, 1998

I have been less than spellbound by the news stories revealing that BMW Manufacturing spent thousands of tax dollars to send executives on white water rafting trips.

Some grandstanding legislators made this tempest in a teapot even worse by calling for the governor to appoint an Independent Counsel to investigate.

This is white water rafting, so get over it. I'm tired of people picking on BMW. Some are obviously jealous, most likely because BMW is a world class company that makes a profit by catering to Yuppies like NASCAR star Jeff Gordon. He's young, handsome, wealthy and married to a beauty queen. So what's not to like?

A rumor floated that BMW sent its executives rafting to become familiar with water. They speculated that BMW hoped to make competitors think it is planning to build a line of upscale submarines.

As for complaints about the state giving away money, I think BMW should spend the money any way it wants. If the truth were known, Governor Carroll Campbell promised the money as an incentive to make sure that BMW would make a profit in South Carolina even if the company didn't sell any cars. Unlike Campbell's other promises, such as lowering automobile insurance, this one was fulfilled. Since the Z-3 and Z-4 models were such hits, BMW had to do something with all that cash. So they went rafting.

And we rednecks had the same kind of reaction as our common law Oconee County cousins in the classic novel (and movie) *Deliverance*. We stood on the banks and took pot shots at the rafters. It would have suited us better if the BMW big wigs had gone innertubing down the South Tyger River or jet skiing on Lake Hartwell. We could understand that. Being unsophisticated, however, we know nothing about how bashing heads on rocks in a raging river builds leadership. We don't understand why those who survived the rafting trip reported to the office on Monday morning.

I do understand why BMW is using the ropes course as part of the company's training program. I was once a Cub Scout, and if BMW execs can learn how to tie all those different kinds of knots, they qualify for the white collar jobs. As the BMW spokesman was quoted, "it's more than a cookie cutter operation out there." And if sales drop off the bottom of the chart, the execs can use the ropes to hang themselves.

If our BMW plant were cranking out Yugos, I could understand the public outcry. And I know that Flagstar, another company that Spartanburg claimed until recently, lost $154 million last year. Maybe they should have invested in a raft.

What's Wrong with This Picture?

What Can We Do About Downtown?
– June 4, 1997

I had an urgent phone call on Friday. A woman on the other end of the line was asking for help. "What do you think we should do about downtown Greer?" she asked in a voice filled with desperation.

The caller wants more people visiting downtown. More warm bodies will be needed, for example, if and when a new civic center is built, or if the present municipal auditorium should dodge the wrecking ball and reopen.

When it comes to re-inflating downtown Greer, you might as well write your ideas on my mind because it is as blank as a clean sheet of paper. I have pondered this question for 35 years, and I still don't have a clue about what should be done.

I do know that the downtown could use some excitement. But the most exciting thing that has happened in downtown Greer during my watch was the painting of the backs of the store buildings on Trade Street. The late S.A. "Bill" Wall was turned loose with his trusty spray gun to do the job. Wall, who was both a fireman and policeman at the same time, only painted on his day off from work. Unfortunately, that happened to be a windy day, so a number of cars parked in the alleys went home wearing a new coat of beige paint.

Downtown Greer has many unique characteristics. Unfortunately, these special traits do not appeal to many people—only a few museum loving types like me.

Since the heart of downtown, Trade Street, is only three blocks long, people see it too quickly when passing through Greer. I'm sure we could slow things down by erecting one-way signs on the south end of Trade to send motorists going around in circles.

Opening six more barbershops adjacent to Bullock's might get more people to stop and stay a while. That also might be overkill.

Wine and cheese parties might not go over either. But I think we should have at least one Grits Tasting Gala if only to test the waters.

The Family Festival has been successful at drawing crowds downtown, although Anne Helton is the only volunteer who would show up to work a festival every weekend.

My current best idea is to make the downtown a living board game and hand out lottery tickets as prizes. For instance, a daily winner would be the person who guesses the correct time. This is not as easy as it may seem because the downtown streetlights come on during daylight hours and go off after dark.

Another guessing game could be "name that store." As the Bradford Pear trees, which were planted for beauty without regard to size, have continued to grow, the business signs have disappeared among the tree branches.

The adventuresome could play street light stump wiring. The winner would be the person who can connect any two matching wires, among the many protruding from the bases where light poles one stood, without getting electrocuted.

The city also could dig the parking meters out of the museum basement and put them up again as a mind game for motorists. Most people would think they are getting away with something when they parked downtown and did not feed the meters.

Total Confusion – Mar. 6, 1991

I am in a state of total confusion after someone rearranged the grocery store. Everything has been turned upside down. The peanut section has been replaced by houseplants. Movie rentals are where the dog food had been located for years.

Suddenly, it's like I am a total stranger in the store. I went in today and didn't recognize a single thing—except "Granny" McKinney behind the register at the checkout counter.

I quickly discovered that you can't buy groceries in 30 minutes when you don't know where anything is located. Now, a shopping trip of there hours would be making good time. I even heard of some people who have been wandering around inside the store for days trying to find something.

Community Cash advertises "It's not a store, it's a family tradition." I have been buying pickles on aisle 44 for a quarter of a century. That's tradition. But the other day, the pickles were no longer on aisle 44.

That was a cause for panic when I started checking items off my grocery list. I was 45 minutes late for an appointment and desperately trying to remember if I had passed the pickles near the paper towel department on aisle 19. So much for tradition.

I concluded that rearranging the grocery store must be a terrorist plot, or maybe it was done to confuse Iraqi spies. But the result has been like re-writing the Declaration of Independence.

I ran into Phyllis Gravley on aisle 56. She had been in the store since early that morning looking for a pizza. Gravley wouldn't budge. She kept mumbling that Leon told her not to come home without a pizza for lunch.

Gravley was munching peanut butter crackers as the lunch hour came and went. She could hardly talk because her throat was very dry, and she was still eight aisles away from the milk department before even nearing the checkout.

175

I went to find the manager to complain about our shopping rights having been violated. Junior Holder said I would have to write a letter to the editor of the newspaper.

Holder also claimed it wasn't his idea to rearrange the store. Besides, he didn't know where anything was in the first place. Holder explained that he had been afraid to learn the original layout because the new owners might close the store on him, and he'd just have to get used to managing another store.

Holder did mention that during the big changeover he had found all sorts of things that no one knew were in stock. So he's having a big sale. The dozens of shopping carts filled with specials interested me, but I did not find a single pair of shoes. I did snap up a can of Spam. We had not dined on Spam in years, so we opened the can for supper. Now I know why I hadn't purchased Spam in years.

I returned home with twice as many grocery items as were on my list. Since you must examine every shelf while trying to find your way through the store, you end up buying stuff that you have never seen before.

As I was checking out, the cashier gave me a map of the new store layout and an emergency number in case I got lost again. I still can't figure some things out, however. For instance, I bought vanilla ice cream on isle 89 so I could make a sundae. According to the map, however, I had passed the chocolate syrup two hours earlier back on aisle 16.

The tires are no longer near the potato chips either. I always enjoyed snacking on chips while waiting for a bag boy to fix a flat.

Rearranging the merchandise aside, my biggest complaint is the new checkout computer. It adds your bill faster than you can write a check. That is an indication of how much times have changed for I can remember bringing cash to buy groceries. But the buggies will not hold the amount of money needed today, and I guess that's another tradition down the drain, too.

No Parking – Mar. 29, 2011

Change is the only thing in life that is certain. But not always—human beings have yet to embrace walking.

I'm questioning why the person who runs five miles a day needs a TV remote control, and why people battle for parking places nearest the door of the athletic club. Once inside, they will jog on a treadmill for an hour. If these fitness buffs would simply walk to the gym, they would tie up the treadmills for only half an hour.

Walking woes have created a never-ending parking issue that dates back to 1876 when Greer became a city. Even then, there was not enough parking on Trade Street to accommodate the horse-drawn buggies that came downtown on weekends.

Greer's parking problem was compounded by the invention of the automobile. My earliest memories include the traffic jams outside the Post Office (now the home of the Greer Heritage Museum) on South Main St. There was no parking lot, nor parking spaces along the curb. Nostalgia may not be what it once was, but I do remember that Dr. F.G. James simply parked his car in the middle of the street every morning, blocking traffic, while he collected the mail from his post office box. That must be the reason why the parallel parking test is the most difficult part of the drivers' license exam.

Greer's city fathers eventually brought order to the downtown chaos by installing parking meters. That became a reliable source of revenue. Several times a week, S.A. "Bill" Wall, who was a policeman/fireman/jack of all trades, emptied coins from the meters into a wash tub on a cart that he rolled along the sidewalks.

Years later, however, the parking meters were blamed for the demise of downtown Greer. Shopping centers sprang up with acres of free parking, and folks flocked there rather than feed the meters.

In recent years, walking woes have spread to the shopping centers and huge supermarkets. Parking there is becoming increasingly restricted to the point that the sore spot is again inflamed.

Although I have not undertaken a statistical study to prove the point, it seems like there are more parking spaces reserved for handicapped motorists than the number of people who are actually afflicted. How often is a truly handicapped person occupying one of the dozens of mostly vacant parking spaces designated for the handicapped?

Seemingly healthy, robust people will pull into handicapped spaces, bounce out of a handicapped tagged vehicle and dash into the store. (No need to write me a nasty letter. I realize a friend or relative may have borrowed the handicapped person's vehicle to run an errand.)

The only two parking spaces outside the Greer Police Department are not reserved for the handicapped but for captured speeders anxious to pay traffic tickets.

The handicapped parking issue pales in comparison to the myriad of other designated parking spaces that have sprung up throughout town. There are rapidly multiplying parking spaces reserved for such groups of: "parents with young children," "shoppers making a quick trip," "mothers with babies," and more.

Those could be just the tip of the iceberg. There are many more categories of special parking spaces to be reserved. After all, signs sprouting in parking lots will make shopping more efficient just like pushing the button numerous times causes elevators to travel faster.

I recommend that shopping centers add such special parking categories as: "Children with very old parents," "Drivers with floating eyeballs in search of a restroom," "Shoplifters anxious to make a quick get-away," "Alcoholics stopping for just two beers," "Smokers needing a quick nicotine fix," and my very favorite "Geezers with gout."

For good measure, perhaps secluded areas of parking lots should be designated for "Couples attempting to start a family."

Of course, the really important folks have their own personalized parking spaces with their names printed on them—under the BIG signs that declare: "unauthorized vehicles will be towed away."

Buses Will Solve All of Our Problems
– May 28, 2001

I really perked up when I heard that the Greenville Transit Authority (GTA) is considering providing bus service to Greer.

I've always had a fascination with buses. It goes back to when I was a kid visiting my grandparents in Dalton, Ga. I would sit in the swing on their front porch and watch buses making their way to the station that was just down the street. Occasionally, my grandfather would treat us to a bus ride to Ringgold or Rocky Face.

I acquired a deeper appreciation for buses when my midget football coach assigned me to play right tackle with the warning "the offensive line is the last stop before the bus stop."

I agree with the Greenville Transit Authority (GTA) that some Greer people could use a ride—especially those who are currently traveling by skateboard or razor scooter.

As I see it, there is only one problem facing the GTA: Greer does not have a bus station. Never has. Which is probably the only reason Greer is inferior to Greenville and Spartanburg.

I do remember when buses once came through Greer and stopped in front of the Wayside Inn Hotel on West Poinsett St. to pick up passengers. Today the Wayside Inn is mostly a parking lot, and more vacant spaces may appear in downtown Greer as the Bradford Pear trees continue to self-destruct and topple over onto the buildings.

Without a bus station, it seems that the best approach would be to give every Greer resident a bus of his own to drive home. The funding could come from the $6 trillion George W. Bush tax cut and no one would know the difference.

What better way to jump-start the nose-diving economy than to get the Blue Bird Bus Factory working around the clock?

What better reason for the government to start drilling for oil in Alaska national parks than to provide fuel for thousands of new buses?

Hang in here with me. A bus in every driveway isn't as far fetched as you might think! After all, some SUVs are as big as a bus. Like a Greyhound is only a tad larger than a Ford Excursion. Bigger is always better, you know. Besides, school bus yellow is one of my favorite colors.

The GTA survey asks: "Would you ride a bus to Greenville?" Probably not. "Would I drive my own bus to Greenville?" Of course!

The late Jackie Gleason was my favorite comedian, especially in the role of Ralph Kramden who was a bus driver in "The Honeymooners" sketches. "How sweet it is!" and "Away we go!", Gleason's favorite sayings, apply to owning your own bus.

Owning a bus has many advantages: You can always park in the reserved spaces for buses next to buildings like the Bi-Lo Rena. You would not have to walk a long distance or wait in a line of cars to pick up your kid at school—simply use the bus entrance.

Bus drivers don't ever get speeding tickets either. When was the last time you saw a bus pulled over by the cops? A bus shows up like the Georgia Dome on police radar, and surely buildings don't do 65 mph. Then too, you would get a kick when some helpless driver is arrested for passing your stopped bus.

Your bus can get out on I-85 and ride along with the big boys—the tractor-trailer rigs—without fear of being herded over to the shoulder of the highway. What's more, Volkswagens don't dart out in front of buses on city streets and live to tell about it.

Trust me: you can acquire immunity to the scent of diesel fumes. Actually, heavy black smoke has many benefits including keeping pollen under control which gives your allergies a break.

Best of all, a bus driver is like the captain of a ship. He can drop a nagging wife off on a desert island in the middle of the ocean or in a strange land like Thornblade.

What's Wrong with This Picture? – April 3, 2008

What's wrong with this picture? Hollywood came to Greer to make a movie, but Greer people are forced leave town to see the finished product. I, old Grump, am in a funk about having to drive to the Camelot Theatre in Greenville to see Greer in a movie.

Forget for a moment that barely one year ago I refused get up from behind my desk to see George Clooney walking down Trade Street. I care just slightly more now, especially since we are talking about shelling out big bucks this Friday night: $75 for a ticket to attend the movie premier and a red carpet party afterwards at The Davenport in downtown Greer.

That price tag merely starts the movie meter ticking. Even though no Oscar will be awarded, renting a tux for the occasion will cost another $100. That requires making three trips to Greenville, first for fitting the monkey suit, then to pick it up, and finally to return it. Coming with the territory is battling congestion and sitting through more than 100 traffic light changes while my gas guzzling Exploder sucks up $50 worth of liquid gold.

I doubt that The Camelot would allow star-struck rednecks to bring picnic baskets filled with corn dogs, pork skins and pickled eggs into the theatre. So there would be no choice but to munch on $20 boxes of buttered popcorn during the movie. And when the show is over, we would look as if we had been wrestling in a mosh pit and ruined our fancy clothes before the big party even begins.

A George Clooney look-alike may provide surprise entertainment for the gala. I have never seen an Elvis look-alike that actually looked like the real Elvis. If a Clooney twin really exists, he will have to arrive in a glass encased "Pope Mobile" to fend off female admirers.

That brings us to today's "keepsake" edition of *The Greer Citizen*, which will have the unintended consequence of forever reminding readers that we never got to see the Leatherheads movie in Greer. I had rather not be reminded of being so disadvantaged as not having a theatre in town, and with any luck my increasingly frequent senior moments will help me forget.

If you think I am demoralized because Greer has declined from three movie theatres in 1950 to zero today, you are correct. Sixty years ago, downtown Greer was a destination for people from far and wide. Part of the appeal was that The Grand Theatre was the only air-conditioned building in town. During the 'Dog Days' of August, an entire family could spend several hours in cool comfort for less than 50 cents.

The Rialto always had the best westerns, and on Saturdays you could see two of them plus a cartoon and serial adventure for the grand sum of six cents. That did not last long, and neither did The Rialto when it doubled the price of a ticket to 12 cents in 1952.

Today, Greer nightlife is barely a cut above the Sixties when we would break out a quilt and a couple of lawn chairs, grab a six pack of Pepsi Colas and camp on the corner of Main and Poinsett Streets to sit for hours just watching the traffic light change.

Over 40 years later, Greer Station's modern day entertainment begins with watching people fumble over the checks in upscale restaurants. After-dinner activities include strolling down Trade Street and peering in the plate glass window to see notables warming up by bending their elbows in the Bullpen.

We may not have the means to acquire a cultural arts center, eight-screen movie theatre or concert hall, but we could strive for the possible: convert three of our precious parking spaces into a shuffleboard court and install park benches where the John McCain generation could sit and talk about old times, as do men while waiting for their wives in the shopping malls.

Lionism in Greer

Lions Not an All-volunteer Outfit - Sept. 27, 1995

The challenges of life can bring out the best in people—especially those members of the Greer Lions Club who are fortunate enough to work in the concession stand at the football stadium.

Truthfully, fortunate is not the correct word. The Lions Club isn't an all-volunteer outfit like the Marines, looking for a few good men. Every Lion is drafted for concession duty. The club even has a drill sergeant, Jack Smith. He calls the roll and reports malingerers to the Tail Twister.

Those who are excused from Friday night duty must work the North Greenville University games on Saturday afternoons. Their mission is to sell everything left over from the previous night. On at least one occasion, that was 'Mission Impossible.' Jack Coggins popped an entire 50-pound sack of popcorn one Friday evening, and the supply outlasted Greer High's 15-game winning streak. Coggins is the only Lion who was ever drummed out of the concession stand.

B.B. "Buddy" Waters brings his kids to work in his place on Saturdays so he will have plenty of time to sample whatever food is available. Last week, Waters began training his youngest, Marie. She will replace an older brother, Gabe, who is doomed to march off to The Citadel.

No one complains about "Buddy" Waters out of respect for someone when he is down. You see, Waters if living proof of Murphy's Law: If anything can go wrong, it will.

Coffee making was the most recent concession stand calamity to befall Waters. He dumped a family size jar of instant coffee into a gallon of water and heated it to a boil. The result was tar-like syrup with the aroma of burnt motor oil. The only customer who drank a cup of the stuff was still sitting bolt upright and wide-awake, glued to his seat in the stands, when we returned to the stadium a week later.

David Beeks habitually goes AWOL at Homecoming to screen the candidates for NGU queen. Otherwise, he serves as the understudy food taster in the event that Waters collapses with heartburn.

Every five minutes Beeks counts the number of hot dogs remaining in hopes that a few will be left over at the end of the game. If so, he gets to eat them. But that rarely happens because Smith has a miserly habit of ordering too few of everything.

Lion Bobby Williams sits in his car and listens to Saturday afternoon football games on the radio. (It has not occurred to anyone that a radio could be provided in the concession stand so everyone could hear the broadcasts). Williams focuses on the Furman games since both Clemson and USC de-emphasized football. Every 15 minutes, he returns to report the scores to the crew that is busily serving customers. Williams does hang around long enough to devour a bowl of nachos (helps keep them from going stale, he claims), before heading back to his car.

Between Williams' updates, Smith passes the time observing football fans that wander up to the window. He has documented that customers who wear extra pounds always demand extra cheese on their nachos. They are related to fans that order a Diet Pepsi to wash down their candy bars.

Then there are fans that cannot be satisfied, like those who want hot dogs with no chili and those who want a straw for their hot chocolate.

But the worst are fans that carry big umbrellas on rainy days. When they lean across the counter, water cascades from their parasols, showering gallant Lions and dissolving the stacks of cardboard food carriers that we have spent hours putting together.

The only saving grace of concession stand duty is that there is never a dull moment.

Get Your Hot Dog Tickets Quick – Sept. 17, 1997

Nov. 2-8 has been declared National Indigestion Awareness Week. It became a nationwide observance after the Greer Lions Club's 1996 Hot Dog Supper at Big Thursday. They are still talking about that debacle.

The really shocking news is that the Lions have continued to host the event. And Joel Thornton stayed on as chairman, although that should come as no surprise since his grandfather was captain of the Titanic.

The '96 Hot Dog Supper ranks alongside all-time Greer disasters including the city's original skateboard park that was labeled the "Downtown Streetscape." And the short–lived Jazz and Candlelight that threatened to erode supermarket beer sales. Not to mention the Strategic Planning Committee that never planned anything.

Many will never forget the occasion when the Lions served hot dogs that faded into the buns rather than melting in your mouth. The entire kitchen crew applied for Lions Sight Conservation rehabilitation on the spot because they couldn't believe their eyes.

Even worse was the canned chili served on those dogs. A CBS *60 Minutes* investigation revealed that the chili actually was not contaminated. It only tasted like something that could grow hair on an egg. No one would touch it, not even the starving multitudes in Ethiopia.

When the chili was donated free of charge, Thornton should have been suspicious. The square root of the digits on the chili can bar code turned out to be the satanic number 666.

I can't say for sure that it was the hot dog supper. But the next day, my appendix blew up. Put me out of work for an entire week.

Even worse, Gary Vaughn suffered a heart attack. His doctors told Vaughn to never again eat anything that grows out of a can.

The 1996 hot dogs began the evening priced at $4 per plate and an hour later they were going for 25 cents apiece.

It was a different story the next year when the price rose to $5. True to Thornton's promise, there was no need for an EMS ambulance to be on standby at subsequent hot dog suppers. He reverted to doing things the old fashioned way. Not only have the hot dogs been genuine, they were also larger than the 1996-variety that were the size of Vienna sausages. The new chili has been the real thing, made according to Martha King's world famous recipe that is guaranteed to keep digestive systems within the speed limits. Even the cole slaw was homemade, not stuff that had been preserved in plastic for months before being served.

And it's a good thing that Thornton lived up to his word. Otherwise, we would have witnessed the first lynching in Greenville County since 1947.

50-Years of Lionism – Nov. 8, 2011

I have just received a 50-year membership pin from the Greer Lions Club. This actually signifies that most of the sand has drained from my hour glass. Another member, obviously off of his medication, asked me to write about my experiences in the Lions Club.

Okay. Here it is: joining the Lions Club is like winning an election. Once you get in, it's hard to get kicked out. I'm just saying…

You learn a lot about yourself by being a Lion. Like, I must be equipped with a cast iron constitution to have survived 1,200 and counting cholesterol-laden Tuesday night suppers without a single swig of Pepto Bismol…I'm just saying.

I have heard talks delivered by all sorts of speakers at Lions meetings: Governors, All American sports figures, war heroes, beauty queens, and captains of industry. But the most unforgettable meeting was a special birthday celebration--I don't remember whose, but I vividly recall that the daughter of our Tailtwister, Dan Leach, jumped out of a huge birthday cake. She was clad only in a bikini—which was quite a shock for an (then) all male audience. In the era before pacemakers, the bikini jump-started the hearts of dozens of geezers, giving them new leases on life. Our current Tailtwister, Ronnie Bruce, bless his heart, hasn't come close to topping that.

The club has had highs and lows…I'm just saying. A low was when we met at the Roger Huntington Nursing Center and were greeted by residents on their death beds. The atmosphere was far from warm and fuzzy, and attendance plummeted. The late R.B. (Beeco) Taylor stepped up to draw a crowd by promising to serve steak at the next meeting. Anyone who knew "Beeco" understood that he was not about to spring for a steak supper. On the appointed night, "Beeco" welcomed each of us with a wooden popcycle stick that he claimed was a "steak." Most Lions threw their stakes in the trash, but to our chagrin, "Beeco" had labeled several to be exchanged for a free potted camellia plant at his nursery.

Some amazing people are Lions…I'm just saying. Like Bob Hoyle who has written several books that he printed and bound himself. Hoyle is an accomplished musician who plays a number of instruments and even recorded and packaged his own CD. Few know about this because getting Hoyle to talk about himself is like pulling eye teeth.

My favorite Lions activity was the now-defunct Broom Sale. Luckily, I was frequently assigned to the late Furman Dobson's team. I'm just saying…. it was good fortune because the neighborhood dogs would always chase Dobson and leave the rest of us alone as we walked door-to-door. We were safe until the year that Dobson decided to ride instead of walk. He drove down the middle of the streets dispensing brooms to his team with the dogs yapping and nipping at our heels.

We found many Greer people waiting, with money in hand, to buy a broom because they had a relative or friend whom the Lions Club had helped by providing eyeglasses, an eye exam, eye treatment or maybe even a leader dog. Selling brooms was how the club raised money for sight conservation efforts—the primary endeavor of Lions International, which is the world's largest service organization. Some folks who bought brooms had no need for them with wall-to-wall carpet in their homes or with last year's unused broom still in the original plastic wrapper.

Lions provide the Big Thursday Hot Dog Supper—another learning experience…I'm just saying. With few exceptions, only South Carolinians put chili on hot dogs. Chili makes a hot dog. But sometimes chili can destroy a hot dog. Like the year Joel Thornton was elevated to chairman and introduced canned chili. Somehow the club recovered from that disaster, but Thornton still hears about it.

Apparently we never knew what we were doing in the kitchen at Big Thursday until the club began inviting females for membership. I'm just saying.... because now we march to the orders of Suzanne Traenkle and Vickie Kennedy.

The State of Greer

State of the Onion – Jan. 29, 1992

I've been in tears ever since hearing the State of the Onion address.

This may not be the same state you're thinking about. I'm referring to the State of Greer. Mayor Don Wall stopped in town between hunting trips and delivered the annual speech to the breakfast crowd at the Food King. I have selected a few highlights to pass along:

The Mayor emphasized that he is still standing, which is more than can be said for the other Wall, the one in Berlin.

Doing something about the high cost of auto insurance is at the top of the mayor's list of goals. The Governor may not be able to do anything, but Wall can. He plans to introduce a law to ban automobiles from the city's streets. It is anticipated that there will be a run on dog food at the grocery store when horses are pressed into service for transportation. Upon hearing that news earlier today, supermarket manager Junior Holder came in from the golf course.

On the political scene, Charlie Williams has called a press conference for Monday at 10 a.m. at Doodle's Exxon to announce his candidacy for Mayor in 1995.

Singleton Gilmore has moved his mortuary into Sylvia Jones' territory. Look for one of them to exit feet first in 1995.

Sen. Verne Smith celebrated his 20th. anniversary in the S.C. Senate with a barbecue on Monday night. Thank goodness it wasn't Smith's goose that was cooked.

On the national scene, it must be a Presidential Election Year because another Democratic Party contender has been caught with his pants down. Well, they don't call it a "party" for nothing, do they?

So far, President George H.W. Bush hasn't made the grade as a Japanese car salesman. Bush keeps saying that when the Japs start buying Buicks, the recession will be over. Now if we can just hang on for another 10 years until that happens….

Even so, most Greer people are continuing to worry about the economy in the wake of the cabbage crop failure on the City Hall lawn. I merely wonder whether I will get a paycheck on Friday.

On the international scene, who would have thought we wouldn't have Communists to worry about any more?

On the local scene, the Greenville County School District will begin testing radons. They must score at least 750 to become eligible to play football in the SEC after graduation.

Not content with having invented the "Eastside" from what was once known as Taylors, *The Greedville News* has relocated the Aqua Tech hazardous waste site to downtown Greer.

AT&T is bracing for possible gridlock since Hayne Griffin got a second wind.

Our preacher friend Alton Bell has mounted a campaign against providing free condoms for Furman students, "Let those rich kids buy their own condoms," Bell said.

Breast implants are out; counting fat grams is in.

Overkill is also in. Clerk of Court Barbara Greer summoned 55 citizens to serve on a six-man jury this week. Then they canceled the trial when the lawyers didn't show up.

A new Greer library is out because the tax increase would have been as much as it costs to rent one movie. But the library isn't taking that sitting down. A campaign has begun to seek alternate sources of revenue. I just received a bill for $148.50 for a book that has been overdue since 1959.

It has taken members of the class of '57 two years to plan our 35th reunion. At this rate, it will take us five years to fill out the forms to get our Social Security started.

The latest Gallup Poll survey of patrons reveals that the most enjoyable aspect of Greenville Symphony Concerts is intermission.

The Greer State of Mind remains confused.

If this report brings tears, maybe that's why it's the State of the Onion.

City To Raise a Flag – Jan. 26, 2000

Every now and then we accidentally stumble upon a pleasant surprise. The word for this is serendipity.

That happened to me on Friday night when I went to a Greer High basketball game, and a political rally broke out. Sort of.

At halftime, Greer Mayor Rick Danner decided to give a "State of the City" address. I think he got carried away in the surroundings which is the closest that Greer will ever come to having an Iowa-type political caucus. It was an indoor gathering of boisterous citizens who cannot sit still—clapping, yelling and making noise.

Anyway, Danner stood up at halftime and started expounding about how things are in Greer. The only reason I am reporting what Danner had to say is because most of the spectators paid him no attention. They were too busy watching Greer's version of the lottery. Dozens of people were trying to win Poke Mon prizes by sinking baskets from mid-court.

That's too bad, because Danner made a stunning declaration. He announced that Greer intends to put up a flag. The City plans to raise the Skull and Cross Bones, white on a solid black background, above City Hall. The flag will serve as a bold symbol that openly declares Greer's former covert annexation policy. After all, Danner said, annexation is no different from the colonists took this same piece of land from the Cherokee Indians.

With that out of the way, Danner echoed Governor Jim Hodges' "State of the State" theme by declaring that education will also be his top priority. Danner called on spirited citizens to organize hot dog suppers to raise $1 million as an incentive to lure Karl Beason back into the classroom. Danner also promised that Greer's SAT scores will improve—just as soon as someone can interpret what SAT stands for.

On the health front, Danner revealed that the city will spread happiness and erase the budget deficit by installing Viagra vending machines in all public restrooms.

When it comes to utilities, Danner is living up to his promise to make the city more user friendly. If the electricity ever goes out for days at a time, as it did this week in the so-called "Electric City" of Anderson, Danner is installing a toll-free complaint line: 1-800-PAR OUT.

Our rhetorically blessed leader went on to promise that downtown Greer will get new Christmas lights. In fact, the new display will be so dazzling that the holiday crowd will not think that lightening bugs are flitting about as was the case last Christmas. The Mayor also plans a trim-a-tree party complete with chain saws for everyone who wants to participate.

The Downtown business district is in the forefront of Danner's beautification plan. It calls for painting murals on the store fronts. The paintings will depict people inside the vacant buildings, fulfilling the Partnership's revitalization dream in one bold stroke.

I thought the only downside was when Danner declared that he intends to lower the speed limit on West Poinsett St. for the third time in six years. His only explanation was that when motorists are plodding along at 15 mph, they will think Greer is much larger than it actually is.

Just as he was about to announce the appointment of a new ambassador to Sugar Creek to succeed Charlie Williams, Danner was rudely cut short. A county mounty suffering with earwax build-up, thought Danner was preaching and escorted him from the building.

People Worth Remembering

My Favorite Mother-in-law - Aug. 2, 2006

My mother-in-law, Elsie Griffin, endured a miserable life for the past eight years. And so, when Griffin passed away at 2 a.m. Monday, July 31st, it was a relief for her, although she will be greatly missed.

The calamities that had befallen Griffin late in life read like a horror story. While strolling on the boardwalk at Myrtle Beach, she suffered a broken pelvis when run over by a teenager playing touch football.

Pushing a lawn mower up an embankment a few years later, Griffin fell backward into the street, striking her head on the pavement and suffering a concussion.

Later, she fell out of bed at 3 a.m. and broke a hip. While recovering from that misfortune in 1998, she fell and broke a leg in the hospital. That led to confinement to a nursing home where, two years later, Griffin fell and broke the other leg while getting out of a beauty salon chair, having forgotten that she could not walk without assistance. The broken bones did not heal correctly, ensuring that she would never walk again. That doomed Griffin to spend the rest of her years lying flat on her back.

The only saving grace for Elsie Griffin was having such a severe case of dementia that she could not remember all the bad things that had happened to her.

Over the last five years, she underwent gall bladder surgery and survived an assortment of illnesses and strange issues that included the collapse of the ceiling in her bathroom.

I would like to forget all those bad things as well and remember that Elsie Griffin was a very devout individual and a fighter who rarely changed her mind about anything. Her life's outlook seemed to be "I'll show them!" That's probably why she lived to the age of 93.

Griffin paid herself, from the household account, to do yard work and set aide that money. Over time, she saved enough money to enable my father-in-law, the late Preston Griffin, to get a start in the furniture business.

One of my first memories of Elsie Griffin was long ago in my high school days when I went to visit my future wife, Margaret. I carried my prize possession, our pet alley cat Tiger, to show the Griffin family. Margaret's mom opened the door, took one look at Tiger and screamed "Get that cat out of here!" Needless to say, there have been no more cats in my life.

Fortunately for me, Elsie Griffin declared much later that I was her "favorite son-in-law" – although that was during the years when I had no competition. Other times, she was silent about the designation.

I have never figured out why, but Elsie Griffin always took my side when any sort of dispute arose between my wife and me. I never knew what she said behind my back, though.

One Christmas, years ago, I tore into a large package under the Griffin family tree to find the most beautiful hand-knitted coat sweaters that I had ever seen. I wore that navy blue sweater nearly every day and received countless compliments. I assumed that my mother-in-law would make me a similar sweater each Christmas from then on. Wrong! She never made another one, not even after I had dropped dozens of hints and even after I had leather patches sewn over the holes in the sleeves. That garment is still hanging in my closet to serve as an example to my other clothes of what a good sweater should be.

Elsie Griffin baked absolutely the best coconut cakes I have ever eaten. It has been 15 years since she baked the last one, but I will never forget them. Or the way she sliced those cakes – so thin that you could read a newspaper through a slice. If we didn't make fools of ourselves by asking for seconds, thirds, fourths and more, one of her cakes would last a month.

Griffin also made countless asparagus casseroles that she knew I detested. And she never wavered in serving one on all occasions, even after I pointed out, more than once, that my mother "would have fixed me something special" in lieu of asparagus.

That independent spirit was still alive on her deathbed. Members of the family had been gathering from across the land and were prepared for a big meal and a wake on Saturday, several days after the medical authorities had assured us that Griffin would have departed. Well she showed them and us. We served the big meal anyway, including an asparagus casserole.

Griffin had quite a sense of humor that she kept until her dying day. For example, there was the day that her oldest son, Hayne, stopped by the nursing home to visit during his lunch hour. When he got ready to leave, Hayne explained, "I have to get back to work," and his mother asked, "Where do you work?"

"Why, Mutual Home Stores, of course," he replied.

She then asked, "Well, who owns that business?"

"You do," he replied.

"Then sit back down. I'm giving you the rest of the day off," she declared.

I never told Elsie Griffin that she was my favorite mother-in-law, but I guess she figured it out. The only one any better has got to be my wife.

How Do You Say Goodbye? – Aug. 19, 1992

"I guess I just don't know how to die," Preston Griffin lamented on several occasions during the past week before he succumbed to the ravages of cancer. But, like everything else he did in life, my father-in-law died with great dignity—with his chin up, his trust in God never wavering, and without a single complaint or wallowing in self-pity.

He showed us how to die in the grip of a horrible illness, just as my parents had done before. And through it all, the most difficult question for me has been "How do you say goodbye?" I don't have a good answer for that one, even after years of searching.

In a sense, we never say goodbye because our loved ones are locked in our memories forever.

Preston Griffin was a self-made man who actually lived the American Dream. His father was killed in a railroad accident when he was four years old, leaving his mother to raise the family of five small children. Preston Griffin did not have the opportunity to get a college education or many other advantages either. But through sheer determination and hard work, he became a self-educated man. He founded a highly successful chain of upstate furniture stores. He became a leader in community affairs, both at the city and county levels.

Although his life's story is truly remarkable, it is not the most important thing about Preston Griffin.

The New Testament writing of the great Apostle Paul reveals that Christianity makes a gentleman out of a man. Using that yardstick, Preston Griffin was one of the greatest Christians of all time because he certainly was one of the greatest gentlemen of all time.

Preston Griffin never had to ask the question "How do you live?" He simply lived the Golden Rule, and lived it as few others have done before. He took great pains to treat everyone fairly and with respect. I never heard him utter an oath or an unkind word about anybody, even on occasions when I would have highly recommended it. He was truly a man without enemies.

I don't think I could have been given a better father-in-law, who was affectionately known as "Pop" to the family. I cannot begin to count all the ways that "Pop" has helped me. We did not always agree on things, like the times I strayed and voted for a Democrat. And when it came to sports, he was a Furman fan, and I am a Wofford alumnus. But we were in total harmony in our appreciation of the finer things in life: golf and ice cream.

Never either, will I forget the smaller things: "Pop" always moving forward with right hand outstretched to greet you; always dressed in a coat and tie because he went everywhere with class; and always getting a laugh with his latest corny joke.

With "Pop's" passing, many family rituals have ended. Whenever he went to a baseball game, "Pop" would concentrate when our youngest son, John David, came to bat, and the result would be a hit. It's true. No one could figure out what happened to John David's hitting when "Pop" became too sick to attend the games.

Then there was the tradition "Pop" had made of taking our third son, Preston, out to lunch every Saturday. They discussed all the great issues of the day and life itself. The younger Preston never made a decision without first asking his grandfather's advice.

How do we say goodbye? I think I have found the hint of an answer from this verse of an old, old hymn. It expresses hope for the future among the bittersweet memories of the past:

Oh joy that sleekest me through pain,
I cannot close my heart to thee;
I trace the rainbow through the rain,
And feel the promise is not vain
That morn shall tearless be.

In Serious Danger - April 2, 2003

There was much hoopla on Thursday night when Greer High and Middle Schools threw an appreciation event for my wife's 20 years of service to the school children of Greenville County as the trustee representing District 18.

A whole bunch of dignitaries, from Senator Verne Smith to Crestview Elementary third grader Ashley McCoy, paraded to the podium to sing Margaret's praises. All of the accolades were well deserved, I might add.

One of the few people in the audience who was not invited to take a turn at the microphone was yours truly. Greer High Principal Marion Waters realized that no one of sound mind should take a chance on what Leland might say in public. And as Rep. Lewis Vaughn puts it, even Leland wouldn't have an idea of what he might say should he be summoned to center stage. In light of many? requests for my thoughts on my wife's 20 years on the school board, however, here are some.

Back in 1982, I would never in a million years have believed it if someone had told me that Greer would have all the wonderful new school facilities that our students enjoy today. When Margaret was first elected, Greer could not even get a crumb that fell from the school district table on Camperdown Way in Greenville. We were still trying to recover from the disastrous Piedmont Schools Project that squandered $3 million in an attempt to discover if students could excel in one-classroom schools.

During her tenure, my wife had to deal with all sorts of contentious, ornery, cantankerous, and snobbish people who were united in their pursuit of wealth and their hostility toward Greer. If I had been in her shoes, I would be still serving time for assault and battery or worse.

Some folks assume I made great sacrifices by "allowing" my wife to devote more hours than a full time job serving on the school board.

It was no sacrifice at all. I merely kept clinging to the hope that someone would call her with the message: "Your check is in the mail." But that never happened.

Even so, I want to thank Margaret for putting aside any urge she might have felt to slave over the hot stove in our kitchen. Otherwise, I would weigh over 400 pounds today.

I am grateful to my wife for tying up our home telephone line for days on end so I would not be harassed by angry subscribers anxious to chew me out for something that rubbed them the wrong way in the newspaper.

Thank you Margaret for staying so busy worrying about the school kids that you never had time to make endless lists of projects for me to do around the house—projects that are just now beginning to surface such as knocking out walls, enlarging a bathroom, moving trees, etc.

Pat Sudduth, the new Dist. 18 Trustee, said, "It's a wonder Margaret hasn't killed Leland for some of the things he has written." Now, however, I may be in serious danger since she has time to read the newspaper.

On the bright side, I guess what this all means is that I will no longer be widely known as Mrs. Margaret Burch.

Mr. Waters extended an olive branch for having kept me out of sight during the program by saying, "When you retire, Leland, we are going to invite all your friends and throw a bash. There should be plenty of room for the crowd in the broom closet on the second floor of the east wing."

Dr. Davis Had Only One Speed – May 1, 2002

Compiling material for our special publication saluting the 50th. anniversary of Allen Bennett Memorial Hospital has brought back many memories, especially of the late Dr. Lewis M. Davis.

Our family was blessed to have been friends with the Davis family for as long as I can remember. When I was growing up, I was in awe of Dr. Davis, and I still am, many years later. Not only was Dr. Davis an incredible person to know, he always seemed to be there whenever any of us needed a doctor—and there were plenty of those times.

Dr. Davis had only one speed—wide open. He could do anything faster, and usually better, than anyone else. That included surgeries. My mother always said that Dr. Davis' patients were better off because they didn't have to stay under an anesthetic very long.

If he had not been dedicated to medicine, Dr. Davis could have had a career driving a car with a big number on the door. He loved fast machines. When the Ford Thunderbird was introduced, Dr. Davis was among the first to own one. Later, he had the first Datsun 240-Z, a five speed. I once asked him how many times he had to change gears from his house to the hospital, and he replied "13" without having to think. He had that trip, which he made in less than two minutes, down to a science.

He later graduated to a motorcycle that could be seen in the wee hours, parked outside the emergency room door.

Dr. Davis' other great love was camping, which was fortunate for us. We went on several camping trips together, and at least two would have been disastrous if Dr. Davis had not been there. At Cherokee, N.C., our youngest and most accident-prone kid, John David, pitched over the handlebars while riding on a bike with an older brother. He landed head first in a graveled parking lot. Dr. Davis patched him up, and knew all the steps to take to prevent his face from being badly scarred.

A few years later, when John David was old enough to ride his own bike, he skidded across the asphalt pavement of a parking lot in Hilton Head, rubbing the skin off a leg and arm. Again, Dr. Davis was there to patch him up.

And Dr. Davis didn't mind helping on those occasions. He never sat still for more than a couple of minutes anyway. One of the reasons he enjoyed camping was because it is an adventure in repairing things that break down, from electrical systems to plumbing. He was forever tinkering, and would gladly repair any of my breakdowns, which were frequent.

Every summer, Dr. Davis headed for the motorized city on the Grand Strand known as Ocean Lakes. He would scout around and stake out a place for me to camp. When we arrived a few days later, he would bring out a box containing hundreds of parts and assemble a screened tent over our picnic table. I never once saw him go into the ocean for a dip or take a sunbath. He was always busy working on some project and waiting for sundown when we would head for the Grand Prix racetrack. We would drive the racecars nearly every night, and Dr. Davis would beat me every lap, even though he was 20 years older.

Dr. Davis would never leave town after having just performed a major surgery on a patient. He would wait an extra day or two, even if it delayed one of our trips, to make sure that the patient was recovering properly.

He also was one of the last doctors to make house calls—and certainly one of the rarest who would even see patients at his own home. People would often come by at night, after the clinic had closed, and he never turned anyone away. That is all the more remarkable considering there were days when he saw as many as 100 patients in his office.

Other than dressing in what my Dad often described as "loud" clothes, Dr. Davis never did anything that called attention to himself.

If a conversation ever turned toward any of his numerous accomplishments, he always changed the subject.

After retiring, Dr. Davis wrote the history of Allen Bennett Memorial Hospital and never mentioned his own name. Hopefully that conception is corrected in our special publication.

The fact is the hospital was largely Dr. Davis' idea—and he certainly made it happen by convincing leaders in both Greer and Greenville to work together for the project. The hospital is one more reason why Dr. Davis meant so much, not just to his patients and friends, but also to the entire community.

Greer Has Lost a Great Treasure - July 14, 2004

The death of Suzanne Greene has left me with a heavy heart and one of the most difficult columns I have ever had to write. She was inarguably the most talented individual that the community of Greer has ever produced, and it was my good fortune to count her as a friend.

Greene was best known, at least in local circles, for her fabulous watercolor paintings. Greene's creations ranged from wonderful florals to landmark scenes of Greer. Each was interpreted in her own unique way using colors that, like everything Goldilocks touched, were not too bright, and not too dim, but just right.

I worked with Greene on many projects, one of which was painting roses that I had grown. In the late afternoons one recent summer, I would cut a few halfway decent roses and rush them over to Greene's house. I always found her occupied with taking care of grandchildren or some chore other than painting. Once those were out of the way, Greene would work into the wee hours with her watercolor brushes to capture the essence of the roses on canvas before the blooms faded.

Lately, Greene began insisting that I write a book and even offered to illustrate it. After a couple of years passed, while I was beating thousands of golf balls into oblivion instead of producing a book, Greene went ahead and drew the illustrations anyway. They are better than any book I could possibly write.

That isn't all she did, however. Greene marched to the beat of someone half of her age. When her contemporaries were retiring, she plunged into creating an artistic masterpiece titled "Women in Time." She later added "a continuum" to the title, and then a subtitle: "female archetypes."

Greene painted well known local and national women who exhibit prominent aspects of the female psyche to illustrate this work. The inspiration for her final project arose from the fact that several published works about male prototypes exist, but there are none about females.

In our last conversation, Greene explained her purpose. "I wanted to show what it is like to be a woman, to go through what women do in life, seeking understanding. If only people knew what I have been through! But most of all, I think a woman should be understood as a soul mate."

Her take on males was: "American men haven't had to do anything after killing all the Buffalo out west. That's why space exploration is the best thing that ever happened to men."

While scurrying to the dictionary to find definitions of archetype and continuum, words beyond the grasp of even one who was a home room spelling champion at Greer High in 1955, I realized Greene's masterpiece may be beyond our comprehension. Even so, the world should be exposed to this marvelous work. And so, a late May meeting was arranged to find a publisher for "Women in Time." That very day, however, Greene was rushed to the hospital to begin one final, lengthy struggle against a pernicious form of leukemia.

That was typical of the disappointments that came Greene's way. She often seemed so tantalizingly close to grabbing the brass ring of national discovery as a great artist. And I think that may happen when her book is finally published.

"I have always thought your artwork is fantastic, and this book is a masterpiece," I told her.

But Greene took little encouragement from my words. "If I am so great, where's the money?" she asked.

"Don't worry." I replied. "The check is in the mail."

As Greene's luck would have it, researchers recently discovered a cure for her form of leukemia. "Only it's too late for me to take the treatment. But maybe others won't have to go through what I did," she said. "If I don't live, I will be satisfied. That's just the way it is."

Greene was already looking ahead to the hereafter during our last visit. "I used to think of Heaven as a sugary place, but not any more," she said to me. "I also used to think the Holy Spirit was a female, but I have decided it is neither male nor female."

As we were leaving her bedside, Greene insisted on giving my wife a portrait that she had done of her some time ago, even though it was not quite finished to the exacting standards the artist was seeking. We tried to pay for the piece, but she exclaimed, "If you pay for this, I will just drop dead right now!"

Suzanne Greene was one of the community's greatest treasures. She was brilliant, funny, extremely talented, accommodating and generous to a fault. Greene founded Greer ArtReach (GARP) to raise money for scholarships. She gave away countless works of art to help churches, Greer Community Ministries, and other worthwhile causes. Some 16 of her watercolors depicting the Stations of the Cross decorate the sanctuary of her beloved Episcopal Church of the Good Shepherd.

Greene may not have been "discovered" nationally, but she was far from a prophetess without honor in her hometown. Friends overflowed the church at her memorial service. And I am certain Greene has been discovered in Heaven where she is surely recreating the same beautiful paintings of angels that she did here on earth.

Few people can match Suzanne Greene's heritage—she left the world a more beautiful place than she found it!

The Season of Miracles - Dec. 31, 2008

Christmas is the season of miracles—most of them unexpected like the December 27th marriage of Hazel Austin, our companion of the last 40 years.

You might say it was a whirlwind romance, and a complete surprise since Hazel had been single for 30 or so years.

"Don't tell anybody, but I've just found out that Hazel is dating," my wife whispered one day, a few months ago.

"Who's the lucky fellow?" I asked.

"He's Irvin the Mechanic," my wife said. "No relation to Joe the Plumber though. He works on Hazel's car."

"Did you have a good weekend?" my wife asked Hazel as they stood in the kitchen one Monday morning several weeks later.

"Yes," Hazel said. "We went to Orangeburg to meet Irving's relatives."

"This romance must be getting serious," my wife said. "Hazel, are you planning to get married?"

"Well…" she replied.

"Hazel, you're my best friend. If you're really getting married, I want to come to the wedding. I don't want you to come in here one Monday morning and announce that you got married over the weekend," my wife warned.

A few minutes later, Hazel returned to the kitchen and declared: "December 27th."

"What's that?" my wife asked.

"December 27th. I'm getting married that day." Hazel explained.

"When did you get engaged?"

"Election night," Hazel answered.

That's why no one else was in on the secret. They were watching the election returns on CNN.

Under the direction of Hazel's daughter, Beverly, the wedding plans quickly grew from a small home ceremony to a major production at the Needmore Recreation Center which, I feel pretty sure, has never hosted an event of such magnitude. Given a few more months of planning, there would have been no choice but to move the wedding to the Bi-Lo Rena.

Then a potential deal breaker occurred as the big day neared. "I don't know what to do about the bed," Hazel confided to my wife one morning. "The bed is up against a wall, and there isn't any other place for it. Neither one of us is willing to crawl over the other one to get out of the bed," she said.

"Maybe you should just call off the wedding," my wife suggested.

"No." said Hazel. "A good mechanic is hard to find."

Two days later, the problem was solved by removing the bookcase from the bedroom. As the wedding preparations resumed, I was dispatched to hack down a magnolia tree for table decoration greenery. Preston, who was to assist Hazel's son, Bernard, in giving the bride away, went shopping for a new Sunday suit since his 10-year-old threadbare outfit might not have made it down the aisle.

The bride spent the entire day before the wedding in her kitchen, preparing food for the 75 lucky people who had been invited plus another 50 who simply showed up with their appetites when the word got out. She baked macaroni pies and hams, fried a hen house full of chickens, boiled green beans, and whipped up a ton of her world's best potato salad.

If that seems miraculous, it was nothing compared to the ice tea that magically turned into fruit punch an hour before the wedding.

The Needmore Center had been rented for two other events that day, leaving only the time slot of noon-5 p.m. for set up, decorating, the wedding ceremony, followed by the formal seated dinner, and finally the clean up.

By the time the ceremony began, I was exhausted from watching volunteers haul in 96 chairs and a dozen round tables which were then covered with white cloths, decorated and set with red napkins and silverware.

At the appointed hour, the place was wall-to-wall with folks dressed to the nines. Fortunately, the Needmore Center's furnace had gone out because it was hot as blazes inside, even in the dead of winter.

The bride was radiant and beautiful, and, as expected, stole the show. The shy groom stood tall and proud at the altar.

My wife breathed a sigh of relief when the minister did not launch into the ceremony by reading the story of Abraham and Sarah from the Book of Genesis. And I assumed that it also must have been an oversight when no one threw rice on the couple as they left, arm-in-arm, a couple of hours later.

Hazel's granddaughters, Amber and Mariah, performed a rhythmic dance to conclude the ceremony, but the happy couple refused to join in for fear for falling and breaking something.

And then the feast was served, topped off with slices of wedding cake.

"Well, Ada, I guess you're next," I remarked to Hazel's sister as we gathered up the remains of the magnolia tree for the compost heap.

"Oh, no!" Ada exclaimed. "I'm not even dating anybody, and you got to date somebody before you get married."

Life in the Nineties - Mar. 4, 1992

I just made a pedal-to-the-metal, five-hour dash up Interstate 26, from Charleston to the top of the mountain, to attend Mrs. Vernon (Matsu) Crawford's 90th birthday party.

Since there aren't many 90 year-old kids on the block, I was anxious about how the incredible lady of Black Mountain, N.C. was holding up. Many folks her age are merely taking up space. But not Mrs. Crawford. She hasn't changed a bit, at least not since her 75th birthday. The former Greer resident is a wonder to behold and a match for people half her age.

"Just because I'm 90, I'm not going to act like an old person," she said, pulling me aside and nodding in the direction of a 70-year-old man who was hobbling along with the aid of a walking cane.

Mrs. Crawford, who could be mistaken for a 60-year-old, has a world-class mind. I have interviewed U.S. Senators, Congressmen, Governors and candidates for President, and all would be hard pressed to match wits with her.

The author of four books, Mrs. Crawford recently wrote to President George H.W. Bush (five pages, typewritten) to inform him what should be done to improve public education in America. She recommended returning prayer and Bible study to the classroom, among other things. She mailed the letter to Barbara Bush, explaining "I knew she would read the letter. President Bush wouldn't. I just asked her to tell him what I said."

The plan succeeded. Mrs. Crawford received a phone call from the White House and written replies from both Barbara Bush and the Secretary of Education.

Resplendent in an aqua suit, orchid corsage and "each one of my hairs in place," the former missionary to Japan was naturally the center of attention at a huge reception in her honor. The birthday party attracted 150 close friends. "I don't even know this many people back

215

in my home town," remarked one of her "adopted" children who had flown in from Florida.

A visit with Mrs. Crawford is like being in the middle of an ETV current events program. You are bombarded with brilliant statements in 30-second sound bites. Each bite is likely to focus on a different topic as she reacts to those around her. You see, Mrs. Crawford's one concession to aging is that she is deaf as a post, so conversations with her are one-way affairs.

One minute Mrs. Crawford recalls the occasion in 1978 when our son John David (then age three) brought out a megaphone so he could "preach" to her. The next minute she is reflecting on the theories in Pat Robertson's latest book.

Mrs. Crawford didn't hear a thing I said. That was okay with me because I didn't say anything worth hearing. I decided that deafness is an asset.

"Come along," she commands, grabbing a flower arrangement with each hand and marching forth from an immense birthday cake that covers a card table. Two out-of-breath 50-year-olds and a startled teenager scurry to keep up. Mrs. Crawford has begun her daily one-mile trek through Highland Farms, the sprawling retirement complex where she resides.

The place is full of retired doctors, lawyers, industrial titans and Indian Chiefs, but not one dares play her a game of checkers for fear of being embarrassed. More importantly, however, she is a rock of faith and a beacon for those around her, just as she was for more than half a century as the wife of a Presbyterian minister, the late Rev. Vernon Crawford.

She has just completed another book titled *Thanks, It's Been Wonderful*. The autobiography is filled with memories from her childhood in Laurens County and stories of missionary life in Japan. If Mrs. Crawford had poisoned five husbands or owned 20,000 pairs of shoes, the book would be a best seller. But it has not been published because she isn't famous.

What does life hold for someone in her nineties? The last thing Mrs. Crawford said to me when I left the celebration was "I have a lot more to say."

When I Grow Up I Want to Be Like the Gastons
July 23, 1997

When I grow up, I want to be like the Gastons, Tom and Kate, that is.

Although the couple recently celebrated their 86th birthdays, they have more energy and wit than most people half their age.

While most of their contemporaries are in cemeteries or nursing homes, the Gastons are busy cultivating one of the Abner Creek area's rapidly disappearing chunks of farmland. They are outdoors from dawn to dusk, working and puttering among hundreds of rose bushes, thousands of azaleas, and two vegetable gardens.

"Gerald (their son who lives next door) didn't want his garden this year. His freezer is full, so we took it over." says Kate Gaston, explaining that they are working a second vegetable garden because they don't like land sitting idle.

Visiting the Gastons is like visiting the Biltmore Estate. You can't see it all in five minutes.

Unlike the Biltmore Estate, the Gastons don't operate a gift shop. Instead, they load visitors down with gifts of flowers and vegetables.

The Biltmore Estate tour guides could learn a thing or two from the Gastons. They provide guests with a laugh-a-minute. It is similar to being in the middle of a television sitcom.

When Mrs. Gaston recently had cataracts removed from both eyes, I inquired if she could see any better. "No." she said, "But the operation was a success."

Kate gives the orders. Tom listens and says very little. Sometimes he follows Kate's orders, and other times he doesn't. "Tom never sprays the roses like I tell him to," Kate complains. "Most days, Tom is up by 6 a.m., telling me to get up, like we have 15 children to feed."

Sometimes Tom even launches out on a project of his own, like repairing his 30-year-old riding lawnmower. "Tom took three weeks to fix it, and the grass was getting about this high," says Kate, stretching up on her tiptoes.

"Tom worried the people at hardware stores trying to get parts for the lawnmower," Kate claims. "We should have bought a new mower instead."

"When he finally got the new bearings, Tom took a hammer to the mower to drive them in," she continues with the tale. "He hit the mower like he wanted to show it who's boss. Well he ended up bending the deck. That made the blade lower in the front and higher in the back. When he finally cut the grass, it was the worst looking thing you have ever seen. Tom and Gerald had to weld pieces to the deck to pull it back in place."

When not overseeing Tom's activities, Kate can be found rooting cuttings of roses and other plants. "Last year, I rooted a climbing rose and forgot about it. A few months later, I looked up and saw it growing up in a tree," she says. To which Tom responds, "Please don't root anything else."

The Gastons have the recipe for a long-lasting marriage. They will celebrate their 67th wedding anniversary on Oct. 16th. Tom tried to schedule his medical check-up on that date—"so I could get a good report on our anniversary." he said. "But they were full that day."

"Not so fast," contends Kate. "I can read Tom like a book. The reason he wanted to go to the doctor on the 16th is because he only wanted to go out one time that week. We would have ended up celebrating our anniversary in the doctor's office."

Celebrating Marlea Rhem's Birthdays
– Oct. 10, 1990; Sept. 26, 2001

It has been generally accepted that bad things happen in multiples of three. Now I can confirm that it's true. Over the past fortnight: an initial terrible event was 911, the outbreak of terrorism in America; the second was the crash of the stock markets; and the third: I wasn't invited to Marlea Rhem's birthday party for the eleventh consecutive year.

Not only that, the big party wasn't even held on Rhem's birthday. It was two weeks early. I assumed that changing the date was intended to disrupt the timing of anyone who might have been planning to crash the party.

Of course, I took it personally even though the last birthday gift I presented Rhem, a rare matching set of Hardee's California Raisins cups, had not have been well received.

I also realized that my next-door neighbor, Thomas Grady, warns everyone not to tell me anything because I will print it in the newspaper. But I would have promised anything for an invitation to Rhem's birthday party, even keeping my mouth shut. Besides, I couldn't have gotten in a word edgewise among the hens.

My imagination has run wild since then. What could they have been doing behind closed doors in the pretentious Poinsett Club? Were the drapes drawn tightly in the Vardrey Ramseur Room to prevent the candlepower from overpowering the dawn's early light? Or was a private screening of "The Best of Backyard Mud Wrestling" taking place? I'm pretty sure that President George W. Bush did not jump out of Rhem's birthday cake, but I could not dismiss the rumor that George Clooney made a special appearance.

I eavesdropped on subsequent phone conversations to get to the bottom of the mystery. Eventually I pieced together the Rhem theory on aging, which is nearly the opposite of doggie years. Here it is: after having celebrated many birthdays far in advance, you will have fallen so far behind your aging contemporaries that you won't have to enroll in AARP or take out a subscription to Modern Maturity until all of them are in nursing homes.

Turn back the clock to October 3, 1990, when I was waiting for life to begin at 40 and people were asking me how it felt to be 50!

Upon reaching the age of 50, my advice is to go out and buy yourself a birthday present. That is exactly what Marlea Rhem did—she threw herself a big party to celebrate reaching the magic age of 50.

I don't know if a flash (hot) came over Rhem, but at the time I advised her not to throw another party. Speaking from experience, you don't need to celebrate more birthdays after 50. Besides, I found it rather depressing to be mingling with all the other old people who attended that party.

It was scary when the candles on Rhem's birthday cake set off smoke alarms throughout the neighborhood. Several of us had to slow down our pacemakers because we had not seen a fire truck with lights, sirens and the whole nine yards, come roaring up in years.

Thankfully Rhem had planned fun games to take our minds off worrying about whether the federal government will discontinue Medicare and Social Security. Our team would have won the bedpan relay if Allen Moore hadn't stumbled at the finish line.

One Who Made an Incredible Difference
– July 25, 1990

This really isn't the place to print bad news and maybe not even a place to be serious very often. But there are times when bad news has to be noted, and the untimely death of Florence Eleazer is one of those occasions.

Eleazer did a terrific job for C&S Bank, managing the branch at the Greenville-Spartanburg Airport. There are countless customers who go out of their way to bank at the airport because of Eleazer.

I often wondered if banking wasn't only a hobby for Eleazer. She always finished work by the early afternoon at the very latest and then was free to plunge into countless volunteer activities that continued the rest of the day and into night.

I have known Florence since we were in high school together, and I never remember her sitting still for a minute, then or now. I never saw her engage in an idle conversation or waste a precious minute of time. She was a bundle of energy, involved in so many activities that it would be useless to try to list them all. Among her favorite endeavors were coaching kids teams and playing women's basketball and softball at Fairview Baptist Church.

That was just the beginning. More often, Eleazer would be out beating the bushes selling memberships in the Greer Chamber of Commerce or overseeing a project for the American Business Women's Association, one of numerous organizations that she had served as president.

Eleazer was active in the Greer High School Booster Club for many years. On one occasion, she served as president and was responsible for considerable progress including obtaining a new scoreboard for the school gym and getting new uniforms for the girls' athletic teams.

All of her activities brought Eleazer into contact with so many people that it would not be an exaggeration to state that she had more friends and acquaintances than anyone in Greer.

What's more, Eleazer seemed to stay younger than most. Perhaps it was because she was constantly involved in doing things for young people including Junior Achievement projects. One of her last efforts was an attempt to organize a teen dance during the Family Festival in May. That was about the time that she was struck down by tragic illness, and the event never quite came together simple because Eleazer had reached the point where she could not do everything by herself.

Eleazer attempted to grow roses but rarely had time to give them much attention. She was one of the original members of the Greer Rose Society, and naturally the club managed to talk Eleazer into serving as president, in spite of everything else that she had to do. I recall that Eleazer once hosted a rose society meeting, providing the refreshments, the guest speaker, and the whole nine yards, and as soon as it was over, she left to conduct the meeting of another organization.

Eleazer was always opening her home to others, even to the point of pain. There was one occasion when she hosted the rose club's annual pruning demonstration, and watched in anguish while Gerald Davis whacked her climbing roses to the bone.

Eleazer always arrived at the rose society's annual shows without any roses to exhibit, expressing no interest in winning ribbons, but merely wishing to lend a helping hand. "Okay, I'm here. Tell me what to do," was her standard greeting.

That was her outlook on life, and it is probably the first thing she announced to St. Peter upon arriving at the Pearly Gates on Monday morning. When something needed doing, you could always count on Eleazer, no matter how busy she was. I can't imagine that she is resting now.

With the death of Florence Eleazer, the bell tolls for all of us because we are greatly diminished. Eleazer will be greatly missed because as many as ten people cannot do the things this one person accomplished.

If there is one thing that can be learned from Eleazer's life it is that one person can make a difference—often and incredible difference—in the community.

My favorite Insurance Salesman - Aug. 24, 1988

I have always considered insurance to be a necessary evil. In fact, I would go so far as to claim that life insurance is a "lose-lose proposition," just the opposite of the popular term "win-win." If you pay out premiums for years and do not die, then you have lost all that money. If you die at an early age, your wife collects. Then she can marry an insurance salesman and live happily ever after on your money. Either way, you lose.

I admire life insurance salesmen for the way they operate. They usually pounce on newly married husbands about two weeks after the wedding. At that point the newlywed, who has just had his wings clipped, is beginning to realize that he isn't going to live forever. In fact, the new husband may actually fear the end is near if his wife is learning how to cook. In that situation, a new husband is easy prey for an experienced insurance salesman.

I don't mean to downgrade insurance salesmen. As Will Rogers probably once said, "I have never met an insurance salesman I didn't like."

One of my all time favorite insurance salesmen is Claude Powell. He spent an entire career working for the post office, then retired and made a million dollars selling insurance.

Powell even started a fire department and did all sorts of other amazing things. This proves that anyone who can soothe folks' nerves about missing mail and the ever-spiraling cost of postage stamps can also sell refrigerators to Eskimos.

Actually, Powell does not attempt to sell insurance. He primarily pushes mutual funds and investments but keeps an insurance policy tucked in his back pocket just for emergencies. I discovered this the hard way when Powell stopped by my office one day trying to interest me in making an investment. After hearing his sales pitch, which by the way, was quite good, I informed Powell that I could not afford to invest any money. When that failed to get rid of him, I added, "what I really need is a life insurance policy" (in the event I was overcome and dropped dead during the heat of another sales pitch).

Powell answered, all too quickly, that he had the very thing I needed. Even though I am 30 pounds overweight, my arteries are clogged with cholesterol, and I have a history of evil kidney stones, Powell said I could get a discounted insurance policy if I promised not to smoke any more cigarettes.

For the next several hours, we debated the merits of this slightly better-than-average lose-lose insurance policy. At long last Powell said, "The only thing I want is for you to be happy." Right then, it dawned on me that I was going to have to buy the insurance policy, because that was the only way I was going to get rid of Powell. And only then would I be happy.

When I started paying the premiums, I became unhappy about writing checks. So I cancelled the policy. Now I'm happy again, and I'm not in the market for another insurance policy. So don't call me, Powell. I'll call you.

Ray Starnes was Appreciated – Mar. 12, 2008

"We live; we die, and the wheels of the bus go round and round." That line was spoken by terminally ill corporate billionaire Edward Cole in the recently released hit movie *The Bucket List*. The movie has much to say about life and the timing of one's death. For example, surveys have found that most people do not want to know in advance the day and hour of their demise.

The Bucket List is the tale of two men who are diagnosed with terminal cancer and wind up in the same hospital room. When physicians manage to prolong their lives by putting their disease in remission, the two make out a "bucket list" of things they really want to do before "kicking the bucket"—things like sky diving, driving race cars, ascending to the pinnacle of an Egyptian pyramid, etc.

The movie hit close to home because it was showing in area theatres on Feb. 28, the day that Ray Starnes, a former long-time employee of *The Greer Citizen*, passed away. Unlike the characters in *The Bucket List*, Ray Starnes did not have an exquisite sense of timing. He died the day after that week's edition of *The Greer Citizen* hit the streets, and therefore, his obituary did not appear in print until the following week. The daily newspapers would not publish Ray's obituary because the family could not afford the cost—an unfortunate situation that also says a great deal about the direction that huge, profit-driven corporations have taken in recent years.

Like everyone who punches the clock in the newspaper business, Ray Starnes was far from the status of the movie's billionaire Cole, played by Jack Nicholson. He was more like Carter Chambers, played by Morgan Freeman, who had spent 45 years "greased up under the hoods of cars."

Starnes lived a hard life that was filled with a multitude of troubles, some of them his own doing. He enjoyed the weekends, especially nights out on the town with his best buddy, Stanley Wood. After downing a few too many, Ray and Stanley inevitably ended up in a fistfight—with each other. They had to settle all sorts of debates such as "better taste or less filling," "paper or plastic," etc. There were a few occasions when Ray showed up at work on Monday morning with a bandage around his head or his arm in a sling. "But you should see Stanley," he would always say. And sometimes his greatly troubled mother would call ahead so we could bail him out of the city's hotel in time to punch the clock.

Years of weekend misadventures added up to a mountain of driving license woes and insurance hikes to the point that Ray simply gave up his wheels altogether and began walking everywhere.

Somewhere along the way, Ray's wife walked out. Starnes spent his latter years attempting to keep his three offspring headed in the right direction.

And while things may have been tough, Ray Starnes, unlike all too many people today, always gave an honest day's work for an honest day's wages.

Starnes grew up in Clinton where he went to work at a very early age in the newspaper shop. Back then, printing was hot, dirty work, not unlike a steel mill. Lines of print were cast on a strip of hot metal and spit out by a Linotype machine, or type was set one letter at a time by hand and cast in a molten lead-tin alloy. A great deal of sawing and trimming was required to fit each page together in a metal framework for printing.

Starnes was a craftsman when it came to producing printing jobs and newspaper pages in metal.

But in the 1970s with the advent of computers and "offset" printing, everything changed. Starnes had to learn an entirely new way of doing things in the "offset" system using computers and film.

Starnes adapted well to the new system. He not only ran the darkroom but also learned other new specialties. As the years passed, Ray did everything in his power to improve the appearance of the newspaper that was gradually getting worse as the printing press was wearing out before our eyes. He undertook all sorts of experiments to discover why photos appeared too dark or too light in print.

Ray Starnes may never have written a prize-winning story or taken the lead in spreading the news to help launch a new community endeavor, such as the Soup Kitchen. But he was dedicated to making sure that this newspaper, with such vital information, reached the citizens of Greer every week. And everyone who worked alongside him will always be grateful.

Remembering Booker
(by Edd A. Burch)

(Editor's note: Off the Record was originated by my father, the late Edd A. Burch, when he was the editor of *The Citizen* in Dalton, Ga., in the late 1930s. He brought the column to Greer when he purchased *The Greer Citizen* in 1942, and continued to write it every week for the next 43 years. Unfortunately, very few of those columns were preserved because a collection of them would have made a fantastic book. However, one reader clipped and saved a particular column "Remembering Booker" that was written in the 1950s. I am reprinting it since the column is a very accurate description of a slice of life in Greer in that time.)

Every town has its characters, and Greer is like all the rest. One of those characters, Booker T. Gunter, a colored man of doubtful age (probably anywhere from 45 to 60 years old) died recently. For years, Booker was a yard man, and for part of that time a good one when he could leave John Barleycorn alone, working for any number of families all over town. He probably left this world owing many of his benefactors various sums from a few cents to several dollars, none of which they ever really expected to collect.

In my case, Booker last "touched" me just two days before he was found dead. He caught me at the office on Sunday afternoon and asked for money to get "an ice cream." At that time, Booker informed me he had quit drinking, and I asked, "When? Last night at 12 o'clock?" But he vowed it had been two weeks. Booker was always quitting, and I remember once several years back when he actually did quit and started saving his money. He wouldn't trust it to the bank, so June Waters and me became his bankers. Finally when he had saved between 50 and 100 dollars, Booker couldn't stand it any longer. He closed his accounts with June and me and the hard earned dollars he had saved were soon "gone with the wind."

Booker claimed he came to Greer from Elberton, Ga., and when he found that we were also from Georgia, he used this to make of us "soft touches." I became Captain Burch, Leland was Little Captain, Walter was "Mister Walter", and Sarah was "the Missus" when Booker was sober. And when he was under the influence, Sarah became "Madam Queen." When Walter was about 12 years old, Booker, while working around the yard one day, began to call him "Mister Walter" and buttered up his childish ego. It turned out later that Booker had touched Walter for a dollar, which probably represented his savings for several months.

When Booker decided he was going fishing, there was no getting any work out of him that day, and you might as well loan him a buck and let him go. He had a way of coming around on Sunday to borrow a dollar to go to a singing. One Sunday we held out on him until he proved that he could sing. His favorite song was "I Don't Know," and the words in the title seemed to have been the only ones in the several verses that he repeated over and over. Finally, when we had to stop working Booker regularly because of his unreliability, when I refused to loan him a dollar, he'd say "Gimme 50 cents then," and if he didn't get that, he'd settle for a quarter and go off around the house in what almost amounted to a trot.

Many incidents come to mind about Booker that occurred during the years we worked him. One Sunday morning, I glanced out the window and there sat Booker perched upon the top of a big pile of compost nursing his Saturday night hangover and waiting to make a "touch." Another time, he dug up all of Sarah's fine Iris and Day Lilies and discarded the plants for weeds. Sill another time, I had told him to come out and cut some dead limbs out of a pine. I looked out the window early one morning and there was Booker perched precariously atop a ladder and busily sawing off tree limbs—dead ones, green wood, and all. Needless to say, he left Vandiventer Drive in a hurry that day, but he was soon back.

When Booker didn't show up for several weeks, we would accuse him of taking a vacation at Travelers Rest (county prison camp for colored), which he frequently did. You had no trouble telling when he was drinking for he would say, "This here's the Book," or "This old N….. ain't goin work today. I wants a dollar. I'se goin fishin."

I must confess I was mad with Booker on plenty of occasions, but the maddest of these was one when I went to Travelers Rest and paid his fine and brought him home to work out the amount he owed. Booker showed up faithfully the first day, but the second morning he didn't appear. Later that day I happened to ride down Miller Street and there was Booker working in Carl Lancaster's yard.

No matter how undependable he got, I don't think we ever turned Booker down. He averaged coming by our house at least once a week (when he was in town) for something to eat, and he was never turned away. Sarah tried to talk him into doing better and I remember once he told her, "Missus, I didn't come here for no lecture. I just wants something to eat."

(Selective) Childhood Memories

Childhood Memories

I have wonderful memories of growing up in Greer in the 1940s and 50s. We lived in a house on North Main Street directly in front of Memorial United Methodist Church. This is impossible to imagine today, but in 1941 there was a field of cotton on one side of our house, and my dad raised chickens in a pen in the back yard.

I grew up making friends with kids in the vicinity including Roy Hefner, Joe Kinard, Rob Hughes, Gene Gibson, Eric Anderson, and Denby and George Davenport. We played cowboys and Indians, and other games.

One of my favorite memories is of diving into mountains of autumn leaves, shed by the (once) towering oak trees on North Main.

Football was so important to some, including me, that I have devoted a considerable chapter to the subject. The first Greer High football game I attended ended in a brawl. I also remember watching in amazement as Greer High players tumbled off the stage during my first ever basketball game at the old Davenport School.

Downtown Trauma - March 29, 2006

Someone asked if I planned to take a stand on the proposal to move City Hall into the Allen Bennett Memorial Hospital. Well, yes, especially after I fired off a letter to Webster's Dictionary to stop the presses in order to insert another line under the definition of the word *disaster*. That would be moving city halls away from downtowns.

I don't enjoy getting caught up in controversies that should never have arisen in the first place. This one has been like a groom leaving the altar to chase a bridesmaid who showed up wearing a bikini. It may have looked good at first glance, but it wasn't the right choice.

No matter what the future holds, downtown Greer will never be like it was back in the 1950s when I was growing up. Back then, you could find everything you needed, from a new car to a casket, in downtown Greer.

Yet that was not always "a good thing" as Martha Stewart likes to say. For I was traumatized (try that word on for size) by things that happened to me in downtown Greer.

One of my earliest childhood memories is my mother dragging me along to The Leader Department Store. The Leader's entire second floor was filled with materials for sewing—hundreds of bolts of cloth, thousands of spools of colored threads, racks and racks of patterns, etc. (That was when women made their own clothes, before they discovered that the Chinese will make garments for pennies.)

Mother's trips to The Leader seemingly took hours. I had nothing to do but crawl around over bolts of cloth, looking for an escape hatch and wishing the Amber Alert would soon become a reality since I was being held hostage.

After one mind-numbing morning in The Leader, mother rewarded me with a fountain Coca-Cola at the Rexall Drug Store across the street. Coca-Colas were served in iconic, top-heavy glasses that were difficult to handle, and mine soon toppled to the tile floor, splattering into a million pieces. I was devastated because back then soft drinks did not come in 64-ounce bottles from the supermarket. Eulalia Walker, who owned the drug store, felt sorry for me and gave me another Coke.

I suffered another psychological shock at The Grand Theatre. Several of us 6-year-olds spent every Saturday morning there, taking in a Lassie movie with a cartoon, plus a segment of a long-running Western serial. During intermission one Saturday, there was a drawing for a prize. The owner, Bill Drace, was giving away a drum that day, and drew the ticket stub with my number.

I wanted the drum, but there was no way I was going to claim it by walking all the way down to the front of the theatre in front of all those other kids. Drace kept calling my number while I slid farther down into my seat. Finally, my best friend, Denby Davenport, grabbed my ticket and yelled. "Here it is! Leland won the drum!"

A week later, my parents declared that I would never be allowed to go to the movies again if I ever won another drum. I did even better. I haven't won a thing since then.

Even more traumatic were visits to the downtown dentist office of Dr. J. Roy Jackson. It was at the top of a seemingly endless flight of stairs on the second floor of a Victoria Street building. Climbing up those steps was as intimidating as "walking the plank" on a pirate ship.

"Open right wide, sweet boy!" Dr. Jackson would command as he drilled every tooth in my head—some of them several times. That was before the widespread use of the pain-killer Novocain.

Teens could get a driver's license in downtown Greer where the road test was given every Wednesday afternoon. I was a nervous wreck the first time I went for the piece of plastic that authenticated one's manhood. So was the highway patrolman whose knuckles were as white as mine. I flunked. What an embarrassment in front of my classmates!

235

Downtown Greer has left me with more emotional scars than emotional attachment. Still, I could not resign myself to the concept of having City Hall located in the colonoscopy Center of the Upstate.

Every Time the Church Doors Opened, I was There

– January 23, 2002

Every time the church doors opened, my parents were pushing me inside. Not that I objected to going to church, my problem was that I could have been the poster child for Wall Flower Anonymous, especially when I was a teenager.

A well-intentioned leader of the Methodist Youth Fellowship (MYF) decided that we should learn to square dance for innocent fun and to serve as an "ice breaker" to become better acquainted. I hated every minute of square dancing. My two left feet continually tangled, causing me to trip over the wooden ladder-back chairs that encircled the social hall where square dances took place. I also occasionally crashed into one of the metal poles that supported the ceiling. Even worse, I always seemed to end up as the partner of the only girl in the MYF who, to put it politely, had a face that could stop a train. I felt as if I was suffocating when the weekly MYF meetings rolled around. But there was no question that I would be present; otherwise I got no allowance.

The Baptists soon got wind that the Methodists were dancing in church and sprang into action to rescue us from eternal damnation. The First Baptist senior high RAs invited the MYF over for a round-table discussion, bent upon showing us the impropriety of our ways. This undertaking must have been the forerunner of youth mission trips that are popular today, for the MYF was a ready-made mission field and a small minority in a region where there are more Baptists than people.

When two hours of spirited discussion failed to convince MYF kids of the "evils" of dancing, our Baptist hosts trotted out sentence prayers as a last resort. That was a shock because Methodists didn't do much praying, especially in public. When it came my turn to pray,

I was at a loss for words with which to beseech the Almighty. The Baptists had already used the best declarations, like offering thanks for food, homes, good health, schools, etc. After turning several shades of red with embarrassment, I eventually mumbled, "I'm thankful we will be leaving this meeting in a few minutes."

A year after that, I summoned the nerve to go back for more. This time, I asked a Baptist girl for a date and escorted her to the Sunday night church service. It was the kind of outing I could afford – no movie tickets or popcorn to buy. Which is the only way that I managed to overcome the feeling that I was as out of place as a terrorist marching in the Washington DC Veterans Day Parade.

I breathed a sigh of relief when we found the back row empty. Things were going too well, but that changed. The service had just begun when the offering plate came around. I had to dig deep to come up with a quarter about the moment an usher stuck the collection plate in my face. I reached out and grabbed the plate, but the usher did not let go. So I turned the plate loose about the same time he was dropping it into my lap.

Horrified, I watched the heavy wooden plate spiral downward toward the brightly-polished hardwood floor. It seemed like a slow motion replay as the plate crashed on its edge with a thunderous noise that shattered the silence, and then bounced up, flopped sideways, and crashed a second time. The noise was amplified by the wooden pews, which acted like sounding boards, and reverberated off the rafters. The sound was deafening, so it seemed, causing everyone in the congregation to turn and stare at me.

I was the first to offer up a prayer that night, thanking the Good Lord that not a single coin had been dropped into that offering plate as it traversed most of the congregation before arriving at my pew. Otherwise there would have been total chaos with dozens of people scrambling over the floor to rake up the money.

My embarrassed date and I were the first out the door, leaving on the first stanza of the closing hymn. I may have run, but I couldn't hide. The next day, everyone in town was talking about my fiasco.

(Selective) School Memories

Remembering Old Central Elementary
– Aug. 21, 1985

My most vivid memory of starting school is one of fear and trembling. Like most first graders, I was quite small and extremely shy. Going to school took a lot of courage, especially the first day. It was like the first time I went to the dentist, which was such a bad experience that I am still petrified every time I must face a dental appointment.

That September morning, my dad pushed me out of his 1946 Chevy, and I started up the steps of old Central Elementary School. Waiting at the front door was the legendary principal, "G" Hayes. In one hand, he had a wicked-looking leather strap that he occasionally whacked across the palm of his other hand, making a loud noise. His voice boomed like a thunderclap, "GOOD MORNING, MR. BURCH!" reverberating throughout the building.

Mr. Hayes' early morning blast made me, a five-year-old, want to turn and run. Only years later did I realize that he was just being friendly. In my mind's eye, "G" Hayes was eight feet tall. Terrified, I scurried past him to the safety of Mrs. Christine Hutchings' first grade classroom.

When it came to discipline, "G" Hayes was a better deterrent than the eclectic chair. I existed in a state of constant terror at old Central, making sure I did not get sent to the office to endure the wrath of the terrible leather strap.

Actually I don't remember if anyone ever felt its wrath. I eventually understood that Mr. Hayes simply carried a big stick to maintain discipline, and he really cared about us kids. I remember how much we missed Mr. Hayes when he retired at an early age.

By the time I got there, Central was getting old, having been built in 1905. It housed all grades in the Greer City School System for 20 years until Greer High was relocated in a new building erected with the help of a generous $500,000 donation from D.D. Davenport. That's when the two story red brick building on School Street became Central Elementary.

Central, like many other schools, may be gone but not forgotten by thousands of Greer students. How could anyone forget those old wooden floors that had been soaked in oil, year after year, to keep dust to a minimum? That made the floors so slick that kids could not run through the halls for fear of falling, which helped maintain discipline. Everyone said old Central with its oil-soaked floors was a firetrap, and it was. Years later, while being used as a warehouse for automotive carpeting, old Central caught fire, and three fire departments could not put out the blaze.

Things Have Changed at Chandler Creek

Buildings may come and go, but one thing that never changes is kids' attitudes toward school lunches. That stood out among glaring changes that hit me when I arrived at the new Chandler Creek Elementary School for Grandparents Day.

Instead of walking straight to the cafeteria, we were required to sign in at the front desk where we were given a nametag—in case we forgot who we are.

The lunch bell rang at 9:30 a.m. I wasn't exactly famished, having downed breakfast only 45 minutes earlier. Grandparents were herded into the cafeteria where I observed that some things never change, like waiting in lines. Which gave me plenty of time to consider the day's menu printed on a large wallboard. Nowhere did I see cornbread and beans. We were served a "bean of the day" at old Central Elementary. Those ranged from limas, to pintos, to green beans, to navy beans, even with English peas thrown in occasionally for variety.

Mashed potatoes were daily fare at old Central. When I made it to high school, the Friday meal of hot dogs and French fries came with enough grease to account for the disappearance of the nation's oil reserves. That was the foundation for the huge clientele of today's heart doctors.

But health conscious Chandler Creek Elementary School served salad. The only lettuce we ever saw at old Central was fed to the pet rabbit in a cage in a corner of our first grade classroom.

Our Grandparents' Day lunch included a toasted cheese sandwich and chicken noodle soup. The fare was very educational, especially for first graders learning to count. They could have added up all of the noodles in their bowls without getting to double digits.

My grandson Eli beat the system, however. He carried a box lunch of pizza roll-ups and pigs-in-blankets but didn't offer to share.

Recess was my favorite activity at old Central. Grandparents were not permitted to go out to the playground at Chandler Creek. The principal patiently explained that the swings and slides were not built for 200-plus pounders. Instead we were ushered into the media center (translation: library) where a book fair was taking place. I don't remember many books, let alone a fair, at old Central. Whenever a book was required, we were marched across the street to extract one from the shelves of the Davenport Memorial Library.

When I was at old Central, the only young, beautiful teacher was Elizabeth Propes. I couldn't help but notice a number of gorgeous young teachers shepherding kids around Chandler Creek. That could be the only time in history that a first grader and his grandfather had a crush on the same female.

Students Had to Sacrifice – Jan. 14, 1998

Having matriculated from old Central Elementary gave us a leg up going into junior high school. That's because old Central had a fire escape. Not only was that handy for getting out in case of a fire, it also served as an invaluable tool for teaching basic rocket science. For example, we learned to calculate time and space travel by taking bets on how fast our 300-pound teacher could descend from the second floor during a drill. We learned about trajectories by kicking footballs across the playground at odd angles so they would land among the group of teachers that sat at the foot of the fire escape to supervise recess.

There were too many students and too few buildings back in 1952. I was in junior high, and we had to share the Davenport building with high school students while a new Greer High facility was under construction. We sacrificed by attending class in the afternoon, arriving at noon as soon as the high school students went home, and we were dismissed at four o'clock.

Attending school four hours a day did not affect our test scores. Truthfully, I don't remember taking any tests—probably because they only gave tests to students who were applying to Harvard or Yale.

I can remember my father saying education had gone to the dogs because I only had to walk a half block to high school. He claimed to have walked two miles to a one-room school back in the Twenties.

My year in junior high was the high point of my public school days. I remember having a good time and very little learning. That later became the formula for the infamous Piedmont Schools Project. My junior high year also saved the budding careers of two new Converse College graduates. If Juanita Guthrie (Rogers) and Avriel Seifert (Patrick) had been saddled with us for eight hours a day, they would have gone into a less nerve wracking line of work, like becoming air traffic controllers.

Since 1952 was before the advent of computers, our eighth grade science class was devoted to learning the colors of the spectrum. General Science was taught by Mr. Leland Cooper who drove the only Henry J automobile that any of us had ever seen. It is helpful to know about the Henry J whenever the name comes up in "Trivial Pursuit," but I have never heard the spectrum mentioned again.

I would not label those years as "the good old days," but I wouldn't trade them either – because I would flunk out of today's high tech classes. Davenport Junior High didn't even have typewriters, those great machines that have become dinosaurs during my lifetime. But we did have some advantages that today's students do not experience. One was shop class where we were taught to make things out of wood using carpentry tools. I suppose the educational theory was that shop class would provide the spark of inspiration to launch the next Chippendale to create noble furniture like hat racks and lamp stands.

Mr. L.R. Duncan taught the shop class in a tin-roofed building out back on the Davenport campus. We thought Mr. Duncan was a preacher because he had a booming voice that could drown out the cacophony of two dozen pounding hammers and a couple of dueling power saws.

Strange as it may seem, Mr. Duncan often lectured during class, and we took notes, huddled around a pot-bellied wood stove on cold winter days. Eventually we were allowed to attempt to make something out of white pine boards, a valued commodity even then. We sold candy bars to raise money to buy wood for the shop class.

Mr. Duncan had a special name for our handiwork that served no useful purpose. He called them "what nots." Technically a "what not" is a one shelf bookrack—a flat board enclosed by two end pieces. It took me several weeks to make a "what not" because I insisted on cutting my pine board with a coping saw. I had been terrified of the electric band saw ever since the day Mr. Duncan demonstrated how such a machine once sliced off several of his fingers.

I used Duncan's miracle ingredient, wood putty, to seal the gaps between the boards in my "what not." Wood putty was the key element of every shop class project, like flour or corn meal that cooks use to beef up numerous dishes. If only I had a can of wood putty now, I might be tempted to pick up a hammer and saw again after all these years.

After that, it was three more years before I advanced to another cutting edge class, Typing 101, at Greer High School. It was reserved for seniors only. It was in that class that I learned a method of typing that can defeat any computer spell-checking program ever created.

The Davenport Junior High locker rooms had cold, damp concrete floors that were primitive in comparison with the ceramic-tiled showers in the North Main Street high school building. And today, the newest Greer High Campus on Gap Creek Road has carried athletic hygiene to an even higher level with a whirlpool bath in the coaches' quarters. That gives real meaning to drowning your sorrows after a defeat.

The high school's new 2,000 seat gym, arguably the finest in Greenville County, is a far cry from the Davenport auditorium that doubled as a gym where basketball players risked tumbling off the stage into the laps of spectators in pursuit of loose balls and crashing into the walls while making a lay-up. Spectators are greeted by a huge redesigned Yellow Jacket at the new Lewis Phillips Gymnasium. Compared with the original version, the new mascot seems downright friendly—which may reflect the demeanor of the school's basketball teams.

The name Greer High appears in huge letters on the new school. For many years, however, the North Main Street facility went unidentified, the logic being that everyone in town knew it was the high school.

Even though it was new in 1953, I don't remember getting excited about the school. I had just discovered girls, which was about three years after girls had discovered boys, but, by then, the girls were no longer interested.

Myth Shattered – Sept. 8, 2010

Anyone who has visited my office knows I never throw anything away. Thus, it was no surprise that while rummaging through the mountain of debris to collect artifacts for the Greer Heritage Museum, I discovered every report card I had brought home during my childhood. The bad part of this not-so-amazing discovery is this highly sensitive material somehow fell into the wrong hands— my grandson's.

The old report cards shattered the long-standing myth that I made all A's in school. Even worse, however, the truth has finally come out about my behavior. I haven't been an angel all my life, according to entries on my report cards in the spaces reserved for "Teacher's Comments."

In 1945-46, Mrs. Christine Hutchings had a lot to say shortly after I had arrived in the first grade at Central Elementary School. "Leland is careless with his food at lunch, spills it on the table and floor. And he refuses to touch healthy foods like chicken, fish and broccoli."

Mrs. Hutchings didn't stop here. In another reporting period she noted, "Leland needs to speed up his classroom work. He is the slowest pupil in class. He should also read eight to 10 books during the summer to be successful in the second grade."

When I arrived in the second grade, my teacher, Miss Eloise Wilson, wrote: Leland is making progress as a student, but he simply will not let the girls alone. He pulls their pigtails during recess."

Miss Mae McClannahan wrote on my 1947-48 report card: "Leland does some good work, but he could do much better if he would only settle down and stop talking when I am speaking."

In the fourth grade, Miss Elizabeth Propes wrote on my report card: "Leland should stick to trying to throw baseballs instead of rocks on the playground during recess."

A 1949 note from Principal 'G' Hayes suggested, "Leland should concentrate on developing other talents. A car is only thing he can hit with a rock or a baseball."

"Leland has a bright future in the business world. He has all of the other children paying him insurance not to throw rocks when they are on the playground," wrote Mrs. Grace Medlock, my sixth grade teacher.

"Leland is the first one out of the building and down the fire escape when we have a fire drill, but he is always the last one back in the classroom," stated my seventh grade teacher Mrs. John R. Harrison.

"Playing pranks such as making footprints on the ceiling in home room is not appropriate behavior," wrote Miss Juanita Guthrie, my eighth grade teacher at Davenport Junior High School. "Leland frequently interrupts the class pulling the girls' pigtails and making them squeal. During lunch, Leland spills food on the table and floor, and he avoids such health foods as chicken, fish and broccoli." Finishing her first year of teaching after graduating from Converse College, she added, "As a result of this experience, I have decided to retire after one year of teaching."

"Because 'stumble, fumble and fall' is not part of the Yellow Jackets' football program, I regret to inform you that Leland did not make the Greer High junior varsity team. I would invite Leland to become the water boy if he could improve his speed enough to get the water bucket onto the field in the allotted time out of 60 seconds."—Phil Clark, Head Coach, 1954.

"As the result of air pollution created by excessive cigarette smoking in the boy's restrooms, Greer High has been forced to hire additional personnel to serve as hall monitors."—B.L. Frick, 1955.

"Leland could do even better if he would sit next to someone who makes better grades."—Miss Ollie Barton, World History, 1955.

"Leland constantly sneaks away to the golf course instead of staying after school to work on the *Greer High Times* newspaper." —Lester Bowles, 1955.

"Leland has a great future in golf—as a caddie."—Eddis Freeman, Golf Coach, 1956.

"Leland is a fine pupil, except he won't leave the girls alone. He keeps pulling their pigtails in my typing class."—Miss Barbara Babb, 1956.

"Leland should read at least 30 books this summer if he expects to make more than 600 on the SAT." – Miss Elfreda Cole, 1956.

"I have enjoyed having Leland in my driver training class. And, at the rate he is going, Leland will be able to pass the exam for his driver's license by the age of 21."—Eddis Freeman, 1956.

The last entry on my final report cards was written in May 1957 by Miss Fronda Rice: "Leland is careless with his food in the cafeteria, spilling it on the table and floor. He will not touch healthy foods like chicken, fish, and broccoli."

Our Senior Trip – May 6, 1987

I have forgotten much about high school, but I will always re-member our Greer High School Senior Class Trip to Washington, DC and New York City.

It was like a dream come true when we finally boarded the Southern Railway streamliner one May afternoon in 1957. That wasn't my first train ride, but it was my first all-night trip. We arrived in Washington at 6:30 a.m. the following day. No one had slept a wink, but that didn't slow us down. We even managed to eat the food, which, until this day, is the worst I have ever been served.

A highlight of the first day was visiting the Washington Monument. Several us decided not to wait in the long line to ride the elevator and instead climbed the stairs all the way to the top. What made that ex-hausting experience worthwhile was dropping a golf ball hundreds of feet to the pavement below. It was the highest bounce I've ever seen.

Then it was on to New York City where we checked into a hotel and carried on "big time." We ordered hamburgers from room ser-vice. The burgers cost $5 apiece, which was a fortune during the day when McDonalds was selling them for 19 cents. After that, we did not have any money left for souvenirs. I scraped together a few coins to send a post card: "Dear mom, having a wonderful time…."

…..even though we didn't see much of the girls in our class be-cause they were housed on another floor of the hotel and closely guarded by a squad of chaperones and hotel detectives. Women's Lib was unheard of back then.

We killed time by riding the New York subway from one end to the other on a ten-cent ticket. I would not have the nerve to get on the subway today.

After sailing paper airplanes off the top of the Empire State Building, we met some girls from Skokie, Ill, on a boat headed for the

Statue of Liberty. We exchanged names and addresses and promised to write them. We never did, and they didn't write to us either.

Leaving New York at Grand Central Station, I purchased the greenest 50-cent Cuban cigar ever made. On a dare from me, I gave the cigar to Ken Coates who lit up and was overcome by one of the worst coughing spells I have ever seen. Our chaperone, Coach Eddis Freeman, was beside himself. That was Coach Freeman's last time as a chaperone, and the school discontinued the trips a couple of years later.

After 35 years, You Can Laugh or Cry
– Sept. 9, 1992

Who are all those old people? At last I have the answer—they are the old folks who showed up at the reunion of the Greer High Class of '57.

Seeing people for the first time in 35 years makes one stop, think and even take the chance of looking in the mirror. After that, there are only two choices: You can either laugh or cry.

So we decided to laugh. But first, we observed a moment of silence in remembrance of our long lost waistlines.

Things went downhill rapidly after that. It rained on our cookout and the 300 hamburgers handmade by Ken Coates. It rained on our reserved seats at the Greer High football game. It rained on our Saturday morning golf outing, and that was the only reason I had organized the reunion—to get someone to play golf with me.

Tension mounted during the Saturday night social hour when Ruth (Lazar) Stokes, bless her heart, was late delivering our nametags. Without those, we were a bunch of strangers in a strange land—the Greenville Country Club.

Fortunately, our beloved principal B.L. Frick saved the day. He pointed out that while we are gaining on him, we haven't caught up—yet.

Stokes' grand entrance at 7 p.m. caused everyone to forget that the band was also missing. We forgot to inform the band of the time and place.

Judging by the number of no-shows, reading must not have been part of our high school curriculum.

Even some of the planning committee members dropped out. They complained about being overworked, trying to keep up with the new husbands and wives that our classmates had dug up since the last reunion.

Nobody in the class is rich and famous, so no one had to tell a major lie to impress everyone. We also did not have to worry about such extra expenses as security guards and valet parking for limos.

Eugenia (Davis) Allen came closest to becoming wealthy, except for a decision she made 30 years ago to move away to Rock Hill and vacate the land that was later sold at an inflated price to BMW Manufacturing.

Head majorette Donna Lynn (Jones) Long returned from California for the first time in 35 years. She even considered staying in Greer for good but returned to California for fear that she would miss the earthquakes.

The prize for traveling the longest distance went to Sara (Duncan) Dominick—she floated in from "La La Land."

Homecoming Queen Lorita (Miller) Perkins finally got a crown she can afford to lose, and Mr. Frick did his part by placing it on her head upside down.

Twins Bobby and Billy Howard were presented a case of Ben Gay to ease the pain of having played football in the shadows of David Boozer and Murray Hall.

Frances (Amos) Leonhardt stole the show with her famous dessert she calls "Better than sex chocolate delight." No one could argue with the name because no one could remember what sex was like. Leonhardt claimed she found the recipe in her church's cookbook, and that caused a stampede to join her in Sunday School the next day.

There were many other highlights such as displaying the Official Class Photo, taken in Washington D.C, during the senior trip. It showed Sen. Strom Thurmond in his original hair.

The reunion souvenir was a car flag embroidered with a wheel chair.

K**ool** Aid **anyone ?**

Tape Measure Came in Handy – Sept. 8, 1999

The next time the class gathered, we actually removed Lavenia Dill from the list of departed classmates. John Eller, now a preacher in Georgia, spent the weekend attempting to find out how Dill came back to life. "It would be great material for a sermon." he figured.

Our fourth grade teacher, Miss Elizabeth Propes recalled that I overturned a glass of purple Kool Ade on Loretta Miller's white evening gown on the night of May 3, 1949. That was during a banquet she gave to teach the class proper etiquette. I did not spill Kool Ade at the reunion. It was Ensure. And I would not have spilled a drop if Bobby Gravley had not slapped me on the back.

Juanita Guthrie (Rogers) summoned the nerve to venture among us again and was reminded of the day that students consumed an entire English class period trying to guess the name of her boyfriend (Joe).

Retired Principal B.L. Frick declared the reunion to be "mighty fine." He also confirmed most of the tall tales, including some antics that earned a summons to his office. Like the time Edward Fox hid in the back seat of Larry Bright's car after a football game. Bright, who had driven the band bus to the game, waited until the parking lot had cleared out before heading home. When he put the car in gear, a voice cried out from the back seat, "I'm not ready to go!" Frightened out of his wits, Bright jumped out of the moving car. It rolled across the parking lot and knocked over the flagpole. Even after all those years, Frick was glad to learn how the pole had been demolished.

Then there was the day Fox was driving Edward Hyatt home from school. Both were looking at girls walking along North Main, and Fox slammed into the back of a truck that had stopped at a traffic light. That was before seat belts, and Hyatt's head shattered the windshield. Jimmy Howell, one of the first on the scene, offered Hyatt a ride to the hospital "provided you don't bleed in my car."

Class President Gene Gibson recalled that it fell his lot to measure seniors for graduation gowns. Nancy (Fincher) McManus remembered the gowns came in only two sizes, 32 or 36 depending on the girls' chests. Faye (Donnelly) Nolan pointed out "most of us still have the same measurements, but in different places."

Gibson became so enamored with the assignment that he has carried a tape measure ever since.

A Religious Experience – June 1, 2000

The gathering of 400 chattering people at the Classes of the Fifties Reunion in June, 2000, was a religious experience. It was as if the old classmates had gone to Heaven, bypassing the Wood Mortuary in the process. At least that's what I gathered from Rudy Godfrey's remarks that were lengthier than most Sunday sermons. Godfrey, who had the inspiration for the reunion, said when we do get to Heaven it's like going into another room and waiting until the next classmate arrives. Hence the crowd assembled at the new Greer High School, which is heavenly by comparison with all four previous locations of the school.

"I see you still want to congregate in the hall," remarked retired principal B.L. Frick. At age 91, our mentor and role model was the focus of the center stage spotlight. To no one's surprise, Frick pronounced the reunion to be "mighty fine."

Those who came back looking for their youth didn't find it. And some came a very long way, like John R. Harrison, Buddy Tinsley and Norden Davis, all from California.

No one showed up wearing the same amount or color hair they had in high school. No one, except Ralph Voyles. And he still has the same hairstyle.

All shared a common bond having been molded by teachers who expected nothing less than the best from us. Or, as Homer Voyles, President of the Class of 1950 put it, "they took kids from the farm, kids from the mill villages, and kids from the city and molded them together into a loyal, dedicated student body." It was no surprise that nearly one-third of all the Fifties graduates returned to be reunited, expressing a genuine love for each other.

We were fortunate to have grown up during the golden decade of the Twentieth Century before Vietnam, drugs, AIDS, video poker, Internet porn and all the influences that can adversely impact today's teens. There was room in our lives for a great deal of school spirit—and it is still there as evidenced by the hugs, laughter and reminiscing that took place at the reunion. It was like a typical day had been lifted from the pages of the Fifties, as if nothing had changed for a few golden hours.

"I'd like to bottle this sprit and pour it over our present student body," declared current principal Marion Waters.

Bill "Butter" Taylor, who breezed in from Summerville to entertain the gathering, noted "every reunion has a Bubba, and this one is no different with Ray Sanderson here."

No one claimed the lifetime achievement award for deciphering the school motto that is emblazoned in the hand-carved crest that graces the new lectern on the auditorium stage. Legend has it that the original crest was misplaced during the move from Davenport to the North Main building in 1953. The crest resurfaced during the move to the new campus on Gap Creek Rd. The motto is written in Latin, and since Miss Elfreda Cole has passed on, no one could translate the meaning of *Parantes Pro Civitae*.

Fifty Years Is a Long Time – Mar. 14, 2007

After seven months, numerous meetings, and much hand ringing, the self-appointed committee announced plans for the 50th Reunion of the Greer High Class of 1957. It is hard to overstate how much work went into the planning process—over 500 man-hours by my estimate. Admittedly we are slow, but I remember making fun of New Yorkers we encountered scurrying along Manhattan sidewalks during our Senior Trip.

We spent much of the committee's work sessions reminiscing and waiting for Class President Gene Gibson to show up. Gibson said he didn't hear about the meetings. That's a legitimate excuse because Gibson is deaf as a post.

Eventually we plunged ahead, passing around dog-eared photographs including one of Miss Elizabeth Propes' fourth grade banquet. The girls were dressed in evening gowns and the boys in Sunday suits. "We were cute back then. I wonder what happened," remarked Sarah (Duncan) Dominick.

"A lot can happen to a person in 60 years," declared Allen West, squinting through a magnifying glass at the class graduation photo. The mass of black robes could pass for a flock of penguins.

Hours were devoted to deciding which classmates are still vertical. We celebrated locating J.C. Hamby in Louisiana after he had been lost in Florida for years. Like apples, however, most of us have not fallen far from the tree.

Our teachers are definitely fewer in number. "They were old when we were in school, and now we are old." I noted.

Libby Davis who created a mailer declaring the reunion to be "a very historical occasion—50 years is a long time" recalled "it seems like only yesterday the boys were pulling my pigtails in the first grade. Eric, Roy, and Gene were always chasing me, and Leland, too," she said accusingly.

"I was the only one who never caught you. I was so slow I couldn't even catch a cold," I said defensively.

After settling on the menu, we inserted a 30-minute break into the program to allow everyone time for a nap. That will be followed by posing for a new class photograph to pass on to hordes of disinterested people—our children and grandchildren. The photo will also appear on a recruiting poster for our class sponsor, The Cottages at Brushy nursing home.

Where Did the Time Go? – Sept. 5, 2007

Fifty years. Time is so fleeting that it seems like only a day or even an hour has passed since 1957. Where did the time go?

When we gathered for the traditional class picture, wearing our caps and gowns, that day back in 1957, I never expected to be around 50 years later to attend a reunion.

Our committee spent an entire year planning the 50th Reunion. It took that long because we relapsed into reminiscing about old times instead of actually planning.

When the big day finally arrived "I...I...I don't recognize anybody," stammered Don Hawkins who had traveled the longest distance, from Seattle, Wash. "That's all right Don," responded Sharon (Reese) Coates. "Nobody recognizes you either."

To commemorate the occasion, Margaret (Hannah) Covington complied a list of important events of 1957, such as Sputnik, the Soviet Russian satellite that started the space race. Then, just like 50 years ago when we were working together to publish *The Greer High Times*, she forgot to bring the list.

I never expected to be standing before the class and speaking, because I never had the opportunity to speak when we were in high school. The Howard twins, Billy and Bobby were doing all the talking back then except for the few times that perennial class president Gene Gibson would insert an announcement, or John Eller would deliver a mini-sermon.

When I finally got the floor, I gave them a piece of my mind—a piece is all that is left. My topic was, "What I have learned in life."

When I graduated, I thought I knew everything. There was no reason for me to have that idea, however, because I would still be sitting in chemistry class if it hadn't been for Frances (Amos) Leonhardt and Eugenia Davis pulling me through. I have learned to be extremely thankful for the blessings showered upon us. We did not choose to be born in 1938 or 1939; neither did we choose to live in Greer nor to attend Greer High School. Those are blessings we did not deserve or earn, but I cannot think of a better time to have been born and lived.

Greer High School sent us out into the world full of hope and enthusiasm. We were not commissioned to conquer the world, but I could travel anywhere and inform strangers with a great deal of pride that "I am from Greer"—not the big city next door for fear that no one had ever heard of my home town. Our state championship football team had put Greer on the map.

Coach Phil Clark declared, "The Class of '57 is the greatest to ever graduate from Greer High," to which everyone applauded. Then he added, "because they dedicated the yearbook in my honor."

As I shuffled out the door toward geezerdom, I released a handful of strings tied to helium filled gold and black balloons. They soared toward the heavens, perhaps as a message to our departed classmates; all of us who started out on life journeys together as first graders in the fall of 1944 will always be forever and unalterably linked in a common bond as the Class of '57.

Football in Greer

A Football Gnome - (selectively recalling the history of Greer High football)

Greer High School completed its 88th football season in the fall of 2010. According to my calculations, a member of the Burch family has been on the sidelines covering the games for the last 68 consecutive years. This tidbit may not be worthy of *Trivial Pursuit* or even a footnote in the game program under the all-time school records, but it should underscore the fact that football is important in Greer.

Actually, football is a matter of life and death because football was Greer's only claim to fame for the entire 20th Century until BMW came to town—and many people still haven't heard of BMW. Football is a bond that connects at least four generations of Greer tribes.

I have been on the sidelines at Greer High games for so many years that I have shriveled into a genuine Gnome. I can tell many tales. Here's one about Steve "Woody" Woodward, not yet that long in the tooth but once the Yellow Jackets' equivalent of Luke Skywalker. That was in 1963 when Woodward thrilled Jacket Backers with the longest kick return in school history, 99-yards.

I wasn't around in 1921 when the first game was played on a vacant field (now a city park) at Victor Mill. According to Greer High yearbooks, the sport got off to a slow start. Most of the focus was on the school's debate team—Greer's best students won numerous championships simply by talking.

The community must have taken notice of football by the year 1929 when the team's record was 6-2. But it took another five years to raise money needed to erect lights at the Victor field so people could attend games at night after they got off work.

The first football stadium was a $35,000 WPA project that was built on Green Street in 1938. When the stadium was completed on October 21, it was the lead story, with a big bold headline in red ink, on the front page of *The Greer Citizen*. The Yellow Jackets even got new uniforms for the inaugural game in the stadium, but lost to Seneca, 16-14.

The first game I remember attending was in September 1947. Woodruff defeated Greer, 13-7. I watched as hundreds of angry Yellow Jackets fans poured out of the stands afterwards and chased the officials through the wooden gates of the stadium. The refs made it to the car and locked the doors, but the crowd overturned their 1941 Ford with them sitting inside. It was 43 years before Greer and Woodruff played each other again.

Another of my earliest memories was riding with my dad on a long journey to Honea Path in the fall of 1948 to see the Yellow Jackets. I remember standing outside the stadium before the game and watching the Honea Path team walk through the gate. They were wearing pink uniforms, which I will never forget. The uniforms were likely a badly faded-shade of red, but I have never seen anything like them since.

Back in the Fifties

It was a Friday night in late October. The year was 1954, and Greer High was locked in a fearsome battle with Hendersonville High. As the Yellow Jackets pushed the ball toward the partisan crowd waiting just beyond the end zone, a time out was called. The head official marched over to the Yellow Jackets huddle and announced, "the Hendersonville end on Mr. McLemore's side of the line is missing three teeth."

It was like a weather report. Enough said. Period. There was no yellow flag, no sermon, and no threat of litigation.

That was a half-century ago, and the sport has greatly changed. Back in the Fifties, you had to be slightly crazy to play football, even on a dare. Darrell Leonhardt played football barefooted. Not because he couldn't afford shoes, but I think Leonhardt simply enjoyed the feeling of freshly mown grass on the soles of his feet. I remember the day the referees told him to either put on shoes or get out of the game.

Yes, football was tough back then. No one was allowed to drink water during practice—that was considered "sissy." Instead, the players were given salt tablets to prevent cramps. That explains why so many of them have ended up on operating tables for triple by-pass heart surgery.

Most football players were wearing false teeth when they walked across the stage to receive their diplomas. That was in the days of cardboard helmets that eventually gave way to plastic helmets. Then the facemask arrived, followed by the mouthpiece. Those inventions threw dentistry into a recession.

Today, NFL stars hold out for more money. In the good old days, another kid would gladly knock your head off just for the chance to wear a football uniform.

Back in the Fifties, football was played in all sorts of conditions, from driving rain to blizzards. The players sloshed around in the mud and came down with pneumonia. Today, games are postponed if a black cloud crosses the sky.

Back in the Fifties, the action didn't always end when time expired. The Hendersonville end retaliated as the players were on the way to the buses. He swatted the back of Leon McLemore's head with a glass Pepsi Cola bottle.

The bad blood with Hendersonville had spilled over from the previous year. Greer had defeated Hendersonville on their home turf and joyfully headed to the post-game meal. Upon arriving at the restaurant to eat, however, the irate owner informed Coach Phil Clark, "We're closed. We aren't serving tonight."

The Yellow Jackets rode home on empty stomachs, and some managed to grab a hot dog at the Carolina Lunch which stayed open until midnight.

Remembering Coach Eddis Freeman

In the mid-1950's, Phil Clark and Eddis Freeman formed the greatest coaching combination in Greer High football history. As a student, I spent more time with Coach Freeman than any other teacher. He was a man of many talents who left me with wonderful memories.

Freeman was "macho" in an era when no one knew the definition of "macho." He was constantly doing macho-type things to get our

268

attention, like unexpectedly slamming a yardstick down on a desk with such force that it splintered into toothpick-size shreds in his general science class. Freeman would, in the middle of a sentence, simply pitch forward toward the floor, extending his hands only at the very last second to break the fall. Those antics made Freeman seem larger than life to impressionable high school freshmen.

We did not have Carowinds in the 1950s, but driver training class with Coach Freeman was the next best thing. It was nearly a thrill (or a scare) a minute.

In the fall of 1954, we had spent the first month of school in the classroom studying the handbook of traffic laws, etc. while waiting for the arrival of the new driver training car that we would use to actually learn how to drive. It finally arrived in mid-October, a brand new (the first delivered in Greer) 1955 Ford, courtesy of D&D Motors. Coach Freeman was thrilled, and enthusiastically pointed out all of the features of the car when we piled in, excited about going for a spin.

Our class was the first lucky group to take the car on the road. It had 23 miles on the odometer as we headed out of the school's rear parking lot. When we neared the gate, a big yellow school bus rounded the corner, sailed through the entrance and hit us head-on. The bus did not have a scratch, but the collision caved in the front end of the new Ford. It was back to the driver training handbook for another three weeks while waiting for the car to be repaired.

That left us with a lot of driving practice to make up, and those adventures became as traumatic as trips to the dentist. Coach Freeman sat with his left arm extended along the top of the front seat. If you made a mistake while driving, such as turning left when he commanded "go right," Freeman whacked the back of your head with his hand, which had a unique way of freezing you like a statue.

Coach Freeman always tried to put everyone in a good mood when were out driving. He raided the cafeteria and arrived at the car with a handful of oranges, apples or goodies from the day's lunch spread. We had no choice but to eat the fruit to keep Coach Freeman in a good mood.

Dickie Gravley, a football hero, was so fearful of making a blunder that he went to great lengths to operate the driver training car as smoothly as possible. One day we were doing double duty, practicing driving and taking Coach Freeman to check on the teen canteen set-up in the Paget Chevrolet building, when Gravley was directed to "park over there near the door." Gravley began bringing the Ford sedan to such a smooth stop that it continued rolling until we hit a utility pole. "What did you think the pole was going to do for you—lay a golden egg!?!?" shouted Freeman as he whacked Gravley.

On the football field, Freeman customarily practiced among the players, blocking and tackling without benefit of pads or helmet. His favorite expression was "a good lick (meaning a hit) is like a good candy bar."

Those were the days when football was more of a game of knocking each other down than finesse and technique. Downfield blocking below the waist, crackback blocking, etc. were entirely legal in the 1950s.

One day at practice, Freeman was showing a classmate of mine, Edward Fox, how to throw a forearm to ward off a blocker. Fox, who was wearing a helmet—but no face mask—had the misfortune of raising his head about the time Coach Freeman delivered the forearm. The blow caught Fox squarely in the mouth, but he did not flinch.

"Are you okay, Edward?" Coach Freeman inquired. "I'm all right." Fox replied. "I just lost a few teeth, that's all" he added as several pearly whites tumbled out into his hand. Fox even apologized for failing to keep his head down.

From that moment, Edward Fox stood tall in the eyes of coaches and his classmates. And I learned to always keep my head down.

The tale of '56

Coach Freeman's finest moment in coaching occurred at Union during the 1956 football season. An undefeated season and the state championship were on the line that night, but Coach Phil Clark was at the bedside of his daughter, Susan, who was gravely ill in an Atlanta, Ga. hospital.

The Yellow Jackets trailed 7-0 at halftime, a situation that inspired Freeman to deliver an emotional speech, urging the team to win for Coach Clark. The players responded in dramatic fashion. Murray Hall returned the second half kickoff for a touchdown to tie the game. After forcing Union to punt, Hall sprinted about 70 yards to the end zone on the next play, running over one of his own teammates, Newt Smith, in the process. And the Yellow Jackets went on to an 11-0 record that year.

It was another 33 years before Greer High won a second championship, during which time Jacket Backers continually rehashed the "good old days" of the '56 season. Not only did the "tale of '56" improve with age, it also had at least one positive benefit. Launching into a spiel about the 1956 team was a sure fire way to get rid of door-to-door salesmen.

The 1956 attack consisted of three plays; Murray Hall left, Murray Hall right, and Murray Hall up the middle.

If the 1956 team had a true secret, it was the offensive line. Your grandmother could run behind that line. Nobody knew how good our line really was. We had big names like David Boozer and Hugh Granade who went on to college fame. There were also unsung heroes like the Howard twins, Billy and Bobby. If the Howards ever ran up against anyone they couldn't handle, they simply talked them into the ground.

We never knew if the quarterback, Bobby Gravley, could throw the ball. I do recall that no one was gifted at pass catching. But Gravley was so adept at handing the ball off to Hall that he never had to throw.

Sports Medicine

Other than Edward Fox's misfortune at practice, no member of the 1956 team got hurt. I have always assumed that was because it was my job to patch up the wounded as the "trainer." Back then, the position was known as a "manager" to my friends and "water boy" to my enemies.

By the fall of 1956, my younger assistant Rob Hughes and I thought we knew everything about "sports medicine," having learned much over several grueling football seasons. We treated the players for every injury imaginable, and we did it without computer-driven diagnostic imaging equipment.

For concussions, loss of teeth and internal injuries, there were "speckle pills" from a gallon jar that Rob had bummed from his uncle, Dr. Jim Hughes, the team physician. We prescribed salt tablets for anything less serious like cramps and fainting spells. That explains why so many of them underwent by-pass surgery in later life. Feeding players salt tablets today would probably get us 10 years-to-life for manslaughter. We also refused to give them water because that was considered a sign of weakness.

We were most skilled at swabbing cuts, scrapes and turf burns with Mercurochrome. Simply opening a bottle of the fiery red substance would clear out the locker room like a fire drill.

Slabs of Atomic Balm were lathered on bruised muscles and wrapped with yards of gauze and adhesive tape. The original symptoms disappeared instantly, replaced by an unrelenting burning sensation. The cure was significantly worse than the injury, so few dared to report a problem. And I ended up with nothing to do, like a Maytag repairman. That's also why my medical school application was rejected.

Unlike today's trainers, we got no respect for keeping the team fit through the glorious undefeated season. Our reward was an old jersey, salvaged from the musty pile of garments that today would be rejected by Goodwill.

the bouncing cap

The Game Constantly Changes

Some things are eternally true, like football taught me how to get out of the way of accidents. The last place you ever wanted to be was on the bottom of the pile.

At the same time, the game of football is constantly in a state of change. Take the offense. At Greer High, it evolved from the single wing attack of Coach Walt Pinson in the 1940s, to the T formation installed by Coach Phil Clark in the 1950s, then on to Coach Jim Few's veer in the 1970s, to the no-huddle, one-back attack of Stuart Holcombe in the 1990s, and Will Young's zone option spread entering the 21st Century.

Despite winning two state titles, Coach Holcombe constantly pressured himself to get a third. That was evident in the 1999 season opener. After a disastrous punting attempt when the center snap bounced back to the kicker like a ping pong ball while two players failed to go onto the field for kicking team duty and the other nine failed to throw a single block, Holcombe threw his cap to the turf in disgust. That gave me an idea for a new invention—a rubber cap that would bounce right back after hitting the ground. I envisioned making millions on this invention as well as preventing coaches from suffering back injuries resulting from bending over to retrieve battered hats. As a side benefit, school districts would never incur a workmen's comp claim.

But Holcombe deflated my fantasy of instant wealth when he declared, "we're not going to punt again. Ever. No matter what!" And the Yellow Jackets didn't. At least not that night. Greer twice converted on fourth downs on their own side of the field.

That's a permanent rule change I'd like to see: no punting. Field goal attempts would be okay, if only to keep the foot in football and to remind us to be thankful that soccer was unheard of back in 1921. Otherwise, Burches would have spent 68 years writing about how fast the grass was growing while waiting for something to happen in a soccer match.

Eastside High Coach John Carlisle once asked a player—a 5-6 320 pounder—to switch positions, from quarterback to left tackle. The kid told Carlisle, "I'll think about it. I'll let you know." Carlisle never got an answer. So another change I'd like to see is for high school players to have agents to represent them. Agents could negotiate issues like how much game time players will get, what positions they will play, and the numbers on their jerseys. Agents could win perks for their clients, like an extra scoop of ice cream in the cafeteria or a front seat on the bus for road games.

It Was a Cinch – 2003 State Championship

I had to wait nine years before 2003 delivered the most amazing football season I ever witnessed. It was not one for the faint hearted as the Yellow Jackets won two playoff games with electrifying finishes en route to capturing the school's fourth state championship. My fingernails emerged intact, however, because I knew in advance how things would turn out. Dr. Joe Wentzky told me.

In September, Wentzky dreamed that Greer would upset Greenville on a big play late in the game. At the time, the two teams were not scheduled to play, but they did meet in the playoffs, and Greer won in overtime.

Realizing that Wentzky was on to something, I asked him about the next game against Union. I was relieved when he said that Greer would surely win and advance to the state finals because he dreamed that he was walking around Williams-Brice Stadium, the site of the title match in Columbia. He was right.

Wentzky also "felt good" when I asked him how the Yellow Jackets were going to do in the state finals against West Florence. Then, minutes before the kickoff, he allowed, "it has come to me that we are going to win 35-14." (The actual score was 33-17.)

Since no one has attempted to name a holiday or a highway in Wentzky's honor, I took the precaution of double-checking with a man who has a direct line to the Almighty, Rev. Steve Watson, the team chaplain. And Watson declared, "Greer is going to bring home a great victory."

With those confirmations, I was much more confident than Bunchy Godfrey who had fretted all the way to Columbia. I couldn't resist reminding Godfrey that he had no choice to stay until the bitter end, no matter what, because he was riding with me. After all, Godfrey was walking out the gate at Dooley Field with three minutes left in regulation in the Greenville game when he heard a great roar from the crowd. Running back, he learned that Greer had caught up with a touchdown on a surprising "hook and ladder" play. The next day, Godfrey phoned to apologize for having so little faith. He also inquired "you aren't going to put this in the paper are you?"

"Don't worry." I replied. "It's strictly off the record."

We picked up our grandson Eli, who was one of the water boys, when the team bus arrived home at 2 a.m. from Columbia. One of his shoes was covered in mud, and the other was clean as a whistle.

"Why are your new shoes like that?" my wife asked.

"Oh—the dirty shoe is a Greer High shoe. It went out there and played hard all night. The other is a West Florence shoe. It didn't do much, so it's still clean." Eli explained.

Yoda on the Sidelines

Greer people expect football victories as if they were an inalienable right. When the Yellow Jackets lose, grief support groups spring into action all over town.

I worried an entire week in September 1997 that Clinton might inflict Greer's third defeat of the young season. Just before the kickoff, Fred "Speedy" Gregory, the world's oldest ball boy, edged over. "You can just feel the tension out here," Gregory declared. "There's pressure on everyone tonight, even you," added Gregory who had taken to painting miniature Block G's on the team's game balls.

He was right. The game was going badly for the Yellow Jackets. Clinton, Greer's oldest football nemesis and a team that Coach Jim Few devoted his career to mastering, took a 7-0 lead.

In the second half, however, Greer was suddenly transformed into the Yellow Jackets of old and scored two touchdowns in less than three minutes.

Twice, Greer recovered Red Devils' fumbles. But the officials said they weren't fumbles, even though I saw clearly that they were from my vantage point on the bench. Clinton kept the ball and scored again.

Coach Stuart Holcombe protested the rulings, to no avail. It's a good thing Holcombe's parents didn't waste money sending him to law school, because I've never seen him win a single argument with a referee.

In my younger days, I would have yelled at the officials for making such glaring mistakes. Over the years, however, I have learned that yelling doesn't do any good because most referees are deaf as well as blind. Instead, I now go into my Yoda mode to influence the outcome of the game and warn the grey-haired official nearest the sideline to be on the lookout. I inform him that a search party from the nursing home has been inquiring about a man in a black and white shirt who wandered away. He barks at me to back off.

Walking backwards, I retort that if the officiating doesn't improve, I will ask Chief Dean Crisp to cancel their police escort after the game.

The Yoda effect finally starts to take hold. John Dobson breaks free down the sidelines with no one between him and the goal line, but he steps out of bounds. I'm sure Dobson didn't mean to—his foot barely touched the white sideline. By the time he reaches the end zone, the referee with Alzheimer's has forgotten that Dobson went out of bounds. It made Greer almost even in the bad calls column, proving to be just enough and barely in time.

Football Fanatic

If anyone has the impression that I am a football fanatic, let me set the record straight. The real reason I make a mad dash to Dooley Field on Friday nights is because of the interesting characters that gather there.

On a typical Friday night, I barely close the car door before being surrounded by teeny-boppers in very short black and gold skirts. "You really should buy a program," one bubbles. "It even has pictures of old ladies in it. You would really like it."

I'm even older than the girl suspects. She doesn't know that I had seen 300 Greer High games before she was born, so I don't need a program to know which team is wearing the gold and black. But I offer a weak excuse anyway, "I look at an old lady across the dinner table every day."

The first person I meet on the sidelines is Terry Medford, the team stats keeper. He asked whether he should stay on the field or go to the press box. "We won the last time you sat in the press box, so why don't you just head on up there," I suggest.

Without being asked, Fred "Speedy" Gregory launches into a recital about his shiniest balls in the upstate. "Polly washes my towels in Downy fabric softener. That's the secret," he explains. The glistening footballs are so slick that nobody can catch one.

No matter. Winning isn't a life or death proposition, especially for Dr. Doug Owens. Like all Easley natives, the team physician never gets excited about the games. Instead, Owens spends most of his time trying to con the cheerleaders out of a couple of miniature footballs— one for his grandson, and one for mine.

"I finally have a deal," he announced, slipping through the sideline fence gate. Opening his jacket to reveal a couple of bright gold souvenir footballs inside, Owens said "your part of the deal is to put the cheerleaders' picture on the front page of the newspaper."

As McGee leads the Greer High band onto the field, Jimmy Hunt expresses fear that the long-time mascot might defect to Byrnes High. "McGee could be leading their 350-member band," worries Hunt who paints the yardage lines on the playing field, "which is bad, because he doesn't have an understudy."

I assure Hunt that the size of the band isn't a problem. "Our band has always been small, but it's still great. You see, Greer just doesn't produce many musicians. Never has. Greer is the reason talk radio came about—people wouldn't even listen to music let alone play an instrument," I explain.

"Two weeks ago, there were 500 little girls on the field learning how to lead cheers, and twice that many boys were wearing football uniforms. Not a single kid showed up in a band outfit."

Steve Watson, the team chaplain, emerges from the locker room at halftime worrying that his prayer got cut short. Watson's fears were confirmed as the Daniel Lions scored four touchdowns.

At one point, Coach Stuart Holcombe calls time out and warns, "You guys are going to put me in the hospital. I'm going straight to the hospital."

Holcombe then attempts to phone his assistant coaches in the press box to find out what went wrong. But he gets a busy signal because Coach Steve Woodward is dialing CRISISline.

No matter. Dr. Owens is anxious to change the subject to his upcoming bird hunt in Nebraska. Claims he will bring back hundreds of pheasants for Thanksgiving.

I swallow this tale with a large grain of salt, never having seen any evidence, such as a photograph, of Owens' big adventures. When I finally get a word in, I volunteer to accompany Owens on the hunt—in hopes that I spot a bird wearing black and white stripes.

A Marked Man

One Friday afternoon I asked my youngest son if he was planning to go to the Greer High football game that night. "No," he answered.

"Why not?" I shot back. "You know I am going to be inducted into the Athletic Hall of Fame tonight. That's almost like going to Heaven."

"Well," he replied, "the only place with a longer list of names than the Hall of Fame is the white pages of the phone book."

Even so, I was honored to be joining the company of famous folks like David Dean Craft and Steve Brown. I felt conspicuous standing in front of thousands of Jacket Backers during the pre-game ceremony. It was like wearing a bullseye. Sure enough, I soon discovered that induction into the Hall of Fame made me a marked man. When the game began a few minutes later, I was watching the Yellow Jackets hammer away at the Eastside Eagles when a center snap sailed over the head of the punter. It was the type of miscue that can change the course of a game.

"What a great photo!" I thought, raising my camera to focus on the scramble for the loose ball. Then into the corner of the picture frame came a referee, quickly filling the entire shot (I cannot count the number of my potentially award winning photos that have been ruined by an official getting in the way). I lowered the camera in disgust, having missed the shot. The referee kept coming. He was looking back at the play while running the opposite direction. Unfortunately the official was not running in a straight line and veered out of bounds, barreling toward me at full steam. I realized the referee was going to run smack into me and instantly regretted the unkind things I had written about officials, their poor eyesight, absence of parents, etc. I could just see the next headline: "Hall of Famer hit, killed by runaway Zebra."

At that point, the sequence of events changed to slow motion like an instant replay on television. My next thought was how to save the company's overpriced camera. Alas, I was also moving in slow motion, unable to turn away before the referee plowed into me, still running full speed in one direction while looking in another. After the camera flew apart, the last thing I saw was my feet going past my head in a backward somersault. Thankfully no one else saw it happen because they were cheering the big play on the field.

The referee and I collapsed in a heap and had to be untangled by a couple of paramedics.

I realized that I had come full circle from my very first venture into football at the age of nine. I tried out for the Greer Midgets with a vision of becoming an All American running back like my hero, North Carolina great Charlie "Choo-Choo" Justice. Although my waistline equaled the number of inches of my height and my foot speed made a turtle seem like a rocket by comparison, Coach Virgil "Grin" Pruitt decided to let me learn the hard way. He handed me a ball and ordered "take off!" I took only a half step before five tacklers piled into me, and

I collapsed like a house of cards. I was under the pile, thrashing about on my back like an overturned roach bug, gasping for air. My day in the sun at halfback was over, and I was helped over to the opposite side of the field where I was reassigned to the offensive line, which is the last stop before the bus stop for players headed out of town.

So everyone was asking, "How did you get into the Hall of Fame?"

During the induction ceremony, it was mentioned that I was a member of the Greer High golf team. Actually I was the fifth man on a four-man team. Unlike other sports, the team with the lowest score wins in golf. When we added our five scores together the total always came up more than the other team's four. Our coach, Eddis Freeman, was totally immersed in football and unconcerned over losing every golf match.

My greatest golf catastrophe occurred when I decided to practice. I sneaked over the fence at the high school to hit balls on a Sunday afternoon because none of the golfers with cars would give me a lift to the country club. My ball striking was in rare form that day. Standing on the upper football practice field, I managed a rare swing that sent a ball soaring almost 250 yards where it slammed into the front windshield of "The Golden Chariot," the football team's hallowed bus.

The next morning, Athletic Director Phil Clark summoned me to his office. "Do you know who broke the windshield in the bus?" he asked, figuring that I might have seen something since I lived next door.

"Yes sir," I said, "but I didn't mean to do it. You see I hit this rare 250 yard drive, straight as an arrow…"

With that, Coach Clark reached for his big wooden paddle that kept order better than a squad of nightclub bouncers. "That will be ten licks." he announced—"not for breaking the windshield, but for telling a lie about how far you hit a golf ball."

No, I did not get in the Hall of Fame for my golf prowess. Maybe it was for football. I eventually made the midget football all-star team.

Some say that as the right tackle on the offensive line, I was a "look-out blocker"—I yelled "look out" to our ball carriers when opposing tacklers charged past me.

Then I decided I was honored for having seen 500 Greer High games, maybe more than anyone in history. "No," said Heather Smith who organized the ceremony. "You made it because there was a blank space on the bottom of the program page for one more name."

DePressed

I owe an apology to the hundreds of people who showed up early at Dooley Field on Friday night, Oct. 27, 2000 in hopes of seeing the Jackettes' latest dance routine or the Golden Lancers Band performing their competition show. What the crowd got was me—standing in the middle of the field dumfounded during a ceremony when some well-meaning folks named the stadium press box in my honor.

I want to thank everyone who had anything to do with this unde-served, depressing recognition. If you haven't guessed why my name is on the press box, welcome to the club.

Robbie Gravley whispered to me the day before that he was "working on" getting the facility named "the Burch Press Box." I realized right away that "the voice of the Yellow Jackets" had run out of material after tacking another hour onto his pre-game radio show that now starts at breakfast.

I assumed naming the press box would be honoring my father who started the tradition of a Burch roaming the sidelines, advising the football coaches and criticizing the officials at every Greer High game.

So I had a big speech ready about how my daddy, the late Edd A. Burch, missed seeing only one game in 43 seasons (1942-84). I recalled that he once matched Steve Woodward step-for-step on a 99-yard punt return to the end zone, and how he habitually threw his clipboard 25 feet into the air whenever the Yellow Jackets scored.

There wasn't time to tell them the story of the night when the Yellow Jackets threw a pass that Easley intercepted. "Why in the heck did you throw a pass?" daddy demanded as he stormed up to Coach Phil Clark. "Look here, Edd," Clark said. "You stick to running the newspaper, and I'll stick to running the football team."

During the ceremony, the wraps came off a sign that declared the facility the Leland E. Burch Press Box. When I recovered from the shock, I breathed a sigh of relief that the sign did not say "memorial" press box.

Then I thought I might have some incurable disease, and they put my name on the press box while I was still around. Or maybe they were telling me it's time to get off the field after 39 years of covering the Yellow Jackets.

"No," explained Principal Marion Waters when I voiced my concerns. "The real reason is that when someone has been around as long as you have, people do things to recognize you, like a perfect attendance award."

That put me in the same category with Harley Bonds, for whom the old Greer High building was renamed when it became a vocational career center. Bonds was 97 years old. Folks congratulating me said I did not look a day older than Bonds. Others wanted to know "what were Friday nights like in Greer before football was invented?" I probably could have told them if only my memory was as good at it used to be.

"I'll bet they start calling the press box the 'Burch perch'," one of my sons declared after the ceremony. Another chimed in "with your luck, Dad, they will move the stadium to the new campus and leave your press box sitting here."

Forever Young – Aug. 26, 2008

Junior Holder, among the most loyal of Jacket backers, has been eating hot dogs for good luck before every football game. In 2005, I put Holder to work rating the quality of the franks served by Greer opponents. I figured this would be a vital service for Jacket Backers because hot dogs have played a key role in Greer High's gridiron success, dating back at least until 1955. Hot dogs were served every Friday in the school cafeteria, and I must say those were the best I have ever eaten. The chili was loaded with grease that disappeared into the buns making the bread a juicy as the wieners. If I ate one of those dogs today, it would set off a gall bladder attack. But back then, those hot dogs fueled what was arguably Greer High's best ever football team.

Arriving at Hillcrest after a snail-like ride down Highway 14, we made up for lost time at the gate when the attendant observed that Bunchy Godfrey and I were so old that there was no need to produce our credentials. Which was good, because Godfrey had left home without his ticket.

"If we don't win tonight, at least we have them beat on the hot dogs," Holder declared a few minutes later, staring at his half-eaten, foil-wrapped frank.

The game was an historic occasion since it marked Will Young's debut as head coach, only the fifth person to hold the job in the last half century at Greer High.

The Yellow Jackets made a lot of mistakes including fumbling several punts. Young finally instructed the kicking team, "don't dare touch the ball, no matter what."

Meanwhile overly-helpful Jacket Backers standing behind the fence on the sideline continually shouted advice to Young, like "Quit running the same play!;" "Change quarterbacks!;" "Throw the ball!;" etc. Young merely ignored the critics, causing me to think, "this guy has really got a tough hide." I later learned that Young is deaf as a post. He had not heard a single word yelled at him.

Not once did Young throw his cap, however. I decided that his lid must be brand new or else Young has arm trouble because cap throwing is a Greer High coaching tradition—in special situations, of course.

I never saw Phil Clark throw his cap, but Jim Few did once, and that got him ejected from a game at J.L. Mann. Stuart Holcombe had cap throwing down to a science. And Travis Perry could sail his cap out to midfield when he wanted to get the attention of the officials.

Greer Baseball

Greer's Own Field of Dreams – July 24, 1996

Greer's own "Field of Dreams" is among one of the community's top ten favorite historical sites, according to a new survey.

Venerable Stevens Field is a rare landmark that has its own personality. Like an obstinate son-in-law, Stevens Field has successfully withstood every effort to change it for the better.

The park is said to have been built in the 1920s for Victor Mill baseball teams, which were about the only thing Greer had to brag about in those days. In the 1940s, American Legion baseball succeeded the textile leagues as the main attraction at Stevens Field.

The J.P. Stevens Co. donated the park to the city around 1942. The City Council gladly accepted, figuring (correctly) that they would not be around a half-century later to worry about the white elephant when the gift became permanent in 1992.

Meanwhile, the original park that was built of wood burned to the ground in the early 1950s. It hasn't been the same since.

Stevens Field was rebuilt with cement and concrete blocks, but the new stands have not withstood the ravages of time any better than wood. Today, Stevens Field looks as if it had been hit by an earthquake with rows of collapsed cement steps and slabs of grandstands buckled at odd angles.

The press box roof leaks like a sieve. There has been no urgency to repair the press box because no baseball is played when it is raining.

The public address system consists of two loudspeakers. One is pointed upward and the other is aimed straight down, apparently to keep both heaven and hell informed of the score.

An underground watering system was installed last winter, but something failed, and the grass turned brown this summer like always.

The new lighting system, installed three years ago, was billed as an improvement. The lights are actually better for certain activities, like doing needlepoint in the stands, because the poles are so short. The infield is dark as a broom closet at night when players must feel their way around. On top of that, some of the light bulbs burn out during nearly every American Legion game.

The bats (not only the baseball kind) come out at night at Stevens Field. That's all the more reason some believe the place is haunted. Besides, no one can account for some of the strange things that happen there.

For instance, an unwanted surprise arrived several years ago. Sewage began oozing up from underneath the stands. An in–depth investigation failed to reveal the source. A few weeks later, however, the foul leak disappeared as mysteriously as it had begun.

The men's restroom was out of order for several years because the commode would not flush. Even so, an over-zealous city employee poured anti-freeze into the non-functioning plumbing for winter protection that year.

The next spring, Rusty Foxhall, who singlehandedly kept up Stevens Field for years, arrived to work at the park, accompanied as usual by Ubu, the family's pet dog. Ubu soon became thirsty in the hot sun, found his way to the men's restroom (which was unlocked because it is out of order). Foxhall's best friend drank the anti freeze in the toilet and died. After that, the commode mysteriously began working again. Thus, Ubu did not die in vain.

Being preoccupied by the annexation wars, the new owner (City Council) has not gotten around to repairing the stands or even plugging the hole in the outside wall.

There is hope, however. Years ago, someone decided the wall should be painted. Bill Groce, who then operated Groce's Lab, donated a truckload of surplus paint he had received from the Charleston Navy Yard to be recycled. The paint was Navy Blue at one time, but is now a faded gray.

Groce's Lab later became Aqua Tech, which went belly up and became the target of a Federal Superfund Cleanup. If the feds would extend the cleanup to removing the Stevens Field paint (with the stands attached of course) as part of making restitution, the ballpark could qualify for another improvement—a dome.

Morning-after Quarterback - Oct. 2, 1985

Morning-after quarterbacks glory in second guessing football coaches. Second-guessing is also popular in baseball and other sports, but have you noticed that coaches rarely second guess each other in their profession?

Second-guessing was one of my favorite pastimes until I was cured during an American Legion baseball game at Gaffney.

Bob Dunlap, one of the finest gentlemen ever to coach the sport, was fighting to stay in the league race with a Greer team that was very long on pitching but very short on hitting. Greer had been losing games by scores of 1-0, 2-1, etc., and Dunlap was beginning to feel the pressure.

In a game at Gaffney one July night, the score was tied 0-0 in the bottom of the eighth inning. Then Gaffney rallied to take a 1-0 lead on a couple of questionable calls, and Dunlap was ejected for arguing with the umpires. As he left the stadium, Dunlap told Team Manager Gordan Wood to take over. But Wood protested, "I can't coach," and looking at me (the only other person from Greer in the vicinity), he said, "Leland, you coach the team."

Lightning had struck, and I had a golden opportunity to get a start at becoming a big league manager like Joe Torre. It didn't work out that way. I quickly discovered that coaching is a lot easier said than done.

Greer's first batter in the top of the ninth inning was the team's largest player who wasn't hitting his hat size. But he happened to make contact with the baseball and drove it over the heads of the Gaffney outfielders. The ball rolled all the way to the fence, which was nearly 400 feet from home plate in that park. The player seemed to lumber forever before reaching second base, and I was yelling for him to stop there. Instead, he never looked at me while continuing to chug toward third base where he was thrown out by a mile.

As fate would have it, the next better got a single that probably would have scored the tieing run. I attempted to get the next batter to bunt the runner into scoring position, but he popped up to the catcher. That left it up to a kid who had already struck out twice. I pushed the last button and inserted a pinch hitter from the bench. He struck out to end the game.

Would I have done anything differently in my one and only coaching experience? I would have, and I did. I wouldn't have gotten into the coaches box in the first place, and in the second place, I haven't been back to Gaffney.

This was a most forgettable experience, except the Greer American Legion Post 115 Commander Bob Polson reminded me of the incident at every opportunity. The only way I got him to shut up was to threaten to publish his photo riding an elephant when a traveling circus came to Greer.

Greer Basketball

It Could Be a Short Ride Home - March 2, 2005

Some observers consider Greer High to be a "football" school, but basketball can, and does, grab the spotlight on occasion. Last winter, the Lady Yellow Jackets were undefeated until they ran into questionable officiating in the Upstate finals. This year, the Yellow Jacket boys blew past Union, Greenville and the striped shirts for a date in the state finals this Saturday night in Columbia.

The late W. L. "LeRoy" Jones was a member of Greer High's first basketball team and could recall games played on the dirt playground of the old Central Elementary School in 1921. Jones and the Yellow Jackets moved indoors when Davenport High School building opened. Unlike today's Lewis Phillips gymnasium, players crashed into the walls at both ends of the court after every layup, a situation that took speed out of the game. Not until 1948 did one of those teams make it to the state finals.

Although I never had enough ability to run and chew gum at the same time, I have always been fascinated by sports. I tried out for the jayvee basketball team in the tenth grade, and I think my dad must have bribed Coach Phil Clark to keep me on the team. Even so, I was stationed so far away at the end of the bench that an extra chair was necessary. I got to play in only two games, both of which were hopelessly lost by the time my name was called.

Then the late Coach Eddis Freeman "suggested" that I should be the scorekeeper instead of trying to play on the varsity. Not wanting dentures at a tender age, I agreed to Coach Freeman's request. I ended up scoring more points with my pencil than my entire jayvee career. I would never have overlooked writing down a basket in the scorebook which was the explanation given for Clover's loss to Greenville High in the recent playoffs.

Speaking of Greenville High, I almost didn't make it out of the old Hughes Gym the night that a melee broke out when the Yellow Jackets whipped the Red Raiders in 1956. The Greenville crowd literally ran us back to Greer—round and round through the neighborhood to our cars. One of my pals, Roy Hefner, actually went through someone's house—they opened the front door and he never slowed down until he ran out the back door—to escape from the angry mob.

Greer High sent six basketball teams to the state finals during the 1950s. Joe Craft, father-in-law of present Greer High Coach Jeff Neely, was a starter on a "close, but no cigar" team in 1954. The 1955, 1956 and 1959 teams won state titles.

Unmatched youth basketball programs at Victor Mill and Greer Mill provided the foundation for those teams, which turned out a host of outstanding players. Steve Brown, Class of 1958, landed a scholarship to USC. There were many others, too numerous to list.

Lewis Phillips coached several of Greer High's outstanding teams including the 1959 state champions. Yet, the one I remember most was the 1963 model that lost a heartbreaker to Chapman in the Upstate finals in the last two minutes when nearly everything that could go wrong did go wrong.

One of the most amazing teams was the 1978 edition that no one gave a chance to get out of the conference. But a last second long-range basket by Jeff Farrington, seemingly falling backwards into the stands, enabled Greer to upset one of Louie Golden's powerful Riverside squads. Those Yellow Jackets, coached by Melvin Gooden, went on to win the state championship with Farrington and a couple of other bright stars, Dempsey Cohen and Ray Smith, who were juniors at the time. Both enjoyed college careers. Smith played professionally in Europe. Cohen returned to Greer and raised a family—his daughter, Tenia, was a member of the 2005 Lady Yellow Jackets.

Neely's 1994 team reached the state finals with Ron Bruton and Derrick Drummond only to be crushed by Eau Claire's future NBA star Jermaine O'Neal.

Firm Grip Did the Job - Feb. 10, 1999

They may have lost a step. OK, I'll grant that the old guys can't even run now. After all, it's been over 40 years since they answered the tipoff for a Greer High basketball game. The bunch of 1950s players who gathered for a reunion Friday night are just as sharp as ever when it comes to memories. The Fifties Yellow Jackets made it to the state finals six straight years and helped put Greer on the sports map.

One of the youngest-looking old timers was Don Jones, although he was known as "Grandpa" in high school. The nickname originated with fans of opposing teams who got tired of seeing him. After losing to Greer and Jones year after year, they took to calling him "Grandpa" from the stands. Other than the late "Pistol Pete" Maravitch, who played for Daniel High, Jones is the only player I know of who started on a high school varsity team for five consecutive seasons.

Jones' specialty was raining long bombs on the enemy from the corners. He routinely scored from three-point range when the shots counted only two points. There's no telling what his scoring average would be today.

One of Jones' favorite memories is from 1956 when the Yellow Jackets won the state Class 1-A title and were invited to an extra event, the Tournament of Champions, which was for the winners in each class. "We weren't supposed to have a chance, but we beat Bishop-England (the 2-A winner) by 20 points in the finals. I guess we showed them Greer was for real."

Mickey Flynn remembered the 1956 season when the Yellow Jackets were battling Florence in the state finals. "The score was 60-60, and I was standing on the foul line with a one-and-one and just two seconds left. I was scared to death. By the grace of God, I made the first shot, which was all we needed."

It was a dramatic turn of events from his sophomore year. When the team arrived at the historic Carolina Field House in Columbia for the 1954 championship game, Joe Craft (father-in-law of current Greer High coach Jeff Neely) discovered that he had left his pants in the hotel room. "Coach (Eddis) Freeman ordered me to give Craft my pants because I wasn't going to get in the game." Flynn recalls.

"There was nowhere to change because the team did not have access to the dressing room in the ancient gym. So I swapped my pants for Craft's warm-ups right there in front of 2,000 people, with just some of the guys holding up towels for a screen."

Leon McLemore recalled beating Byrnes High in the upper state finals two years running, both in overtime, in games at Presbyterian College in Clinton. "In 1955, there was no way we were supposed to win. But somehow we did. It was hot in that old wooden gym, and most of the Byrnes cheerleaders fainted. We had to help carry them over to the infirmary after the game."

Everyone had an Eddis Freeman story to tell—"he was at least 20 years ahead of his time in coaching." said Steve Satterfield. "He brought the Greer Mill and Victor Mill kids together to play as a team."

"Everyone was afraid of Coach Freeman," recalls Butch Miller. "In 1955 we were playing in a tournament in Spartanburg when Dickie Gravley and Jack McKinney did not get to play in the first half. They decided at halftime that if Coach Freeman sent them to go in the game, they would not go. It wasn't long after the second half started that Freeman called on McKinney, and he didn't budge. So Freeman sent him to the locker room to get dressed— he was off the team. Then Freeman told Gravley to go in. And Gravley didn't waste a second. He went out on the floor with the warm-ups on."

Harold Durham's favorite memory was from 1954—the invention of Firm Grip, which was a resin-like substance guaranteed to eliminate slippery hands. "Firm Grip was new stuff, and we were all rubbing some on our hands before the first game. I noticed Rudy Godfrey was wiping Firm Grip on the seat of his pants, so I asked him what he was doing." Godfrey replied, 'I'm putting it where it will do the most good for where I'll be during the game.'"

Priceless – March 5, 2009

$40 for tickets; $5 for parking; $12 for soft drinks—priceless!—even for tightwads like me to see Greer defeat heavily-favored J.L. Mann in a 76-74 thriller to win the upper state 3-A basketball championship.

It was one of the great games in Greer High School's storied 89-year basketball history. It came on the heels of an equally amazing game four days earlier when the Yellow Jackets rallied from 20 points down at intermission to knock off favored Daniel High, 88-86.

An estimated 8,500 cheering spectators, many like us with knees jammed into our chests in rows designed for elves in the Bi-Lo 'Rena, created a great atmosphere. The game had us jumping up and down like thousands of yo-yos bobbing in unison. They could have evacuated the crowd at intermission and charged everyone full price to come back in for the second half.

Years from now, at least 100,000 will claim to have seen the Mann game like the countless number who boast of having witnessed Frank Selvy's famous 100-point scoring feat against Newberry in the old Textile Hall in the early 1950s.

Last week's victories were on par with Greer's dramatic playoff win over cross-town Riverside in 1978. That game is remembered for Jeff Farrington canning the winning shot from the corner of the court while falling backwards into the bleachers at the buzzer. That was before the 3-point shot era, and kids who fired from 25 feet away were usually yanked from the game. Today, it is known as "The Shot," and folks still bring it up whenever Farrington, now an assistant football coach at Furman, is in their midst. That win broke the Warriors' stranglehold in the hoops rivalry and propelled the Yellow Jackets to the state title.

James Dean was also a member of the 1978 team, and his youngest son Chris is a key player on the 2009 squad. Much more than a chip off the old block, Chris can do just about anything with a basketball.

He proved it against Daniel by stealing the ball with a few seconds left and taking it the length of the court for the winning score.

"I can't bear to watch," groaned my wife who buried her head in her hands after Dean tied the Mann game at 74-all with a free throw, and the Patriots were working for a final shot. So she didn't see Dean making the most remarkable play of this, or many other seasons, as Patriot star Damien Leonard was going up at close range for what seemed likely to be the winning basket. Dean jumped higher, stuffed the shot and took the ball away in the same motion. That was insult added to injury, since Dean had stolen the ball in the closing seconds of the third period and took it in for a slam-dunk that swung the momentum Greer's way.

Chandler Hash, grandson of super proud Grayson Hash and a scoring machine with all the moves of Davidson standout Stephen Curry, then soared above a couple of taller Patriots to score the deciding basket with 2.6 seconds left.

Fouls called in the last three seconds are rarer than a March snowstorm in Dixie. But Hash was whistled for a Mickey Mouse foul with .09 left, and Leonard went to the free-throw line with the chance to send the contest into overtime. When Leonard missed, someone said I had tears in my eyes. Actually, my eyeballs were floating because I dared not take a restroom break for fear of missing a single minute of the action.

Greer will battle Camden for the state 3-A championship in Columbia this Saturday night in the school's 11th trip to the finals. The Yellow Jackets have a 5-5 record to show for their previous 10 title games dating back to 1939, so the 2009 team could put GHS ahead in the win column.

With the exception of the 1955-56 squad, this team is different because there is no dominant big player in the middle, like Ray Smith in 1978 and LaRon Dendy in 2005. The 1978 champs also had a couple of super players in Dempsey Cohen and Timmigo Burnett, plus

Farrington and James Dean who's oldest son, Jamar, by the way, was a starter on the 2005 title team.

The 2009 team also plays defense, an attribute missing in the 2005 state finals when Greer's 100-97 win over Lake Marion broke the event's all-time scoring record. No one expected so much from these underdogs, but they have proved the experts wrong, first by winning the Region III title and later dethroning defending champion Greenville High in the second round.

Louie, Louie - March 31, 1993

Riverside High's Louie Golden, who is fast becoming a legend in his own time, was "roasted" the other night. Not that Golden needs the recognition. He is arguably the best active basketball coach in South Carolina.

The "roast" must have been intended to let a little air out of Golden's balloon. Because a bunch of people are necessary to roast someone of Louie's girth, they even called on me to say a few words.

That got me to thinking. I have been Louie Golden's press agent for 20 years, only I didn't know it.

I came to another conclusion: Louie Golden is not a coach. He doesn't have to coach. Louie Golden is the world's greatest con artist. Golden wins games before they start, some of them even before the season starts. I say he's a great con artist, because it has taken me this long to figure it out.

Golden dragged his crying towel over here way back in 1973. That was a few days before Riverside opened, and he's never put it down. I get Golden's crying towel treatment every year when I interview him about the upcoming season. I ask: "Louie, what kind of a team are you going to have?" And, with crocodile tears in his eyes, Golden has given me the same answer for 20 straight years. This is how it goes:

"Oh, man. We are really hurtin' this year. We're slow, and we're short.

"Oh, man. We only had two kids to transfer in this time. One of them is 6-11, you know, the one who moved in with me. Just because he's taller than anybody else in the league doesn't mean anything. The other one—well he got cut from the U.S. Olympic team. If he couldn't keep up with Michael Jordan and Charles Barkley, he probably can't help us either.

"Oh, man," Golden would continue, "all these other teams are really improved. We don't stand a chance. You take Greer. Now they have three players who can really dominate a game."

I can't imagine what kind of game Golden is talking about unless it is checkers—because most years, Greer has not been blessed with three players who could even make Louie's team.

By the time the season opens, Golden has put out the word in all the right places. Then he starts working on the opposing coaches, calling them before the games and feeding them the same line. He is still talking when the other team gets off the bus. By game time, the opposition is so confused they don't have a prayer.

Am I complaining? Heavens no. It's easy for me to write about Riverside basketball now. I just get out last year's article, change a few names, and reprint all of Golden's standard quotes.

But we came to bury Golden and not to praise him. So I also pointed out that he is infected with a mutation of the infamous "Chicken Curse" (the USC Gamecock disease which makes coaches disappear). In this case, however, Golden makes entire schools disappear.

Golden began his career at Sterling High School, and it burned down. His next stop was at Beck High—now a middle school slated to be closed. He then went to Carolina High—on the newest list for closing, and Riverside High may soon be merging with Greer High.

Even with all his faults, I'm thankful for Louie Golden. I'm especially thankful that Golden doesn't sell cemetery lots because I would have bought a dozen of them already.

Greer Golf

It's Spelled f-l-o-g - Jan. 21, 1987

If the annual Super Bowl game turns out to be like many of the previous affairs, it will be a "super bore." Even though no one asked my opinion, I have decided to defect from the TV set to the golf course this Super Sunday, since golf can be more exciting than football. There is always the thrill of seeing your ball fly away in unexpected directions on nearly every shot. Golf is also challenging, especially when one has to look under rocks, behind tree trunks, etc. to find errant balls.

I grew up playing golf during the early days of the Greer Country Club in the mid-1950s. Apparently my gang learned the game backwards—spelled that way, it's f-l-o-g—because we had all sorts of strange adventures.

One of my earliest recollections of the country club was when a group of members decided to remove the rocks from the fairways. About 25 men started out early one morning, walking abreast along the first fairway, scooping up rocks and throwing them into a dump truck. They hadn't gone 50 yards before one of the men keeled over dead as a doornail with a heart attack and everyone immediately went home. The rocks remained for years, but made golf interesting by sending balls bouncing from the middle of fairways off into the woods.

I recall an incident that occurred late one afternoon when several of us teens happened to find a small dead snake on the golf course. About the same time, we spotted Dr. J. Roy Jackson, our dentist. Whistling and humming to himself, Dr. J. Roy was out for a round by himself, striding along an adjacent fairway and carrying just two or three clubs that he always used.

It struck us that this would be a great opportunity to repay Dr. J. Roy for the many hours we had endured him grinding cavities out of our teeth without the benefit of Novocain. So we dashed ahead of the good dentist and carefully positioned the snake in the cup of the green he was approaching. After replacing the flag, we darted behind some bushes and anxiously waited for Dr. J. Roy to get the scare of his life.

Well, the joke was on us. When Dr. J. Roy reached the green, he never bothered to putt his ball into the cup. He simply picked it up and whistled his way to the next tee box.

My only athletic claim to fame was playing on the Greer High golf team, which was easy because I was one of only 4-5 kids in the student body who owned a set of golf clubs.

Our coach, Eddis Freeman, knew no more about golf than the rest of us, which was practically nothing. He gave each of us a sleeve of 3 balls to start the season, and I lost mine the single afternoon on the course. Freeman's only advice to us about how to play the game was to stop running up and down the hills at the country club to save our energy. After that, we were on our own.

We even had a few laughs, like the other kids gave me the nick-name "Piney" because I hit so many balls into the woods. I topped that by once blasting a wayward shot clear through Eric Anderson's golf bag.

Anderson, like most of us, sometimes let his temper get the best of him. One day Anderson hit such a poor shot that he flung his golf club in disgust. The club struck a nearby tree on its balance point and wrapped itself neatly around the trunk—a feat that I have never seen duplicated.

The End is Near - May 15, 2008

Some believe that the current U.S. Presidential election campaign is a sign of the end of time. More substantial proof can be found in the Bible where the same prophecy is written twice, in the books of Joel and Acts: "In the last days, God says ... Your old men will dream dreams ..."

Having accomplished most of my life goals, except to be elected President, I am living proof of an old man dreaming dreams as a member of a group of elderly hackers envisioning that our golf games can actually improve. I am clinging to this dream after spending a fortune in a futile attempt to buy a better game. I have the newest clubs guaranteed to correct one's faults, golf balls that fly farther than ever before, and shelves filled with golf improvement books. After none of those helped, the only thing left was to put this sagging bag of wrinkles back into prime physical condition as it may have been 40 years ago.

Such a feat could become one of the Seven Wonders of the World, but stranger things have happened. I turned to SSI (Serving Seniors in Denial) which is offering a geezer golf program. Actually, no one uses the "G" word there. The program is officially described as a weekly exercise class designed to strengthen golf muscles.

SSI is an oasis of amenities like a Thornblade on Wade Hampton Blvd. "Age Before Beauty" is inscribed over the entryway.

Security is tight at the check-in (it's PG-70, no one under 70 is admitted without parental consent). There you are photographed and issued a key for a locker to store all of your important accessories such as an I-pod, cell phone, Depends, Viagra, Flomax, etc.

At the appointed time, class members are gathered up by our trainer, J.T., who also teaches group classes for kids. J.T. says there isn't much difference between geezers and the kids. Both groups have short attention spans or they can't hear, they don't understand the instructions and forget what they learned from one week to the next.

While we exercise, J.T. regales us with stories of when he worked as a caddy on the PGA tour. His favorite is the day that Vijay Singh spent four hours practicing hitting shots out of sand traps. J.T. had to retrieve all 100 golf balls more than a dozen times.

Last week we got the shock our lives at the check-in desk where we were informed, "Lance is waiting for you."

Lance is a co-owner of the place. He explained that J.T. was tired of babysitting and left on the spur of the moment to return to caddying the PGA Tour, which is like going from a Little League game at Century Park to Yankee Stadium.

Lance knows all the exercises vital to build golf muscles but confessed that he has no answer for the muscle between our ears. He leads us through a one-minute warm-up of twirling our arms, after which we have to take a break.

You need good balance to play golf, so we try to stand on a huge ball. We do one pushup and hold the position for 15 seconds or collapse, whichever comes first. Then we swing a "speed stick" that shows us how fast we can swing a golf club. I was timed slightly ahead of the post office's snail.

I hate doing sit-ups and trying to touch my toes. You have to be flexible to play golf, but I am no rubber man. If I can touch my knees it is like the game of horseshoes—there is some merit for coming close. This exercise brings us face-to-face with the reality of the "I've fallen and I can't get up" syndrome. Classmates with artificial knees, hips and other bionic parts do better at picking themselves up than my originals with expired warranties.

Based on my first six months in the class, it will be another 15 years before I shoot my age, which will be 83 by then. "No." Lance assured us. "You will really see great results when we get to the lessons about improving your score keeping."

It's Thanksgiving

I'm Thankful – Nov. 23, 2005

It's Friday at 12:20 p.m., and I am surrounded by gray haired folks huddled around knee-high tables. No, it is not the Roger Huntington Nursing Center. It's Chandler Creek Elementary School, and this is Grandparents Day.

We are devouring a meal of pizza, lima beans and whole-kernel corn with a miniature cup of pink applesauce on the side. Some gray-beards are speculating that if master chef Gerard Cribbin ever discovers that such competition exists in the marketplace, it will cause him some sleepless nights. Others said if the Pilgrims had known 350 years ago that we would be eating like this, they would never have gotten off the boat.

But I digress. I am here primarily as the proud grandpa of Eli.

"Were you ever called Eli?," asks his teacher whom I mistook for a teenager when we were introduced. "I've been called a lot of things, but never Eli." I replied.

"Well, Leland is his real name too, isn't it?," she continued. "Yes, but he can't help it." I said.

"Are you here doing your practice teaching?," I asked, quickly changing the subject. "No," she huffed. "I've been on the faculty here for five years."

The highlight of the day for Eli is the Book Fair because he loves to read. Since he was loaded down with cash from all of his grandparents, I expected Eli to emerge with an armload of books from the racks of new publications in the media center. Instead he bought only one. "Why didn't you get more books?," I asked.

"I'm putting the rest of your money in the bank," Eli explained. It struck me that the kid is going to grow up to be like his great uncle Walter.

I was especially thankful that Eli is no longer in kindergarten, because at that age, the kids eat lunch at 10:30 a.m.

And since this is the season, I'm thankful for many other things:

…..that Greer has a rock star. His name is Merle State.

…..that our bathroom scale is no longer in working condition.

…..that we don't have reservations for Thanksgiving dinner at the same place as last year. It was only last month when I finally finished paying off the credit card for that meal.

…..that my wife has only one house to redecorate.

…..for grandchildren—I never have to worry about loose change in my pockets.

…..that I am not a member of Greenville County Council.

…..that Pat Robertson is not calling upon God to punish Greer.

…..that it takes only 15 minutes to drive out to my favorite new store, Hobby Lobby.

…..that I had to wait only one hour to get a flu shot last week. The pneumonia shot was worse than the wait, however.

…..and I'll be thankful when Turkey Season is over—I will feel safe again when going out in public.

Still Thankful - Thanksgiving '09

My bit of wisdom this week is that things could always be worse. For example, have you ever considered what we would be eating this Thursday if the Indians had given the Pilgrims a donkey instead of a turkey that first Thanksgiving?

Yes, I am thankful for that and a whole lot more. I am especially thankful that the folks at the newspaper office clipped my photo out of the holiday issue of *Greer Then* magazine so that I did not have to show up in person to be the target in the annual community turkey shoot.

As a resident of the state that leads the nation in obesity, I'm thankful that Governor Mark Sanford has been setting the example to encourage physical fitness by hiking the Appalachian Trail.

I'm thankful to be able to avoid Black Friday by staying in bed all day.

I'm thankful that my cell phone is an unlisted number.

I'm thankful that the fire marshal has limited the occupancy of Bullock's Barbershop to 50 people.

I'm thankful that Republicans are saying no to everything—it reminds me of the way I was brought up.

I'm thankful for the daily blizzard of junk mail advertising pouring in since September because it reminds me Christmas is right around the corner. Therefore, I'm also thankful that our mailbox did not collapse under the weight of the four-foot-high stack of shopping catalogues that my wife has received this month.

I'm thankful that UGA VII went to the Big Kennel in the Sky before having to watch the Georgia Bulldogs stumble, fumble and fall to Kentucky on Saturday night.

I'm thankful that we don't have Lou Dobbs to kick around any more.

I'm thankful that Jerry Bruce hasn't planted a railroad in my front yard.

This is not a Tweet because thankfully no one has taught me how to Twitter.

I'm thankful that Greer does not have a bus station; otherwise we might be a stop on the Sarah Palin rogue elephant book tour. I have a hunch that Jenny Sanford's book will be much more enlightening.

I'm thankful that I am always appropriately dressed for Tacky Day.

Becoming a curmudgeon has its perks, like no longer having to worry about identity theft, for which I'm thankful.

I'm thankful that I don't have to worry about when to get a mammogram.

At the age when one can no longer conjure up a wish list for Christmas, I should be thankful about the Christmas bonus I am about to receive. Which means I can also give thanks for having eluded the scouts from the nursing home for another year.

With friends like Ronnie Bruce, I'm thankful for enemies.

I'm thankful the swine flu does not leave its victims oinking.

We have had an abundance of rain recently, which means I'm thankful that our latest CPW water bill did not deliver its usual shock & awe.

I'm thankful that our bathroom scales don't panic—yet—whenever I approach them.

There are only a couple of posts about me on A.. book, the network for anti-socials at the opposite end of cyber space from Facebook—and for that I am thankful.

The world was agog last week when Oprah announced plans to wind down her TV show, and I was just as thankful because an entire day passed without anyone mentioning Michael Jackson.

I'm thankful that I don't feel the urge to see a vampire movie this holiday season, and that I am wearing my Halloween mask 24-7-365.

318

I'm thankful our representatives in Washington, D.C., are fighting to prevent national health care. Such a program would cause all of our emergency rooms to go out of business.

I'm thankful that James Paget is keeping the publishing industry afloat with another book.

I'm thankful for the therapist who provides counseling for my addiction to salsa and chips at Mr. Salsa.

I'm thankful that Wayne Cole isn't an airplane pilot.

I'm thankful that possums are on the Endangered Species List.

Turn about: I graciously accept thanks from the thousands(?) of readers who are grateful because this column is about to come to an end.

Finally, I'm thankful that I have another two years for worrying before the world ends in 2012.

Annual Letter to Santa

Dear Santa - Dec. 19, 2001 (an excerpt)

Christmas is just not the same this year. I can't seem to get into the holiday spirit after the city fathers whacked down the magnificent Bradford Pear trees on Trade Street—it just doesn't look like Christmas.

The tree massacre has sparked an appalling chain of events in downtown Greer. Without tree limbs, there was no place to hang the city's holiday decorations, which consist of three strands of twinkling miniature lights. Several street lamps came down, too.

Things got so dark that the CDGC, the GDCG, the DCGC, not to mention the CGDC, all got up and walked out, even refused to sponsor the annual Christmas pageant.

Some enterprising folks did wrap the chest-high tree stumps in ribbons. But these wrappings are in non-seasonal shades of yellow, which expresses hope for the trees to be rescued from the landfill where they have been hijacked.

So Santa, topping my list of Christmas requests for the good? little girls and boys of Greer, S.C. is that you promote Rose Marie Jordan to First Sergeant of the Downtown Beautification Police.

Bring Mayor Rick Danner a larger closet so he can invite more people to his secret meetings.

Since Wryley Bettis has blown his chance to advance from parking lot attendant to a Wal-Mart greeter, perhaps you could get him on as a driver for Papa John's.

Dear Santa - Dec. 22, 1999

'Twas the night before Christmas and all through the city, not a creature was stirring, not even the Annexation Committee...

...when out on the lawn I heard such a clatter, that I sprang from my recliner to see what was the matter: Theresa "Granny" Williams was perched on a ladder, shaking pecans from the top of a tree for her fruitcake platter...

And then it hit me. I forgot to mail my annual letter to Santa! So here it is.

Dear Santa:

Of course, bring "Granny" pecans—loads of them. Her nut rolls are naked and cold. And the rest of us are suffering toasted pecan withdrawal this Christmas. Let me explain.

Reaffirming that advertising pays has been the number one project for the millennium at the newspaper office, and with Granny's help we have proved it! It happened without warning on Monday when the first call of the day was a customer requesting a classified ad in the paper. It read: For Sale - shelled pecans, $3 per pound.

When Granny took down the ad, she got so excited that she called all of her friends to let them know about the pecans. The telephoning took the rest of the day, nearly eight hours. Between calls, Granny made plans to go after a few bags of pecans for herself. She started by obtaining a map to Riverside High, a landmark near the pecan trees. She did not know the location of the school, since it's only been here for 27 years, and it isn't on Highway 414.

When five o'clock finally arrived, Granny jumped in her car and eventually managed to find the pecan lady's house on Suber Road. There, she got the shock of her life. The woman had sold out of pecans. Granny's friends had beaten her to the pecans and snapped up the woman's entire crop of 38 pounds of nuts!

As for the rest of our staff: Scottie Mooney needs medication for tension and heartburn arising from his first taste of dealing with customers. He could also use a chain to anchor the printing press to the wall in case Sanford & Son tries to haul it away for recycling.

I really hate to bring this up, Santa, but since you are well over 150 years old, you must have a touch of Alzheimer's. You left a Kenner Easy Bake Oven for Julie Holcombe last Christmas, and she has since learned how to cook, ensuring that she retains her title as Most Valuable Employee. There is just one minor technicality, however, Julie still needs a house for the oven, and you failed to deliver one last year as promised.

Wes Skinner needs a video of last year's national championship football game because his beloved Tennessee Vols aren't going to be there this Jan. 1.

Kris Gordon needs an insurance policy for her newest prized possession, the actual hot tub that was used in filming the movie Titanic. If that porcelain Lake Murray were to spring a leak, it would create a real river at Riverside High.

Office manager Donna "Tater Tot" Dawley could use a Humvee for traveling the many roads under construction. On a recent trip to Greenville, Dawley sideswiped all the mailboxes on Edwards Road. The mailboxes were relatively unscathed, but her car was $2,000 worth of bodywork worse for the wear.

Please introduce Joel FitzPatrick to some good ole Southern teams like the Braves, Falcons and Panthers. They at least make the Big Dance occasionally, in contrast to his Detroit also-rans: the Tigers, Lions, and Pistons.

Angela Mathis needs a secretary to keep up with her millennium appointment schedule: the entire Winston Cup NASCAR circuit; seven Clemson home games and 26 weekends on Lake Hartwell.

Sherrie Campbell, who recently broke the old attendance record set by former sports editor Mike Burns, needs a whole pad full of doctors' excuses.

Gala Mickle seems to be trapped between a rock and a hard place—marriage and teaching school. Perhaps a superhero such as Batman could come to the rescue.

Speaking of superheroes, Gena Jackson is the newest Wonder Woman on the staff. She could use lead ankle weights to keep her in one place for more than two minutes at a time.

Bring Eddie Burch another Kids Planet, Family Fest Fishing Contest or similar project that gives him something to do when there are no fires to put out.

Ray Starnes, who thought he was semi-retired, needs a key so he can get out of the building. Here lately, he's been locked in for 12-hour shifts at a time.

Please, no more new automobiles for Lori Sondov! With her schedule of housekeeping in Spartanburg, PTA at Chandler Creek Elementary and Boiling Springs High, meetings at Greer Relief Agency, and trips to Rilla's in between, the girl needs a helicopter.

Preston Burch would like to be appointed as a judge for the Miss America Pageant. He has acquired plenty of experience photographing local beauties at every opportunity while they are engaged in playing basketball, softball, tennis, volleyball, soccer and at swim meets.

Walter Burch could use a roll of quarters for making a token contribution toward his free cup of coffee every morning at CB&L.

As for me, since the newspaper recently filed a Freedom of Information suit against the city, I would like to know whether we are hereafter known as the suer or the suee. My second request is for new spell check software. No one believes me when I explain that the spelling mistakes are made by the computer.

…And I heard Santa exclaim as he drove out of sight, "Merry Christmas to all and try not to stay uptight."

Leland and the CRYSTAL BALL

Gazing into the Crystal Ball

The Future Ain't What It Used to Be - Jan. 3, 2000

As it turned out, nearly everything was Y2K compliant when the clocks struck midnight on Friday to signal the start of a new century, except the toilet in the women's restroom of the newspaper office. It failed to flush after Theresa Williams dropped her toothbrush into the bowl. Don't ask how it happened.

An even more alarming failure was my crystal ball. I had to wait until today to be sure, but nearly everything I predicted last New Year's Day failed to come to pass. With one exception—that no new subdivisions would be built without the most important piece of infrastructure, a Waffle House, already in place. This proved to be accurate when the city zoning board recently turned down a 600-home development on Gibbs Shoals Road.

For the coming year, I have a new crystal ball. Wal-Mart guarantees that it is Y3K compliant, but the warranty includes a disclaimer stating that the new millennium does not begin until Jan. 1, 2001. In other words, the following predictions may not come true for at least another year. And if that is the case, I will not have to change anything in this column come next January.

Considering the multitude of inventions of the past 100 years-- computers, televisions, telephones, airplanes, automobiles, microwave ovens, radios, nuclear power, Velcro, twist ties, etc., I find it amazing that no one has improved upon the crystal ball. I am having a very difficult time seeing what 2001 will bring. My cloudy crystal ball keeps flashing a message that was originally delivered by Yogi Berra: "The future ain't what it used to be."

We are entering the "Information Age." Unfortunately, it is occurring just when Virtual Reality is replacing actuality with dreams. With Virtual Reality, things can be something other than they seem. For instance, Tab's Flea Market is actually Times Square when visited through Virtual Reality.

Virtual Reality is the answer to that famed TV commercial question: "Where do you go to work out that important muscle between your ears?" You can experience anything wearing a Virtual Reality device over your head and allowing it to submerse you into new adventures. This has all sorts of possibilities. Instead of plunking down

$100 for a pair of 50-yard-line tickets, the annual Clemson vs. Carolina game can be played inside your head. With the right programming, you can make that game come out any way you like.

Video poker will disappear from the scene in 2000. It will join GARP, Jazz and Candlelight, and the Strategic Planning Committee in the dustbin of history. And it would remain there except that Truman Henderson will have the brilliant idea of resurrecting them all, combined into one neat package: GALOOTAVPP.com. It stands for Greer Artists and Luminaries' Overwrought Outreach to Alcoholic Video Poker Players.

On the political front, J. Van Collins will continue his meteoric rise that began during the '99 mayoral campaign. His next write-in bid will take place in a few weeks in the S.C. Presidential primary campaigns. J. Van offers a clear alternative to the current slate of wooden candidates in three-piece suits. Although J. Van will not win this time either, don't count him out in the '02 race to succeed Strom Thurmond. Provided, however, that Thurmond doesn't make history by being cloned so that he can remain in the U.S. Senate for another century.

How will we measure success in '00? The upstate homemakers' homemaker, Nancy Welch, super glued herself to her kitchen floor during the holidays. It's true. No one can touch that for dedication to cooking during the coming year.

As for me, I am starting a Greer Chapter of Grumpy Old Men and cordially invite you to become charter members.

About the author

 Leland E. Burch, Sr. grew up in Greer, South Carolina where he attended public schools, graduating from Greer High School in 1957. After graduating from Wofford College in 1961, Burch married his high school sweetheart, Margaret Janice Griffin, and returned to his hometown to begin a lifelong career in journalism with the family's weekly newspaper, *The Greer Citizen*.

Active in community affairs, Burch has served as a Greenville-Spartanburg Airport Commissioner since 1985. He is an Elder in the First Presbyterian Church of Greer, past President of the Greer Lions Club, a founding board member of the Greer Heritage Museum, a director of the Greer Christian Learning Center, a co-founder of The Greer Rose Society and a past President of the South Carolina Rose Society.

Acknowledgements

This book would not have been possible without the devotion and encouragement of my wife, Margaret Griffin Burch, who has been an inspiration throughout my adult life.

I am extremely grateful to friends who provided invaluable assistance in helping me bring this book to fruition. Marilyn Hendrix and Bobbie Burns patiently proofread the entire book and ferretted out numerous errors that habitually creep into my work. Their contribution has resulted in much more professional publication.

Julie H. Holcombe and Gloria Fair spent a great deal of time retyping numerous columns that were written before the era of backing up our work on discs. Their efforts saved me untold hours of slaving over the keyboard.

Award-winning photographer Eddie Burch (my son) provided the photos that grace the cover and several interior pages of the book.

And I deeply appreciate the technical information and invaluable advice shared by a pair of authors with Greer roots, Bill Piergiovanni and Mickey Beckham.

Index

26226831R00200

Made in the USA
Charleston, SC
30 January 2014